THE SHORTEST HISTORY OF SEX

Other Titles in the Shortest History Series

The Shortest History of China by Linda Jaivin
The Shortest History of the Crown by Stephen Bates
The Shortest History of Democracy by John Keane
The Shortest History of Economics by Andrew Leigh
The Shortest History of India by John Zubrzycki
The Shortest History of Israel and Palestine by Michael Scott-Baumann
The Shortest History of the Soviet Union by Sheila Fitzpatrick
The Shortest History of the Universe by David Baker
The Shortest History of War by Gwynne Dyer

THE SHORTEST HISTORY OF SEX

DAVID BAKER

PICADOR INDIA

First published in Australia as *Sex* in 2023 by Black Inc.
First published in India 2024 by Picador India
an imprint of Pan Macmillan Publishing India Private Limited
707 Kailash Building
26 K. G. Marg, New Delhi 110001
www.panmacmillan.co.in

Pan Macmillan, The Smithson, 6 Briset Street, Farringdon, London EC1M 5NR
Associated companies throughout the world
www.panmacmillan.com

ISBN 978-81-19300-07-5

1 3 5 7 9 8 6 4 2

Printed and bound in India by Replika Press Pvt. Ltd.

MIX
Paper | Supporting responsible forestry
FSC www.fsc.org FSC® C116313

Dedicated to Viktoria Evans

CONTENTS

FOREWORD

Simon Whistler

Sex. It's the reason we're all here, isn't it? It's a topic that captivates us all yet often remains shrouded in mystery and taboo.

For my generation, sex education was limited to a few lessons in biology class, with the girls separated from the boys and awkward discussions about our developing body parts and what we might one day do with them. 'Uncomfortable' might be the best word to describe that experience.

Perhaps if my teachers had communicated the facts with the ease and clarity of *this* book, I would have got better grades in those lessons, although I imagine the education department might have objected to such sentences as 'Scat fetishes are uncommon; due to issues of hygiene and odour, piss is roughly six times more likely to be used than shit.' Though the statistic, in itself, is intriguing to know. Other books in this genre might lean towards the dry, but David Baker's certainly does not. Rare is it to find a piece of writing where 'bukkake parties' are mentioned in the same breath as DNA replication.

In *Sex*, Baker takes us on a journey that begins with the origins of life, travels through the chaotic evolution that created human sexual anatomy and instincts, and delves into every stage of human history, showing how deeply sex has shaped almost every aspect of our society. He then leads us to troubling questions about the state of sex and romance in the twenty-first century and some bizarre questions about technology and sex in the not-so-remote future, painting scenarios in which we could be (a) sexless machines living in transhumanist 'clouds', (b) immortal studs and babes with enhanced genitals and perfect physiques or (c) lonely, isolated people making love to intelligent robots designed purely for companionship and sex. The machines, at least, seem inevitable. Supply and demand, after all ...

Here is a comprehensive, engaging story that will captivate readers from start to finish, which is really rather impressive for a book of its considerable length. This book is not afraid to tackle even the most unconventional aspects of sexuality, making it an eye-opening and informative read for anyone curious about sex – which, let's face it, includes most of us – and its unique blend of humour and scientific rigour dispels many myths and misconceptions surrounding this complex and fascinating topic. In short, this book is sure to enlighten, entertain and challenge our understanding of human sexuality. It opens up for the reader a much wider world concerning humanity's most whispered-about and intimate subjects. What we *think* we know about sex is just the tip of the iceberg.

INTRODUCTION

I hope the reader of this book doesn't blush easily. They're in for a bit of a wild ride. The aim of this book is to explore sex from the 'ground up' and hopefully give the audience a clear idea of where all the facets of human sexuality came from, and why humanity's baffling array of passions, impulses and fetishes are the way they are. We'll start at the creation of sex approximately 2 billion years ago and chase it down our evolutionary family tree until we arrive at the present.

While thousands of books on sex have been written over the years, this is the first book that seeks to weave together the grand narrative of sex in its entirety. Especially in so short a space. My colleagues and I have jokingly referred to this work as 'The Grand Chronicle of Fuck'. Its scope will go beyond that of most similar fare. For one thing, there is an entire genre of history devoted to exploring the cultural expressions of human sexuality over the past 5,500 years. But this book isn't about exploring in detail 'what the Ancient Greeks liked to do with their dicks' so much as *where their dicks came from*. Furthermore, there is a genre of natural history that explores our sexual instincts, but it usually starts with primates, where sex is already extremely complex, dropping us in the deep end, trying to figure out where the bizarre habits of chimps, bonobos and gorillas came from in the first place. Moreover, these primate profiles are rarely linked to an in-depth historical exploration of sex in the 315,000 years of human history. This book attempts to convey the phenomenon of sex as a totality, from start to finish, from the basic chemical process of two microbes sharing DNA to things as bizarre and convoluted as foot fetishes or bukkake parties. Given where sex started, that is one hell of a transformation, and it is a story that deserves to be told in full.

As a result of weaving all this history into a single narrative, the reader will hopefully emerge with a clear understanding of one of the deepest and most abiding forces of human nature. Zooming out gives us a new perspective on sex and society. We look at how sex changed for humans across the foraging, agrarian and modern eras, and how we arrived at a period in history where the present nature of our sex lives has no historical or evolutionary precedent. We then briefly look at the horizon to figure out where current trends may lead us in the near future, as every human on the planet with a libido tries to navigate this brave new world. But instead of predicting one such future, we survey several.

I have always found the practice of a historian using the magnitude of a grand narrative to stand on their soapbox and preach at people to be highly repulsive. Therefore, aside from telling a unified history of sex, this book has no gimmick or obnoxious thesis advocating for either the universal practice of promiscuity or a return to strict monogamy, like some other works on sex have done in the past. I have endeavoured to present the chaotic mess of our sexual history, warts and all, so readers can reflect on what it means to them. To my mind, there are no easy conclusions. And as 'just some guy', of limited age and life experience, currently sitting here, alone, writing in his pyjama pants, I have no right whatsoever to prescribe anyone advice on how to conduct their sex lives. Or to start waxing philosophical about what sexual behaviours would overall be the most conducive to maintaining a healthy, modern, democratic society. That would be the height of hubris, and no one would listen to me anyway. So, you are cordially invited to draw your own conclusions from this story rather than be force-fed my own. In most places where my perspective shines through the cracks it is for humorous effect or to provoke independent thought, rather than to deliver some cringeworthy 'moral to the story'.

Speaking of humour and provoking thought, this work is intended to be both informative and entertaining, and I hopefully have not failed miserably in the latter regard. There are a few cheeky jokes, a bit of foul language – for that, given the subject matter, I pray I will be forgiven. Furthermore, in every chapter I have attempted to convey some unusual information and burst a few popular myths, along with providing a few historical vignettes purely for the reader's titillation.

The book's structure is straightforward. **Part I: Evolutionary Foreplay** explores the slow construction of the fundamentals of sex from the origin of life to the extinction of the dinosaurs. **Part II: Primate Climax** takes a long, hard look at the journey that led to the complex tangle of human sexual instincts. **Part III: Cultural Afterglow** examines how the evolutionary trends identified in the previous two sections interact with humanity's tremendous capacity for creating a diversity of cultures and ideas, and how the dance of Nature and Nurture played out in the three major eras of human history: foraging, agrarian and modern.

All this is in service of showing how we got to where we are, before providing some provocative information about the current state of play. We then briefly turn to a survey of the potential utopias, dystopias and doomsday scenarios of the future. From there, the reader will likely collapse into an exhausted heap, consumed by feelings of anxiety and foreboding. At which point, if possible, it is probably a good idea for them to take their mind off it with a bit of sex.

I very much hope you enjoy reading this book as much as I have enjoyed writing it.

Milestones in the annals of sex

EVENT	DATE
Origin of life	3.8 billion years ago
Evolution of sex	2 billion years ago
Evolution of multicellular sex	650 million years ago
First gonochorism and non-hetero sex in our lineage	525–510 million years ago
First penises in our lineage	330 million years ago
First mammary glands	270 million years ago
First live births in our lineage	160 million years ago
First external genitalia in our lineage	125 million years ago
The pan-placental orgasm	66 million years ago
Increased sophistication of the clitoris	66–50 million years ago
Diversification of masturbation	60–40 million years ago
First confirmed anal sex	55 million years ago
Promiscuous or polygynous Old World monkeys	40 million years ago
First monogamous apes	17 million years ago
Reversion to polygyny in our lineage	15 million years ago
First harems in great apes	10 million years ago
Multi-male, multi-female promiscuity	6 million years ago
Bipedal changes to breasts, penises and sex positions	4 million years ago

Evolution of flirtation	2.3 million years ago
Monogamy in our lineage, less competition and sexual dimorphism, the shrinking of balls and thickening of dicks, the pair-bonding orgasm, the evolution of love	1.9 million years ago
Sexual practices diversify due to culture, abstract thinking enables the origins of kink, strategic infanticide slows population growth	315,000 years ago
Agrarian cultures favour high birth rates, heavily restrict female sexuality and brutally enforce fidelity	12,000 years ago
Global trend towards outlawing polygyny and homosexuality	500–100 years ago
The Modern Revolution facilitates the growing independence of women, spread of birth control and decriminalisation of homosexuality	100–50 years ago
Promiscuity increases, marriages and birth rates decrease to an all-time low, the number of lonely and sexless people reaches an all-time high	50 years ago – present

PART I

EVOLUTIONARY FOREPLAY

13.8 BILLION TO 66 MILLION YEARS AGO

1

AN UNFUCKABLE UNIVERSE

13.8 billion to 2 billion years ago

Wherein the ingredients for life emerge from an inanimate cosmos • Those ingredients make their way to a newly formed Earth • Life evolves at the bottom of Earth's oceans • DNA begins its endless quest to replicate itself • Numerous catastrophic disasters compel the evolution of an unlikely, inefficient and slightly absurd process – sex.

Despite its somewhat suggestive name, the Big Bang created a Universe that was both sexless and lifeless for most of its history. As far as we know, for roughly 10 billion of the past 13.8 billion years, the cosmos was devoid of life and thus lacked any potential for sex. Yet all the ingredients for life were there at the very moment of the Big Bang 13.8 billion years ago. All the particles that make up every living thing that ever was – or will be – were trapped in the ultra-hot singularity that existed at the beginning of space and time. That fledgling matter has merely changed form since then, in a cascade of cosmic and biological evolution, with tiny particles coupling and decoupling, drifting across thousands of light years to become part of a newly created Earth. And the cream of the crop of those lifeless elements, bubbling away in Earth's early oceans, became the living, sexually intricate beings about which this story is written. It is in that sense that the matter in your body is 13.8 billion years old, whereas sex is a somewhat more recent invention.

Sex has played a pivotal role in the transformation of species in the past 2 billion years since it first evolved from microscopic asexual creatures, impregnating the natural world with its rich and brilliant diversity of forms, and making us humans the sexually complex (and confused) creatures that we are today. By travelling straight down our evolutionary lineage, we can find the origin of every blush, moan and tingling sensation that reminds us we are alive, along with many of the instincts (both good and evil) that reside in the deepest, most innate parts of our being. By understanding how we transformed from such simple inorganic material into complex living beings, with convoluted body chemistry and fragile neurology, we can understand the heart and core of the overpowering human need for intimacy, love and sex.

DATE	EVENT
13.8 billion years ago	First hydrogen for DNA
3 min after Big Bang, 13.7 billion years ago	First carbon, oxygen, nitrogen and phosphorus for DNA fused in the belly of stars
4.5 billion years ago	Formation of the solar system and Earth
4 billion years ago	Formation of the first oceans
3.8 billion years ago	Evolution of the first life
3.4 billion years ago	Evolution of photosynthesisers
3–2.5 billion years ago	The Oxygen Holocaust
2.2 billion years ago	Formation of the ozone layer
2 billion years ago	First Snowball Earth, the first eukaryotes, the evolution of sex

A LITTLE HOT UNDER THE COLLAR

At the core of all sex is DNA, an unassuming dollop of acid, a chemical that creates a panoply of instincts and peculiar bodies in its blind, single-minded effort to reproduce itself. And the core ingredients of DNA are the fundamental elements hydrogen, carbon, nitrogen, oxygen and phosphorus, none of which existed at the start of the Universe. We begin our story by explaining how that innocuous glob of acid – which eventually became responsible for every breathtaking, body-spasming, toe-curling orgasm that has ever been experienced (or faked) – came to be.

At 10^{-35} seconds after the Big Bang, the first tiny pinpricks of matter that make up your entire body were created from pure energy, then mind-bendingly hot, at around 11.3 octillion degrees Celsius. Over the next 10 seconds, in a game of musical chairs, matter and antimatter particles met and exploded in a massive burst of energy, leaving only one-billionth of the original matter that existed at the Big Bang to carry on for the rest of history, alone, without an antimatter partner. It is from this surviving sliver of existence that we are descended. After 3 minutes, that remaining fraction of matter transformed into hydrogen and helium, still super-heated, at around 10 million degrees, in a Universe dominated by violently destructive radiation.

So, in just the first 3 minutes of existence we have the emergence of hydrogen, an ingredient of DNA, and the simplest, most common element in the cosmos. In fact, hydrogen makes up approximately 75 per cent of all matter in the Universe to this day.

After a whopping 380,000 years of cooling down, to a balmy 2800°C, great plumes of gas – giant clouds trillions of kilometres long – began to fill the Universe. There was a brilliant flash, as light was able to move freely through the expanding cosmos for the first time. And we would remain in the form of clouds of hydrogen and helium gas in a lonely, lifeless cosmos for many millions of years.

Over the next 50 million years, the Universe grew dark and freezing cold. Then those wispy clouds slowly began to clump together into dense pockets, and the gas at the centre of them began to generate a ferocious heat. The resulting fire-cloud was so heavy it allowed gravity to suck in even more hydrogen and helium from the surrounding area, further building the temperature. At the core of the tempest, atoms began to be packed tight, ruthlessly forced upon each other in a process known as nuclear fusion. The pressure became so intense that hydrogen and helium atoms started to smash together, letting off continuous nuclear explosions, creating brand new elements. Thus, the stars ignited and burst forth into existence, warming the Universe again for the first time in millions of years.

These stars were so massive that they burned extremely hot and exhausted themselves after only a few million years. In their cores, they used up all their hydrogen and helium fuel and began to fuse together heavier and heavier elements, such as the carbon atoms vital to every cell in your body, the ones that all other chemical combinations into a patchwork of bone, skin and sinew. Also fused in the belly of the first stars, only a few million years after the Big Bang, were the oxygen, nitrogen and phosphorus atoms that would one day complete the double helix of DNA. We now had all the ingredients for sex, in separate atoms at the core of a giant, disorganised lump of gas we call a star.

When these giant stars could no longer take it and could no longer fuse any more atoms, they collapsed and exploded in blinding supernovas. The immense heat from these explosions created the rest of the naturally occurring elements, such as silver and gold. And while these heavy metals played no role in DNA or sex itself, they have been known to play a role in many a seduction. Supernovas thus created all the naturally occurring elements in the periodic table and scattered them across the cosmos.

We now had the building blocks for life and sex. They just all had to get in the right place at the right time to form DNA, create living creatures and eventually have some of those creatures evolve the desire to have sex with each other.

For countless eons, our atoms travelled across the vast stretch of space that, roughly 10 billion years ago, became our Milky Way galaxy. Then, about a light year away from where we are now, gravity sucked most of our matter back into a dense cloud again, creating a second-generation star, seeded with the ingredients for future life. Then, roughly 4.6 billion years ago, that star also exploded in another furious supernova, converting even more hydrogen into heavier elements, and sowing them across the patch of space where our solar system now resides.

GIVING BIRTH TO EARTH

The elements hurled into our solar system by the supernova rapidly got sucked together into a third-generation star, the grandchild of the oldest stars in the Universe. The resulting Sun was born approximately 4.567 billion years ago. With a surface area roughly 12,000 times that of Earth, the Sun devoured 99.8 per cent of all the matter in the solar system. The remaining 0.2 per cent swirled around it in a cloud composed of a fine dust, like the grey ash left after a fire. The dust cloud stretched on for over a light year in every direction. The matter that currently makes up your body floated as specks of dust in the vacuum of space.

The future Earth made up no more than 0.15 per cent of that dust cloud. And the specks of dust that would later come together to form all living things on our planet was a little less than 0.000015 per cent of that cloud. If we include the Sun, all the material for life on Earth thus constitutes roughly 0.00000003 per cent of all the stuff in the solar system, in a galaxy with 200 to 400 billion such solar systems and in a Universe of at least 400 billion such galaxies. Only a further fraction of that life (roughly half) actually has sex. That hopefully gives you an understanding of how rare and wonderful sex is when we are lucky enough to have it ...

As the dust of the solar system clumped together to form objects the size of rocks, then boulders, then mountains, their collisions became increasingly violent. Within 10 million years, the solar system had thirty proto-planets on a collision course with each other. Within another 15 million years, roughly 4.54 billion years ago, it had eight large planets, of which the newly formed Earth was the third rock from the Sun. The final planetary collision, where a proto-planet about half the size of Earth, named Theia, gouged out a huge chunk of Earth, created the planetary fragments that over the next 30 million years coalesced in Earth's orbit into the Moon. During these many apocalyptic collisions that created Earth, there was absolutely no way anything as fragile as life could have existed.

Similarly, the early Earth 4.5 billion years ago would have obliterated any life that tried to form. Every day, Earth was pelted by asteroids as large as the one that wiped out the dinosaurs. Often larger. Volcanoes many times the size of Everest erupted on a regular basis. The surface temperature of Earth could have melted lead. There were massive tsunamis composed not of saltwater but of oceans of lava.

So where were the ingredients of DNA? The hydrogen, carbon, oxygen, nitrogen and phosphorus were heated into the form of gasses and ejected out of cracks in the frail surface of Earth as steam. This was because, as Earth differentiated and heavier elements sank through the molten sludge to the core, lighter elements like those that constitute DNA bubbled to the top. In other words, we began our history on Earth as clouds. We swirled around in Earth's angry atmosphere, in a sky of blood red.

THE ORIGIN OF LIFE

Around 4 billion years ago, the surface temperature of Earth fell below the boiling point of 100°C. The steam that had been belched out of Earth's crust into the atmosphere began to fall back to Earth as rain, in a torrential downpour that continued ceaselessly for millions upon millions of years. The trenches and low-lying areas of Earth began to fill up with water, producing the world's first oceans. Among the raindrops that fell to the surface at this time were the ingredients that would soon form into life: the same organic materials that have been recycled over billions of years and that currently form your body. They found a home in the swirling chemical soup of Earth's virgin seas.

Earth 4 billion years ago was still riddled with volcanoes pumping out the carbon dioxide that formed the majority of the early Earth's atmosphere. Levels of pure oxygen in the atmosphere were negligible at best. At the bottom of Earth's oceans were underwater volcanoes and piping-hot sea vents, emitting extreme heat from a still newly molten planet. The surface of Earth was still grey, rocky and lifeless. Not a single creature, not an inch of greenery. Nothing. It more closely resembled the Moon than the verdant, luscious Earth of today.

Then, approximately 3.8 billion years ago, somewhere in the depths of the sea, the first life began to form. Organic chemicals clung together as they floated around in the swirling oceans of Earth's primordial soup. Eventually, these chemicals began to form highly complex chemical configurations, taking the shape of microscopic cells. These microscopic creatures were heated at the bottom of the oceans by underwater volcanoes. If they had ventured towards the water's surface, much less tried to stray onto land, they would have immediately been destroyed by the Sun's radiation in a world that did not yet have an ozone layer.

We can assign the date 3.8 billion years ago to the start of life because of organic chemical signatures found in rocks dated to that period that could only have been left by life. By 3.5 billion years ago, life was leaving tiny fossil imprints, etched in stone, that can be seen by a microscope. So, we can say with some confidence that life on Earth began around that time, only a few hundred million years after Earth itself formed from a fireball.

But the precise physical process and lucky sequence of events whereby organic chemicals on Earth transformed into the first living organisms remains a blank page in our history. If we knew the process, we could repeat it ourselves, and give birth to new life in every laboratory across the globe.

However, we have a pretty good idea of the 'when and where' of the story. Life emerged at the bottom of the oceans, which was far enough away from the deadly radiation of the Sun. More specifically, it emerged on the edges of underwater volcanoes. This was an ideal spot to keep life warm, and to give it the initial energy to kick-start a microbe's metabolism. We know from recent testing that the DNA held in common by all life on Earth is very similar to that of the microbes that still exist at the edge of underwater volcanoes to this day. So, it seems probable that the Last Universal Common Ancestor of all life was an organism not dissimilar to these microscopic blobs.

These ancestral microbes were carbon-based, as all life on Earth still is today. Carbon is the most flexible of all elements, forming a vital link in the chain for about 90 per cent of all chemical combinations that exist in the Universe. But these blobs also contained the elements of hydrogen, oxygen, nitrogen and phosphorus that were becoming woven together in increasingly tangled and complex chemical formulas. One of those configurations would spawn evolution and – after a spasm of transformation – sex.

THE DOUBLE HELIX

The first self-replicating organic chemicals may not have used DNA itself, but may have had a more primitive, sloppier form of reproduction that has since been lost to time. But once DNA emerged, it quickly overtook all other forms of life on Earth. As a result, literally every living thing on Earth has DNA and has a common ancestry dating back to approximately 3.8 billion years ago. That is why you share

98.4 per cent of your DNA with a chimpanzee and roughly 40 per cent with a daffodil.

The organic soup that congealed at the edges of Earth's underwater volcanoes was composed of atoms of hydrogen, carbon, oxygen, nitrogen and phosphorus. As individual atoms, they were lifeless. But by pure physical chance, they began to arrange themselves into a kind of acidic sludge. This sludge was made of nucleobases composed of the deoxygenated phosphates of adenine ($C_{10}H_{12}O_5N_5P$), cytosine ($C_9H_{12}O_6N_3P$), guanine ($C_{10}H_{12}O_6N_5P$), and thymine ($C_{10}H_{13}O_7N_2P$). Each of these chemicals are cobbled together from lifeless atoms to become the fundamental ingredients for DNA, or deoxyribonucleic acid. History's sexiest acid.

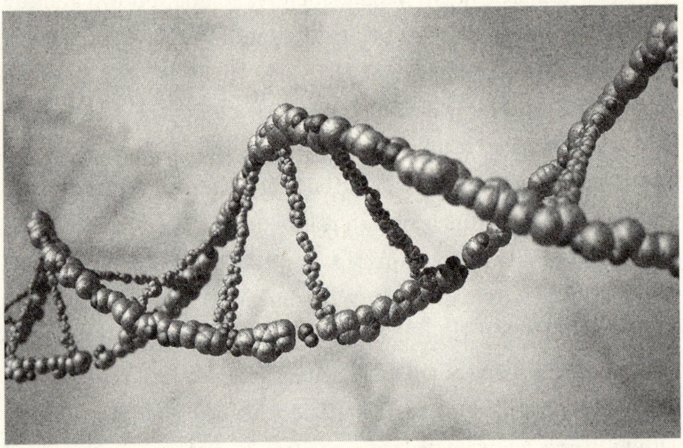

The double helix of DNA

When different elements come together in different chemical combinations, they trigger some sort of chemical reaction. For instance, think of the elementary school 'volcanoes' that result from mixing vinegar and baking soda, suddenly unleashing an eruption of foam. The arrangement of various chemicals into a double helix of

DNA is a little more complex and tangled but essentially no different. And the chemical reaction that results from an arrangement of DNA is self-replication.

In other words, the nucleic acid blindly copies itself like a mindless, eternally running fax machine. One living cell splits into two cells, and on and on it goes. This simple reaction is responsible for eons of evolution and sex: every sexual attraction, fetish and orgasm you have is the end result of a chemical reaction that has been ongoing for billions of years. At its core, sex is the result of a process not so different from mixing vinegar and baking soda. Both chemical reactions eventually produce an eruption of one kind or another.

We'll briefly dig into how that chemical process works, but do not feel stressed if, despite my valiant attempts to boil it down and my forthcoming 'metaphornication', it still sounds like technical gibberish. The main takeaway is that DNA in a living thing acts as the 'software' that tells the wider body what sort of traits a creature should have and how that creature should behave. The DNA provides the marching orders and the rest of the body carries them out by shaping the anatomy and instincts of the creature in question. In a nutshell, DNA is what makes living things look and act the way they do. From fangs to freckles, from growling to laughing.

A blob of DNA is built upon twin microscopic strands tied together in the shape of a double helix. DNA also has a companion solitary strand, called RNA (ribonucleic acid – still a nucleic acid just without being 'de-oxied' by experiencing a loss of an oxygen atom). RNA is the 'hardware' of the living cell. It unzips the double strands of DNA and 'reads' it for information, much like an Xbox reads a game disc. The RNA looks at the pattern of adenine, guanine, cytosine and thymine, which were constructed from chemical elements that had previously travelled across the Universe, in the same way computer hardware reads a binary code of ones and zeros.

The precise arrangement of these chemicals in a strand of DNA tells the RNA what the living creature is supposed to be. The RNA then takes the instructions from DNA and delivers them to parts of the cell that produce proteins (tiny factories in the cell, called ribosomes). And these proteins carry out the grunt work of 'building' the creature and imbuing it with certain traits and instincts.

To use another metaphor, DNA is the architect who develops the plans, RNA is the construction manager who barks out the orders, and proteins are the tradies busily at work riveting together the steel beams, hammering nails into walls and slapping paint on the finished product.

Everything to do with life, evolution and sex radiates out from that chemical process. If the blind, automatic machinations of DNA can be likened to dumping vinegar into a bottle of baking soda, then the origin of species, the evolution of cocks and vaginas, and the sensations one feels when confronted with a bit of lude sexual imagery are collectively the wild, messy foam that spurts forth.

THE HEART OF EVOLUTION

Provided that the living creature survives, the DNA it carries will copy itself in order to continue giving 'building instructions' to the rest of the body for the duration of its lifetime. When a cell copies itself, it splits in two. Most of the time the DNA replicates itself flawlessly. But one time in roughly a billion, there is a 'copying error' or mutation, which slightly modifies the DNA's instructions, and thus creates a slightly different living creature.

It is those accidental mutations that eventually, over many generations and hundreds of thousands of years, give rise to different species. Yes, it is actually an error that gives rise to all evolutionary history. If 'copying errors' did not occur, there would be no evolution; life would have remained exactly as it was 3.8 billion years ago, huddling in microscopic blobs on the edges of undersea volcanoes.

Some of these random mutations are deadly to an organism,

adversely affecting the creature's health and cutting its life short. Some mutations don't affect survival one way or another. And some prove quite useful for survival, providing an edge over competing organisms in a harsh environment where death is always just around the corner. Those mutations that work the best in a specific environment continue to exist. If not, they (and the organisms possessing those mutations) die out.

For instance, let's say you have three wolves. One wolf has a random mutation that makes it be born without legs. It will likely not survive and its DNA will no longer be able to copy itself. Another wolf has a tongue that is 1 centimetre longer than average. That mutation is unlikely to impact its survival one way or another. The third wolf has a mutation that makes its fur a greenish colour, which turns out to be handy camouflage in the leafy forest where it lives. The third wolf will thrive. Yet, after several generations, if the environment changes and leafy forest gives way to snowy tundra, then being a 'green' wolf suddenly would become a detriment to survival. Those wolves that evolved white fur would slowly outcompete the previously successful 'green' wolves, driving them to extinction.

That is how DNA is the core of evolution: the random mutation of a creature's genes and the natural selection of those mutations that allow DNA to survive and continue copying itself. In short, random mutation and non-random elimination. And as environments change, so do the mutations that work best.

Thus, 3.8 billion years ago, microscopic blobs living on the edge of underwater volcanoes began to survive and evolve. They were kept warm by the heat of Earth. They chomped down organic chemicals in the primordial sludge around them. And these microbes split themselves again and again and again, in an endless process as their DNA copied itself.

But these microbes did not fuck. They merely cloned themselves asexually.

THE DISASTROUS ORIGINS OF SEX

The first life 3.8 billion years ago was relatively simple. They were creatures known as prokaryotes: single-celled microscopic organisms where DNA strands floated openly around the cell, increasing the risk of it getting damaged. But they survived, and the bottom of Earth's oceans began to become overcrowded with living little blobs.

To overcome the shortage of 'real estate' 3.4 billion years ago, some prokaryotes evolved to live near the surface of the oceans, no longer keeping themselves warm with underwater volcanoes. Instead, these new microscopic blobs evolved to use the Sun's energy. They used photosynthesis, converting water, sunlight and carbon dioxide (CO_2) in the atmosphere to feed themselves. Just like plants today. And just like plants today, they pumped oxygen (O_2) into the atmosphere as a waste product. The problem is that oxygen is highly turbulent, can create violent chemical reactions and in large quantities could kill fragile primitive life like those ancestral microbes that had evolved on an early Earth where there was very little oxygen in the atmosphere.

By 2.5 billion years ago, microscopic photosynthesisers had increased the level of oxygen in the atmosphere from next to nothing to 2.5 per cent. This nasty chemical killed off scores of microbes in an event known as the Oxygen Holocaust, Earth's first known mass extinction event and one of the only mass extinction events (before humans) kicked off by living organisms rather than an asteroid impact or a super-volcanic eruption.

The surviving microbes evolved an increasing tolerance for oxygen in the atmosphere. Some of them even evolved the ability to consume oxygen instead of carbon dioxide, reversing which chemical was food and which waste. These were the first aerobic species, microscopic creatures similar in that respect to humans and other animals. We inhale oxygen, we exhale carbon dioxide.

But photosynthesisers remained the majority of living things on Earth and continued to create unmitigated disasters by pumping out oxygen. Enough O_2 had gathered in the atmosphere 2.2 billion years ago that the oxygen atoms began to group together in threes, creating ozone (O_3). The resulting ozone layer that blanketed Earth reflected a lot of the Sun's rays back into space. While we desperately require the ozone layer to protect us from solar radiation today, in the short term 2.2 billion years ago, this was not a good thing. Photosynthesising life continued to increase the thickness of the ozone layer. As a result, Earth got colder and colder. The oceans froze at the poles. Then the ice spread down towards the equator, encasing the entire planet in a frozen prison, in the first 'Snowball Earth' event, roughly 2 billion years ago. The average global temperature would have been around −50°C.

Snowball Earth imposed a strain on the microbes living in the now ice-covered oceans. As a result of the strain, a new kind of microbe evolved: the eukaryote. These are 'beefier' cells, 10 to 1000 times the size of prokaryotes, which also evolved to protect their DNA by keeping it in a central nucleus instead of letting the strands just float around the cell. We humans are descended from these eukaryotes, as are all the ancestors and descendants in the evolutionary tree of the plant and animal kingdoms. And it is these tiny eukaryotic blobs that were the first creatures to have sex.

In the same disastrous Snowball Earth period, these microscopic eukaryotes began to engage in carnal relations with one another – as does 99.9 per cent of all eukaryotic life today. The habit stuck and has grown only more thrilling and perplexing. But the question of how and why our microbial ancestors began to feel compelled to exchange genetic information, in the same way two people might exchange phone numbers at a bar, remains shrouded in mystery.

SEX, STARVATION AND HANNIBAL LECTER

There is very little question that sex first evolved around 2 billion years ago as a response to the pressures imposed on our tiny ancestors by the harsh and unforgiving environment of Snowball Earth. Or a similar catastrophe that has since been lost to the passage of time. Otherwise, sex makes very little sense for living things to do. From an outsider's perspective, then as now, sex was a somewhat absurd and costly process.

Imagine that you are a strand of DNA. Your one goal in the Universe is to copy yourself relentlessly. Therefore, why share space with a different strand of DNA from another organism? When you clone yourself asexually, as all living things did from 3.8 billion to 2 billion years ago, you copy 100 per cent of your genetics. Well done. Mission accomplished. But once you combine your genes with those of another microscopic blob, you only successfully copy and pass on 50 per cent of your genes. In other words, this is directly against DNA's raison d'être. A living creature would not have evolved to behave that way unless it was forced to by outside circumstances.

Furthermore, as an asexual creature that just clones itself, you do not require a mate to produce offspring. You can just keep pumping out a huge number all by yourself, potentially creating a colony of hundreds or thousands of offspring in a matter of hours. Again, mission accomplished: that's a lot of copying. However, once you throw sex into the mix, population growth inevitably slows down. It now requires two organisms to create offspring, and it takes time to locate such a mate and to exchange DNA with them. The first evolution of sex thus only makes sense in constrained situations where having a large, fast-growing population was a negative thing and having too many offspring would risk starving everyone. Like a family of fifteen in a famine rather than a family of three. Instead, the act of sex managed to impose population control by slowing down the pace of reproduction in an environment where food and resources were scarce. Just the sort of conditions that would have prevailed on Snowball Earth.

A third problem arises from the fact that mixing the genes of two organisms in sex creates more genetic variation. This means a DNA copying error is more likely than in asexual cloning. And this increases the risk of a microbe 2 billion years ago being born with a mutation that would have killed it or reduced its chances of survival. Remember, not all genetic mutations are good. Many of them can kill you. The only scenario in which switching to sex and greater genetic variation would be an advantage is in a disastrous situation such as Snowball Earth, where living things needed to roll the genetic dice as fast and as frequently as possible to evolve useful evolutionary traits that would allow their offspring to survive in a hellish, starving environment. To put it slightly more crudely, 2 billion years ago our ancestors felt so much pressure from the environment that they needed to fuck in order to survive.

But how would the act of sex have physically emerged in the first place in a world where only microbes had existed, happily cloning themselves, for the previous 1.8 billion years? How and why did the first sexually charged eukaryotes have such a bright idea? The proposed answer may disturb you.

A credible and compelling theory is that the first exchange of DNA between two living things may have been accidental. Two billion years ago, Snowball Earth may have reduced the food available to our eukaryotic ancestors to such an extent that some microbial blobs may have started to eat each other. In a word, cannibalism. When an asexual eukaryotic cell consumed another one, there may have been an accidental exchange of DNA. The strands of the devoured victim may have become intertwined with the DNA of the hungry predator.

The offspring of such a grisly union may well have possessed some slight advantage in a frozen environment. What that precise advantage was, we cannot be sure. But the process of sexually reproducing, thus producing more frequent mutations, allowed these eukaryotes to speed up evolution and adapt faster to their grim environment.

All that was required of these microbes was for the continued shortage of food and the grotesque cannibalistic exchange to occur several more times in a starving colony of microbes over a few short years before it became naturally selected. From there, the habit of sexually reproducing and combining two sets of DNA was no longer an accident but an evolutionary behaviour that two organisms were driven to do.

Let me take a moment to extend my deepest apologies to the reader for revealing that some of the most intimate and romantic experiences of their lives may in fact have their origins in a desperate act of cannibalism.

Regardless of how the first sex act emerged, once it was naturally selected for in a small population of eukaryotic blobs, it took off like wildfire. Despite the numerous disadvantages in the short term, once sex got into our DNA (literally) its evolutionary advantages became immensely potent in the long term.

SEX IS WONDERFUL

The first major advantage to sex is the greater genetic variation that comes from having two parents, which can speed up the pace of evolution and adaptation. Sure, genetic variation can increase the odds of getting a mutation that can kill you, and this risk would have intimidated our asexual ancestors from daring to do the devil's deed prior to 2 billion years ago. But once that Pandora's box was opened and living things were forced to deal with the risk of passing on bad mutations, they also leaned hard into its potential advantages in order to compensate. When you combine two strands of DNA, you may get a combination of physical traits and instincts that would not have occurred by a mere copying error from cloning. To use a simplistic example, a child who inherits his father's rakish good looks and his mother's profound intelligence may well be more fit for survival and to have children of his own one day. If the child had merely been cloned from his father's DNA, he would simply be a beautiful idiot.

A second advantage is that sex can increase the odds that unhealthy genes are eliminated, if the genes in question are recessive rather than dominant, in the same way that red hair is recessive and black hair dominant. If an asexual creature has a mutation that endangers its survival, the trait may simply be cloned again and again and again, until the creature goes extinct. But if a sexually reproducing organism has a negative mutation and then a sexual partner imports more dominant and healthy genes, they may eliminate the 'bad' set of genes. To use another simplistic example, let's say a child's father has a greater risk of heart disease in his family history. And let's say what causes this malady is a recessive gene. Then a mother comes in with a more dominant gene from a family of healthier, more robust hearts, and the dominant gene replaces the recessive one, just like dark hair replaces red hair (no offence to my redhead brethren, you are all beautiful and sexy, I am just using a common example of recessive genes). Again, there is a clear evolutionary advantage in combining two sets of genes rather than simply cloning oneself. In a nutshell, when it comes to sex, it pays to share.

A third advantage is that sex imposes moderation on evolution. Cloning can copy even the most wild, dramatic and grotesque DNA mutations, whereas sex tends to filter these mutations out because sex requires a viable partner. For example, let's say our poor hypothetical child was born with a mutation that gave him eight spider-like legs, eighteen yellow eyes, and a 26-foot-long penis with a dagger-like stinger at the end. If the child reproduced asexually, that dramatic mutation would be cloned. But being a sexually reproducing creature, it is unlikely that child will find a mate willing to risk having sex with him, so the wild mutations will die with him. In wider nature, mutations that are too dramatic generally don't find compatible mates, which prevents a flood of dramatic and potentially deadly mutations from being thrown into the more gradual process of evolutionary change.

A fourth advantage is that sex between two creatures can confer greater resistances to viruses and diseases. An asexual organism is only capable of developing immune resistance to a disease by a random mutation during cloning. Two sexual organisms potentially bring different lineages with different resistances to disease and combine them, building upon them with each generation. Again, to use a simplistic example, dad brings with him a resistance to smallpox and mum brings with her a resistance to bubonic plague. Their child may potentially inherit resistances to both. As such, sex may provide an immense advantage in the evolutionary arms race between parasites and their potential hosts.

And so, once sex took off in our evolutionary timeline, it proved enormously useful for evolution. Sure, DNA had to make the sacrifice of only copying 50 per cent of itself and combining with the genetics of another creature. But in exchange, it increased the odds of its own survival – you can't keep copying yourself if you are dead and your species goes extinct.

Furthermore, sex bequeathed upon those hardy, horny eukaryotes the potential for rapid evolution into increasingly complex species. From tiny, microscopic blobs existing in Earth's oceans to relatively gigantic multicelled creatures that evolved into fish, amphibians, reptiles and mammals. In the next chapter we shall see how, alongside this greater biological complexity, sex also became increasingly intricate and bizarre. And amid the chaos of copulation, we can discern the lineage of our own sexual anatomy, physical sensations and romantic instincts. The origins of these things are evolutionarily distant from us – on timescales of thousands and millions of years – but they are unmistakably and unquestionably part of what makes us human.

2

UNDERWATER FUMBLES AND TUMBLES

2 billion to 375 million years ago

Wherein recurrent frozen disasters spur the evolution of multi-celled life • In bodies composed of trillions of cells sex specialists called 'gametes' appear • The hermaphroditic worm-like ancestors of vertebrates begin '69ing' • These worms evolve into Cambrian fish with primitive brains • Fish in our direct line of ancestry evolve gonochorism • Our ancestors adopt the rather dull practice of external fertilisation • Sexual competition and the 'battle of the sexes' evolve in vertebrates • The earliest tetrapods decide to crawl out of the oceans and have sex on the beach.

The tyranny of the first Snowball Earth 2 billion years ago, which had compelled the evolution of our eukaryotic ancestors and the origin of sex, was eventually broken by the forces of geology. New volcanoes emerged out of Earth's crust as a result of shifting plate tectonics. They pierced through the sheets of ice covering the planet and began pumping tonnes of carbon dioxide into the atmosphere. This reversed the process of oxygen-heavy cooling, and the gigantic ice sheets receded and then disappeared. Earth became warm and temperate once again.

However, the only living creatures inhabiting the planet were still microscopic and single-celled. There was no reason for these tiny organic blobs to evolve into anything larger or more complex. That transformation would require a great deal of energy to sustain, and larger size would induce a fragility that could endanger a species' survival. Life tends towards simplicity unless it is forced to do otherwise. And for the next billion years, our microscopic ancestors survived, more or less, just fine.

Meanwhile, the existential threat of Snowball Earth loomed, as the clash between carbon dioxide and oxygen for dominance in the atmosphere bounced the planet between phases of extreme cooling and temperate warming. Photosynthesisers still existed on the surface of Earth's oceans, and periodically began guzzling carbon dioxide and emitting oxygen as a waste product, cooling the planet yet again. This process was exacerbated by regular Milankovitch cycles, when Earth tilts further away from the Sun, spurring along more moderate ice ages, just like the last one humans experienced 115,000 to 12,000 years ago. That ice age was bad but was nowhere near as devastating as a Snowball Earth.

As a result of cycles of extreme cooling, in the last billion years we have experienced two more Snowball Earth phases, when glaciation has met at the equator and entombed the planet. One occurred approximately 700 million years ago. Not long after Earth had recovered, a second one began 650 million years ago and ended 635 million years ago. This was the last Snowball Earth, thus far, in natural history. It provoked another profound change in the history of life, and irrevocably changed the nature of sex, transforming it beyond a mere exchange of DNA between two tiny blobs.

DATE	EVENT
650 million years ago	Evolution of multicellularism and gametes
635 million years ago	Ediacaran 69ing worm hermaphrodites
525 million years ago	Cambrian fish with brains
510 million years ago	Evolution of external fertilisation and gonochorism
400 million years ago	Intensification of vertebrate sex strategies
375 million years ago	The first tetrapods on land

FRIENDS WITH BENEFITS

For the past 3 billion years, microscopic life lived in colonies of thousands, even millions, of cells in the ocean. Each were separate and distinct organisms, but nevertheless thriving in a community. Some of these blobs even developed symbiotic partnerships with each other, to increase the odds of both surviving. This went double for sexually reproducing eukaryotes, who already depended on exchanging DNA with each other in order to perpetuate their various microbial species and keep the DNA replication process going.

When the last Snowball Earth phase struck 650 million years ago, these communities of symbiotic microbes became ever more dependent on one another in order to survive the sub-zero conditions. Time is fleeting for living creatures, and a single-celled organism only has enough energy to do a limited number of things in any given day. During Snowball Earth, different microbes began to fulfil different functions for each other. Some set about breaking down food, some focused on discarding waste products from that food, and others spent their time solely on the act of sex and the replication of their DNA.

This last (fortunate) group of cells specialised in the process of meiosis and fertilisation, where the cell is initially split with half the chromosomes from its 'mother cell' and then is fertilised with half the chromosomes of the 'father cell' to complete the sex act. From there, a new organism is born. Whereas in the previous 1.4 billion years all pairs of microscopic blobs performed the sex act, now, increasingly, only a select few cells operated in this sphere – canoodling while other microbes in the colony were busying themselves at less titillating work. These lucky reproductive blobs are called the gametes, otherwise known as the sex cells of the body. The microbial world's courtesans and gigolos. In humans, these gametes are the sperm and the eggs. Not every cell in the human body can reproduce. Your hair follicles aren't going to be impregnating anyone anytime soon. That is the specialist role of the gametes.

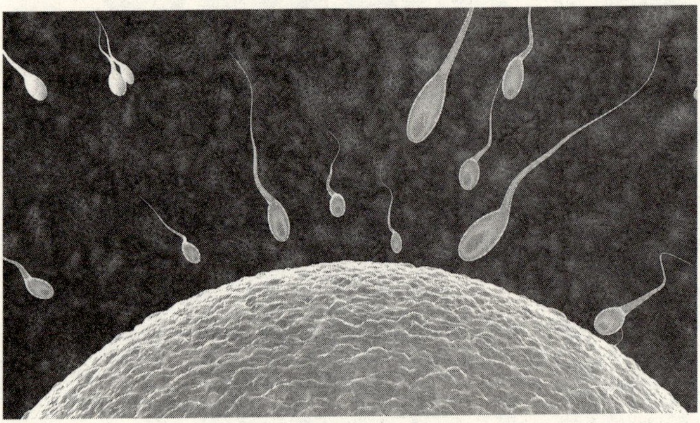

A meeting of gametes

Thus, as symbiosis intensified under the pressures of Snowball Earth, it was as if all the tiny blobs were suddenly working in a giant office building. Some of them worked the mail room, some in accounting, some took out the trash and some of them, to stretch the metaphor, focused solely on banging in the stationery closet or on the conference room table.

Eventually different cells became so intertwined and dependent on each other that if one group of specialists died, the rest would die. And it was through this excessive co-dependence, an immoderate amount of symbiosis, that the first multicelled organisms (the eukaryotic ancestors of plants, animals and fungi) were born.

You are a multicellular eukaryote. A giant corporation of 37 trillion individual organic cells. That is roughly 100 times the number of stars in the Milky Way galaxy. But these cells don't just live in a giant colony where they act symbiotically towards one another. They cannot live without each other. Your liver doesn't just have symbiosis with the rest of your body. It cannot act independently and crawl along behind you when you go to the shops. It is such an inextricable part of your being that you are, for all intents and purposes, one structure, one organism.

And so, between 650 million and 635 million years ago, multicelled creatures with sexual anatomy and the capacity for increasingly intricate sexual instincts emerged. Until now, sex represented little more than a stale chemical reaction between organisms that we cannot even see with the naked eye. But after the final Snowball Earth and the emergence of multicellularism, it was only a matter of time before penetration, masturbation, lust, jealousy, orgasms, oral sex and (more distantly) bukkake parties entered our evolutionary lexicon. But each of these evolved in stages and in building blocks in the line of our ancestry.

WORMING ONE'S WAY INTO SEX

The Ediacaran era dawned 635 million years ago with a warm climate, thanks to volcanoes pumping CO_2 into the atmosphere. At this time, all multicellular life existed in the oceans. And because multicelled beings were as yet evolutionarily untested, a bizarre array of forms emerged that would have done H.P. Lovecraft proud for their outlandishness. For instance, Aspidella were strange disc-like creatures that sat on the ocean floor and had no mouth or anus, instead absorbing food and shitting it out again through pores in their skin. Strange eukaryotic multicelled plants also began to make an appearance.

The ancestors of humans, and indeed all animals, in the Ediacaran era is currently thought to have been a worm-like creature less than a centimetre long: not much bigger than a grain of rice. These ancestral worms burrowed into the soft sand on the floor of the ocean and moved by contracting their muscles and stretching them out again as they slithered along. What scaffolding existed inside these worms was simply soft tubes filled with fluid. They also likely possessed a primitive mouth, anus and digestive tract.

The bodies of these worms would have had sense receptors to detect nearby environmental stimuli, but because those nerves had not yet clustered into a brain at one end or another, they did not have an identifiable head. And because they lacked a brain, they had extremely limited self-awareness and next to no consciousness, and would have reacted only to immediate stimulation from the environment. Not unlike the single-celled creatures from which they were descended. This means that when our Ediacaran worm ancestors had sex, they were not able to contemplate it, let alone experience pleasure. And they had no sexual instincts. Their copulations were mechanical, knee-jerk and thoroughly uninspiring. But we all have to start somewhere.

Ediacaran worms were soft-bodied, meaning they leave very little trace in the fossil record. This deprives us of a direct glimpse of their sexual anatomy. However, looking at their evolutionary precursors and descendants, it seems highly probable that each worm possessed both sperm and eggs, being capable of filling either reproductive role. In other words, the common ancestors of the animal kingdom may well have been hermaphrodites: both biological sexes at once. The worms would carry their eggs in a pouch located on their bodies, along with having an imperceptibly small hole or pore from which would ooze the equivalent of 'worm-sperm'. They had no penis to speak of.

After being born and passing the few weeks required to reach sexual maturity, these worms would have bumped into one of their compatriots somewhere underground and mechanically begun the process of primitive copulation. The two worms would likely '69': that is to say, line up alongside each other so that each partner's mouth and anus were at opposite ends. The two lovers would press tightly up against each other, and the sperm would trickle out of one worm and enter the other via pores in its egg sack.

In this way the eggs would be fertilised. All of this would take no more than a few seconds before each worm slithered along its merry way in search of the day's food (tiny nutrients within the ocean floor). The impregnated worm would carry the fertilised egg for a brief period before sliding it out of the sack (possibly protected by a cocoon) and leaving it safely burrowed in the sand of the ocean floor.

After the baby worm matured inside the egg, it would hatch and start the process of DNA replication all over again. While Ediacaran sex amounted to a rather uninspiring tryst, it did have the virtue of being efficient. The same can be said of innumerable passionless human marriages today, so who are we to judge?

Worms 69ing

EXPLOSIVE SEX ON THE BRAIN

The Cambrian period began 541 million years ago, and within 2 million years there was a proverbial explosion of different species, rapidly evolving and filling new niches in the environment. The Cambrian Explosion began approximately 539 million years ago and is so-called because of the sudden appearance of a wild diversity of new forms in the fossil record within the next 15 million years, until all available ecological niches in the Cambrian oceans were filled (the land remained uninhabited). This acceleration of evolution is referred to as an adaptive radiation.

It was around this time that our direct ancestral line of vertebrates (literally anything with a spine) split off from the lineages of several other animal groups. Namely, the arthropods (trilobites, scorpions, spiders, lobsters, etc), the echinoderms (starfish, sea urchins, sand dollars, etc), the molluscs (snails, octopi, clams, etc), the Cnidaria (jellyfish, corals, etc) and roughly three dozen other smaller phyla of animals. In this book we zero in on our line of descent, in order to showcase everything the human sexual experience is built upon. We don't have room to explore the sexual predilections of every creature on Earth (that little romp with Mother Nature will have to wait for another book).

At the time of the Cambrian explosion, our direct ancestors were still looking decidedly worm-like, and still only a few centimetres long, but with a few important differences. First, they no longer spent most of their time burrowing into the sand on the ocean floor. Instead, our ancestors likely swam like miniature eels, swishing their tails back and forth, propelling themselves through the ocean. They sought nutrients in open waters rather than sheltering on the ocean floor.

Second, and perhaps more strikingly, by 530 million years ago, our ancestors had developed a primitive spine. A simple rod running along the length of the worm, around which various nerve endings gathered to tell the worm about the surrounding environment. This was still very basic information: various changes in water temperature, whether there was food directly in front of them ready to eat, whether there were any other animals (possible predators) swishing about in the nearby water, and, of course, the possible presence of sexual partners. Initially, the same game of 69ing continued between these worm-like creatures, but this was soon to change.

All stimuli (food, predator or sexual partner) would still produce kneejerk, mechanical reactions in these worms. They had very little in the way of self-awareness, and no consciousness whatsoever. However, since the worms were now swimming through the oceans rather than burrowing in sand, they constantly had one end of them facing forward. This had profound results.

One end of the worm was usually the first to encounter food, danger or sex. This led to the process of cephalisation, where sensory nerve endings are increasingly grouped at one end of the body: what would soon evolve into a 'head'. Those nerve endings become so tangled at one end of the worm that the resulting fleshy knot came to resemble a brain. As part of their mounting senses, they also evolved a pair of eyes they could use to detect movement in the waters ahead of them. And in order to aid their propulsion through the waters, they evolved fins. By 525 million years ago, within just 5 million years, we had evolved from worms into primitive jawless fish.

And this is where the evolutionary history of sex gets very fishy indeed. Both figuratively and literally. There was an explosion of different sexual methods and anatomy that makes it difficult, but not impossible, to discern the order of our evolutionary lineage. We shall endeavour to reconstruct things based on the best currently available information.

GUYS AND DOLLS, GUYS AND GUYS, DOLLS AND DOLLS

Much like the Ediacaran worms that came before them, the first Cambrian jawless fish were likely hermaphrodites, carrying both eggs and sperm. From there, some fish remained hermaphrodites but, instead of being two sexes at once, evolved the ability to become one sex or another. In other words, at one stage in their life they carried eggs only, and then after a period of growth the same fish carried sperm only. Instinctually, these fish were capable of transitioning between fertilising and egg-laying behaviours and the sex practices that go with them. Traits of either 'simultaneous' or 'sequential' hermaphrodism were retained by numerous deep-sea fish and evolved again many millions of years later in some exotic shallow-water fish that began living in complicated hierarchies. By and large, however, hermaphrodism in fish gradually fell into the evolutionary minority, but one that still encompassed numerous species.

It seems a split happened fairly early on, approximately 510 million years ago, where increasing numbers of species of Cambrian fish adopted gonochorism; in other words, they became either biologically male or female throughout their entire lives, a trait held by most fish species to this day. This evolutionary tendency increased as their sexual equipment became more intricate and took more energy to grow, thus disincentivising the practice of growing both. Only a powerful inverse evolutionary incentive would cause a fish to retain or re-evolve hermaphrodism.

As such, most Cambrian fish evolved more defined and recognisable sexual anatomy. Male fish initially evolved one testicle, located in the middle of their bodies. Similarly, female fish initially evolved one ovary. Gradually, over the next 100 million years, fish doubled their chances and males and females evolved to have a pair of balls or ovaries, which is a common trait in numerous types of vertebrates.

However, random genetic mutations in DNA still occur that produce hermaphrodites with fully functioning sets of both genitalia in many gonochoristic vertebrate species in our direct ancestral line, at estimated rates of one in every 100 million to 10 billion, depending on the species. A considerably larger proportion of individuals in typically gonochoristic species are born with ambiguous or intersex genitalia: an estimated one in every 10,000 to 1 million, depending on the species. In the latter group, rates of infertility are fairly high, which is why once a species becomes gonochoristic, the species leans heavily in that direction.

We also see the start of bisexual behaviour almost from the start of sex differences in vertebrates. Because of the gradual evolutionary transition from hermaphrodism to gonochorism, the shift away from having sex with any other individual in the species towards only copulating with the opposite sex was equally gradual. This was aided by the fact that early Cambrian sensory development was not so far advanced to permit primitive fish to always reliably distinguish between male and female sex partners, even if homosexual encounters did not produce offspring.

As such, an instinct towards strict heterosexuality did not accompany the shift towards gonochorism. Far from it. Some individuals within gonochoristic species copulated with both opposite-sex and same-sex partners in their lifetimes. This is reinforced by the fact that bisexual activity exists in most vertebrate species (that have not subsequently evolved to be asexual again) to one degree or another, implying that bisexuality is a common trait that is half a billion years old. We also see a parallel emergence of bisexuality in Cambrian arthropods, suggesting that bisexual behaviour is practically evolutionarily inherent to any form of gonochorism. In other words, where there are sex differences, there is sex other than the hetero stuff.

As for exclusively homosexual individuals in a species engaging only with same-sex partners throughout their lifetimes – and seldom or never with opposite-sex partners – we have indication of this in vertebrates descending from the Carboniferous, roughly 200 million years later. However, absence of evidence thus far is not evidence of absence, and it is highly conceivable that exclusively homosexual individuals in gonochoristic species go as far back as sex differences themselves, just like bisexuality does. Watch this space for future research.

As for why non-hetero sex might be evolutionarily passed down through vertebrate species for half a billion years even though it does not result in offspring, there are numerous explanations and it is currently a subject of intense study. The prominent hypotheses centre on pre-birth hormones or genetics – or a mixture of both. The hormones theory posits that while an embryo is still developing in an egg, hormones may produce non-heterosexual instincts in a minority of individuals (the actual rate varies wildly depending on the species). Regarding genetics, there is no discernible 'gay gene', but rather homosexuality likely emerges from a combination of many interwoven genes. Many of those genes influence receptiveness to pre-birth hormones, hence the possible mixture of the two factors.

Regardless of the precise cause, non-hetero sex has existed for hundreds of millions of years, because there was never any reason for natural selection to rule it out. First, many individuals in a vertebrate species who engage with same-sex partners also engage with opposite-sex partners. And while average rates of offspring are slightly reduced for such individuals, they are not reduced anywhere near to zero. Second, even those individuals in vertebrate species who are exclusively homosexual have close relatives with very similar DNA. Their hetero and bisexual siblings and cousins produced offspring and were carriers of the same factors that produced non-hetero activity. In other words, no species has ever gone extinct from having gay, lesbian or bisexual relatives. So non-hetero activity has likely been a fixture in multicellular species as long as the very gonochoristic sex differences that define them have been. Two sides of the same coin.

A FISHY WAY TO HAVE SEX

When it came to doing the deed itself, an early transition made sex decidedly less fun for fish – even less fun than mindless worm-sex. Gone were the days of 69ing. At least for now. Early jawless Cambrian fish appear to have adopted a method of sex that did not involve bodily contact, much less penetration (something yet to appear). Instead, fish evolved a system of external sex. A female fish would unleash its gelatinous squishy eggs into the ocean, and a nearby male would swim up and squirt sperm upon them. A rather impersonal form of insemination, much like using a sperm bank but cutting out the middleman. In the case of homosexual encounters, numerous externally fertilising fish exuded sex pheromones or initiated mating behaviours and displays usually reserved for the opposite sex.

As disappointing as external fertilisation may sound to human ears, slightly kinkier is the fact that small primitive Cambrian fish likely practised external sex in groups rather than as couples. A piscine orgy, if you will. A group of male and female fish would approach a patch of water and lay eggs and ejaculate sperm. With so many gametes in the water, it was less likely that they would all be eaten by other creatures in the Cambrian seas, allowing some fertilised eggs to survive until they hatched. The evolutionary downside of this is it made it less likely for an individual male to guarantee his specific DNA code would be replicated and carried on. And, as we've already explored, the primary goal of any kind of sex is to carry on the fundamental chemical reaction of a glob of DNA replicating itself.

Accordingly, some larger fish species evolved some semblance of monogamy, where a male and a female fish would scuttle off into more private waters and carry out the deed between themselves. This guaranteed fertilisation of the eggs by a specific male. But it also made it necessary for fish to be more careful of their eggs being eaten by predators, and led to a certain a degree of sexual competition between males for access to mates – a contest that was usually (but not always) settled by body size. This led to one of the earliest examples of sexual dimorphism in vertebrates, where there are significant physiological differences between biological sexes. In this case, male fish in some species steadily grew to be larger than females, and better at warding off smaller males from pushing in on all the fun.

This kicked off an arms race of sexual selection, where larger males sometimes had an advantage in breeding. The evolutionary incentive started to spawn larger and larger fish species as the millennia went by. Without this competition, it is difficult to say whether vertebrates would have evolved the way they did, perhaps negating the entire history of our family tree from 500 million years ago onwards. Preventing the vertebrate colonisation of the land, and erasing amphibians, reptiles and mammals, and perhaps even confining us to being rather small jawless guppies in Earth's oceans to this day.

In the initial stages of our evolution, early Cambrian fish remained quite small (a few centimetres long) and thus did not require much energy to grow into full size. The leftover energy could be used to spawn new eggs and sperm frequently and to have sex on a semi-regular basis. Lucky fish. But as they began to increase in size, there was less energy to be devoted to producing gametes, so sex for some species became less and less frequent. Perhaps only once a year. However, fish didn't grow too old to mate during their lifetimes, meaning that unlike many species they did not become barren or impotent. Once a fish became sexually mature, they stayed that way and continued popping out eggs or shooting out sperm until death.

Unfortunately, regardless of the method or frequency of sex, it is unlikely that Cambrian fish experienced awareness of it, let alone pleasure. They held very limited consciousness – some would argue none at all. Cambrian fish brains were extremely primitive, lacking a cerebral cortex. Fish reacted to all stimuli reflexively. Predator nearby? Run away! Female laying eggs nearby? Go and squirt! It is highly unlikely that things went beyond that. Consciousness resulted from a build-up of sensory detectors and a tangle of nerve endings in the brain – all that perceived information being relayed to the brain led to a sort of 'movie' playing in the creature's head, allowing some degree of awareness and self-reflection. But we are many, many millions of years away from that point. Sex remained, for now, a highly mechanical and passionless act.

THE DIVERSIFICATION OF FISH-FUCKING

As the Ordovician period dawned 485 million years ago, the climate became warmer, due to ten times the amount of CO_2 being pumped into the atmosphere by volcanism and other sources. The ocean was extremely favourable to life, with average temperatures ranging between 25°C to and 40°C. This was good news for the evolution of our fishy ancestors. Overall, the number of marine species quadrupled. It was also during this period that the first plants and fungi began to colonise the land.

However, the Ordovician period ended in a mass extinction 444 million years ago, with a cooling period that killed off many warm-water species, followed by another rapid warming period that killed off many of the cool-water species that had recently adapted to the change in environment. All told, approximately 70 per cent of all marine species went extinct. But extinction events generally had a tendency of accelerating evolutionary change, as the niches in the environment were filled again by intrepid new species.

The Silurian period that followed this extinction event saw the further expansion of plants and fungi on land, penetrating deeper into the rocky terrain from coastlines and river valleys and gradually turning the surface of Earth green for the first time. The arthropods (exoskeleton-shelled ancestors of modern bugs) soon joined plant species on the surface, feeding on the plants. Meanwhile, our vertebrate ancestors were not yet ready to venture onto land.

In the oceans, our fishy family had evolved jaws, more elaborate nervous systems and slightly larger brains. The sharks also evolved at this time and split off from our family tree. Fish increased in size and biological complexity, which inevitably impacted the evolution of sex. Some fish species began 'nesting' on one patch of the shallow ocean floor in order to protect eggs from predators (mostly larger fish) and to enforce monogamy in some species.

Sometimes the male fish would be tasked with creating appealing underwater nests by carving burrows and shapes in the sand. If the nest was appealing enough, a female would swim up and deposit her eggs, ready for fertilisation. This is an early evolutionary example of males wooing females by showing off their worth as desirable mates who could facilitate reproduction. In other words, maximising the likelihood that DNA would be copied and some of those offspring would survive to have children of their own. Thus making that particular sex session worth a female's while. A male fish, by and large, was able to rapidly fertilise many eggs, whereas a female fish invested more energy in producing them and thus had to be more choosey about who she mated with. Such were the beginnings of 'the economics of gametes', the horse-trading between males and females over access to sex in exchange for the time and energy each mate invested in their sex cells.

The economics of gametes has influenced the evolution of many sexual instincts and rituals in countless species over the past several hundred million years. For example, if you have ever wondered why, among humans, a man's job seems to be an important criterion in dating for most women, yet a woman's job seems to factor into the average man's affections to a considerably lesser degree (speaking very generally about the dating population as a whole – in a species as intellectually complex as humans there are always exceptions to the rule) the economics of gametes is a big part of why. We shall return to the tangled web of human negotiations over sex in due course. But it all started here, half a billion years ago.

One could say that the Silurian period produced the first glimmer in vertebrates of the proverbial battle of the sexes. But the process of courtship was not always cut and dried. Some female fish evolved the tactic of swimming up to a decent nest and merely pretending to lay eggs, in order to attract nearby males who had not built the nest but might prove genetically more attractive mates for actual reproduction. Thus, in our distant vertebrate ancestry we also see the first glimmers of cuckoldry, whereby a male bids to be selected as a 'nice guy' mate, only for the female to benefit from that work but select a more attractive male interloper instead.

In other cases, female fish would lay sterile eggs mixed with fertile ones, hoping that the best of the competing male mates would be able to distinguish between the sterile and fertile ones, eating the former and inseminating the latter. At a bound, sex became a great deal more complicated and the barriers to successful copulation were erected higher and higher, in the interests of making sure only the finest male specimens were permitted to reproduce. In other words, evolutionary history is strewn with the fossils of extinct 'incels'.

Meanwhile, roughly 400 million years ago, the fishy cousins in our family tree grew more varied in how they had sex. Whereas our direct line of ancestry retained the use of external fertilisation (that is, the dropping and insemination of eggs without penetration) for now, other fish began to become more inventive. Some species began to use internal fertilisation, whereby a male inserted the sperm into a female, prior to her ejecting already fertilised eggs. In order to facilitate this, male fish evolved a somewhat forebodingly named 'clasper', a sort of primitive penis. Male fish would penetrate females and ejaculate their sperm into the female's cloaca, an opening containing unfertilised eggs in a fleshy kind of sac. This also heralded the return of 69ing in some species. Male fish did this in order to prevent the wastage of sperm, which occurred when jets of the stuff were merely sprayed out in the middle of the ocean in the general direction of the eggs.

From the perspective of voraciously self-replicating DNA, the sentiment also works on an evolutionary basis.

The separate line of Silurian sharks also developed claspers, but their mating process could be a bit more violent, as males sank their teeth into female sharks to hold them still as mating took place.

Some female fish ejected eggs not long after they were fertilised,

A shark 'clasper'

to germinate as usual in the ocean or in a nest. Mothers and fathers often guarded the eggs carefully to avoid them being eaten, wasting their sexual investments. Other times female fish would allow the eggs to develop a bit before ejecting them out into the ocean's waters, reducing the amount of time the fish larvae would be vulnerable to the outside world. Again, in the divergent line of sharks, some species only ejected their eggs when they were pretty much matured and ready to hatch.

Sometimes when female fish or sharks retained fertilised eggs inside themselves for an extended period, the eggs would actually absorb and consume other eggs in the cloaca for food, in an act of cannibalism. Other female fish fed their eggs directly by feeding them their own blood. And a rare few other fish and sharks evolved to become asexual again, fertilising their own eggs in a process of parthenogenesis, or a 'virgin birth', in order to side-step the increasingly messy, complicated and risky act of pairing up with a genetic partner.

For the most part, however, most species of fish retained the practice of external fertilisation where females would drop unfertilised eggs and males would inseminate them without need for penetration or bodily contact. And this remains the case for roughly 95 per cent of fish species to this day. No need for claspers either. Our direct line would continue on in evolutionary history, dick-less and without penetration, for a little while longer.

SEX ON THE BEACH

As the Silurian period gave way to the Devonian 420 million years ago, the world was balmy and warm, with no ice, not even at Earth's poles. Tropical and wet temperatures prevailed, except for a few arid deserts forming under the blistering heat of the equator. Ferns and mosses began to colonise the land, as Earth continued to grow greener. By the end of the Devonian, the first true forests would exist, standing at massive heights. These forests were populated by progressively larger insects and arachnids of all kinds.

In the oceans, fish had fully come into their own, with some of them reaching between 3 and 7 metres in length. Our ancestors likely only clocked in at a more modest 1.5 metres. But still, as far as fish are concerned, that length isn't anything to sniff at. And it is quite a bit of progress from the handful of centimetres our worm-like ancestors used to be.

Then 380 million years ago, something revolutionary happened in the direct line of our ancestry. Our ancestors began to inhabit shallow waters and coastlines in search of food. As such, they evolved the capacity not only to exist in water but also to breathe air in order to emerge from the water for brief periods of time. Our ancestors developed a hole on the top of their heads that was angled so air could flow into their primitive lungs. Concurrently, they evolved strong front fins, which they could use to drag themselves out of the sea and along the beach in pursuit of food. By 375 million years ago, a mere 5 million years later, they had strong front and back fins, and primitive hips that allowed them to pull themselves along the land fairly efficiently.

This creature was the common ancestor of the tetrapods, the first vertebrates to colonise the land. It was the ancestor of all frogs, dogs, cats, horses, lizards, bears, snakes and, yes, humans. The first terrestrial vertebrate had four limbs and five digits on each limb. We humans, in our current evolutionary form, have retained these features. However, using x-rays we can even see the vestiges of these unused fingers on the limbs of horses – or, to use an extreme case, signs of limbs in snakes, shrunk to be so small they are almost imperceptible.

Over the next 15 million years this air-breathing fish evolved into the first amphibians (ancestors of frogs, salamanders and so on). Sexually, our direct line of ancestors still used external fertilisation and needed to return to the water to lay their eggs. Otherwise, the squishy, gelatinous bundles of joy would dry out and die. Our direct amphibian ancestors also lacked proper penises. However, much of this would change with the next round of evolution, as the members of our family tree began having sex all over the surface of Earth.

3

TYRANNOSAURUS SEX

375 to 66 million years ago

Wherein our amphibian ancestors evolve rich sex lives • They evolve into reptiles with shelled eggs and proto-penises • They split from the ancestors of dinosaurs • Our cynodont ancestors evolve proto-tits • The Permian Extinction relegates our ancestors to the evolutionary fringes • They evolve into mammals • They begin having live births • Our placental mammal ancestors split with the marsupials • The Cretaceous Extinction wipes out the dinosaurs, causing the rapid evolution of mammalian sexual practices, instincts, fetishes and behaviours.

The Late Devonian period 375 to 358 million years ago saw our ancestors having sex on solid ground for the first time. As our fishy tetrapod ancestors ventured onto land, they found a surface that was already populated by new sources of food for them to munch. Namely, the plants and bugs that had colonised the land before them. However, early tetrapods had quite porous skin and were in danger of drying out, so they clung to the coastlines, river valleys and lakes. Anywhere near water. Not only to rehydrate their damp, slimy skin, but to lay their eggs, which – similarly – would dry out if they were plopped on terra firma.

Within a few million years of first making landfall, our ancestors evolved from something that closely resembled modern lungfish into full-blown amphibians. In terms of sex, at first things did not change terribly much. If it ain't broke, don't fix it. Early amphibians still used external fertilisation and still laid eggs in water like fish do. Once those eggs hatched, the larvae had to stay entirely in the water for the first stages of their lives. These little quasi-tadpoles would remain in the water until they grew the lungs and limbs required to survive on land as adults. From there, they'd hop along the land in damp areas seeking either plant life or small insects to eat.

While the vast majority of amphibians continued to use the rather impersonal egg-laying and sperm-spraying method of external fertilisation, including those in our direct line of ancestry, certain amphibians split off to use more creative methods. Some amphibian species, like the ancestors of modern salamanders, had a male squirt a blob of sperm into the water, which a female then came along and collected like a package delivered by Amazon. She absorbed the sperm into her cloaca (an opening leading to her eggs) and held the semen inside her until the eggs were fertilised. She then ejected the eggs back into water.

Additionally, a rare minority of amphibians evolved a phallus very sexily dubbed an 'intromittent organ', which allowed males to insert themselves into female cloacas and fertilise the eggs directly. Thus, the diversity of amphibian sex resembled the diversity of fish-fucking we had just left behind. There was certainly a slight tendency in evolution towards the internal fertilisation, penetration and penises that are more familiar to humans. But most amphibians 360 million years ago (including our direct ancestors) still retained duller habits of doing the deed externally.

However, these minority cases in fish and amphibians imply that penetration is a common evolutionary strategy that manifests itself in many different branches of the family tree. The reason for that is that internal fertilisation high up in a female's cloaca can prevent the wastage of sperm and increase the odds that DNA continues to get replicated. And, as we've previously covered, the replication of as much deoxyribonucleic acid as possible is the ultimate mission in sex and for life in general. In other words, when push comes to shove, Mother Nature is perfectly happy to introduce a bit of cock into the equation. But for now, our ancestors would have to be patient.

What is perhaps most intriguing about this phase of sex diversification is that the disadvantage of laying eggs in water became readily apparent as amphibians moved into new environments. For instance, if they were to move deeper into humid rainforests without immediate access to a river, creek or stream, they could not give birth. As such, another tiny minority of amphibian species evolved the ability to lay eggs without the need for a pool of water, provided the climate was damp enough to keep the eggs hydrated. In order to make this evolutionary strategy viable, these amphibians evolved to have the larvae/tadpole phase happen entirely inside the eggs. This meant that by the time the amphibians hatched, they would already have the lungs and limbs required to transport them around the forest. And while this strategy remained rare for the time being, it was a tantalising hint of the many transformations to come in our own direct line of ancestry.

DATE	EVENT
375 million years ago	First tetrapods on land
360 million years ago	Intensification of sex strategies
358 million years ago	The Devonian Extinction
330 million years ago	Evolution of reptiles, shelled eggs and proto-penises
270 million years ago	The evolution of mammary glands

252 million years ago	The Permian Extinction
225 million years ago	First mammaliaformes
201 million years ago	The Triassic Extinction
160 million years ago	Mammalian live births
125 million years ago	The placental/marsupial split
66 million years ago	The Cretaceous Extinction

STRATEGIC SEDUCTION AND AMPHIBIOUS ATTRACTION

The brains of Devonian amphibians weren't that much more developed than those of Silurian fish. Debates rage among biologists about the extent to which amphibians were/are conscious. Some say they are *not* because they lack a neocortex – the thinking part of the brain capable of self-reflection. However, the nervous systems of frogs seem to be sufficient for them to observe their surrounding environments and even to learn to avoid doing things that cause either danger or harm. While amphibians do not have a consciousness in any significant sense, their brains could deploy some rather crafty methods in sexual competition. Combined with sexual instincts inculcated into amphibians over millions of years, the result we see is the immense complication of sex amid our vertebrate ancestry.

First, consciously or not, amphibians experience pleasure sensations upon a successful egg-lay and sperm-spray exchange. Dopamine trickles into an amphibian's tiny brain after such activities. But a tiny pleasurable feeling to incentivise reproduction of DNA is a far cry from a full-blown orgasm, which our amphibian ancestors did not have. A vertebrate can have a dopamine surge in their brain after a lot of vital activities – from eating food (also good for survival) to calming down after an adrenaline-charged fear response. They even have an injection of dopamine after taking a shit. So, in that respect, a little sensation of pleasure from froggy-sex is not such a big deal. Nevertheless, our amphibian ancestors were at least vaguely cognisant of the feeling of pleasure during sexual activity. Thus, the Devonian marks the start of a slow evolution of sexual pleasure as our ancestors became gradually more neurologically complex. In the meantime, full orgasms would have to wait.

When it came to sexual strategies in our direct ancestors who still engaged in external fertilisation, things would generally go like this: A male would stake his claim to a patch of water used as a breeding ground and wait for some females to arrive. While he waited, the dominant male would drive off other males from hanging out in the area. Sometimes these forcibly ejected males would linger nearby, hoping the dominant male would leave so they could steal the prime breeding real estate. Already this displays a fair degree of sexual competition, opportunism and duplicity on the part of the fellas. Alas, not much has changed.

Then the female amphibians would show up. If they liked the look of the dominant male hanging around the breeding ground, they'd lay their eggs and the lucky male would fertilise them. The female amphibians would then depart and leave the eggs to hatch and grow up on their own. As a result of the fact that most larvae/tadpoles received little motherly attention, the female would lay dozens or hundreds of eggs in one go, increasing the odds that some of the hatchlings would survive to adulthood. The overwhelming majority of larvae would not. In some amphibian species, males lingered to protect their newly sired offspring, ensuring the copying of their DNA. This led to females choosing to breed with males who looked like they could defend the area from other jealous males who may want to commit infanticide, and fathers who were also capable of herding larvae from one part of the water to another with more food or better conditions.

Since females just show up, drop their eggs and have them fertilised, most amphibian species are promiscuous. Female amphibians are choosey about which males they permit to fertilise their eggs, but they frequently have a new attractive male mate each time they drop a new batch. It's as if the dominant form of mating in humans was women getting pregnant by one-night stands with highly desirable gentlemen, each pregnancy issuing from a different father. But what makes a male amphibian attractive to a female? Well, as with female attraction to human males, there is a huge number of possible answers to that question. The most common (and brutish) one is the ability of a male amphibian to defend their patch of water (ideally one with appropriate water temperature, remote from potential predators and with enough tiny aquatic plant life for the hatchlings to feed on) against other males.

Unlike our fishy ancestors that dwelt solely in water, amphibians can take advantage of their ability to breathe air on land to 'vocalise'. Some male amphibians let out calls to let females know that they are nearby and ready for a bit of rumpy-pumpy. Those amphibians with the 'sexiest voices' tend to attract the most mates. For instance, in many frog species, males with the deepest, most resonant-sounding ribbits enjoy the most success. Hence their calls have evolved to take on an almost musical quality, becoming as attractive as a soulful guy with an acoustic guitar at a party.

Another gentler strategy is that male amphibians may take care to constantly remain in a female's line of sight, tailing her and lingering until she decides to drop her eggs. I leave it to the reader to decide whether this behaviour is doting or stalkerish.

But the methods of attraction are not entirely one-sided. Female amphibians in many species have 'come hither' vocalisations and movements that signal to a male they are interested in a bit of gamete-sharing. These movements can draw the attention of a desirable male and, in turn, seductively stimulate the male's own sexual behaviours.

In essence, arousing the males enough for them to make a move, come over and fertilise the eggs.

Another sexual advantage to being out of the water is the intensified use of pheromones. Primitive fish used pheromones in the water to send each other information about their locations, the presence of predators or the desire to have sex, but in the fresh air the last of these practices went into overdrive. Male amphibians exude strong smells that attract nearby females, trigger their egg-laying and allow those females to recognise their mate again, should they be temporarily separated. The use of sex pheromones can make the difference between a failed and a successful amphibious seduction.

The use of sex pheromones remained incredibly important throughout our direct ancestral line, right up to humans. So crucial are pheromones, if a human has a sudden change in body chemistry (either induced by drugs or by age) and they become less receptive to those pheromones, a person that they previously found irresistible might suddenly lose their sexual lustre. So, the next time you sniff the pillow, shirt or blanket (or, in pervier circumstances, underwear) of your recently departed lover, remember you are experiencing an intense and primal form of sexual attraction that is over 360 million years old. And we are just at the beginning of drawing throughlines for sexual behaviours that are hundreds of millions of years old but still hold a bewitching sway over us today.

All these things were the result of sexual selection, which is the evolution of physical traits, instincts and behaviours that do not help immediate survival in the wild (that is, natural selection) but do increase the odds of successfully procreating. For instance, the croaks of a frog do not aid survival from predators or help a frog find food, but they do attract a mate, thus allowing for DNA replication. And the pheromones wafting from a frog will not help with food or avoiding predators either (in fact, a froggy stench may attract some predators). But the smell does increase the odds of drawing in a vivacious froggy lass who wants to lay some eggs. The forces of sexual selection shape the most powerful traits of a species. And, as we shall see, that statement even applies to our own species.

THE REPTILIAN TRANSITION

At the end of the Devonian period 358 million years ago, disaster struck. Plants and photosynthesising bacteria pumped so much oxygen into the atmosphere that they cooled and dried out the planet again. This was bad news for amphibians (the only tetrapods/vertebrates currently on the surface of Earth) who relied on the humid, damp and tropical climates of the Devonian period for survival. Bereft of lush river valleys and rainforests, and assailed by encroaching deserts, many of these amphibians died off in a mass extinction.

So devastating was the impact of this change in climate that roughly 95 to 97 per cent of all amphibians were wiped out. When one considers that all vertebrates on Earth are descended from these Devonian amphibians – from humans to dogs, birds and crocodiles – this mass extinction nearly wiped out our entire lineage. As it is, we are descended from the 3 to 5 per cent of amphibians who survived. And, as is common in the aftermath of mass extinction events, evolution took a sharp turn in another direction.

The Carboniferous period dawned 358 million years ago with plants going absolutely batshit crazy by growing massive and spreading everywhere. Earth became covered with dense forests. Some trees were 50 metres in height. Oxygen levels in the atmosphere increased to 35 per cent. For perspective, today's oxygen levels are around 21 per cent of the atmosphere. The increased oxygen levels allowed terrestrial arthropods (insects and arachnids) to grow to enormous sizes: dragonflies with metre-long wingspans, two-metre-long scorpions, spiders the size of golden retrievers, and cockroaches the size of crabs. As a result of this nightmarish dominance of bugs over the animal kingdom, amphibians remained relatively small and stayed out of the way, quietly biding their time in what few damp areas were left.

The immense levels of oxygen pumped out by giant forests caused other disasters. Oxygen is a highly reactive material, which means even in our own atmosphere of just 21 per cent a bit of friction on wood can lead to a fire. At 35 per cent, these giant trees were the source of their own demise. Gigantic forest fires increasingly ripped across entire continents, leaving behind the coal beds which we use today, and which put the carbon into Carboniferous. Meanwhile, the oxygen in the atmosphere continued to dry out the climate, leaving deserts where many forests once lay. As the main constituent parts of the supercontinent of Pangea came together, it became increasingly difficult for coastal storms and moisture to penetrate its massive interior.

In response to the drying climate, 330 million years ago our ancestors evolved to not be so dependent on water for survival. We became reptiles. Unlike amphibians, reptiles have much less porous skin so water cannot escape as easily. This enabled reptiles to live in the increasingly arid climate that prevailed at the end of the Carboniferous. They could head away from water and rainforests, set up shop in deserts and survive just fine.

Moreover, reptiles had evolved a new kind of egg – the amniotic egg. Unlike amphibian eggs, which are squishy and gelatinous and have to be laid in water, reptile eggs come with a shell encasing yolk and egg white, just as chicken eggs do. It may seem commonplace today, but 330 million years ago this was revolutionary stuff. It meant that reptiles could lay their eggs literally anywhere. The world was their proverbial oyster. Thus, the first reptiles strode forth into evolutionary history – the ancestors of the dinosaurs and, yes, also of future mammals and humans.

As mentioned in the last chapter, the Carboniferous is the earliest epoch to which we can currently tie the phenomenon of homosexuality: it definitely existed by the subsequent Permian period. And it may have arisen as early as the Cambrian era.

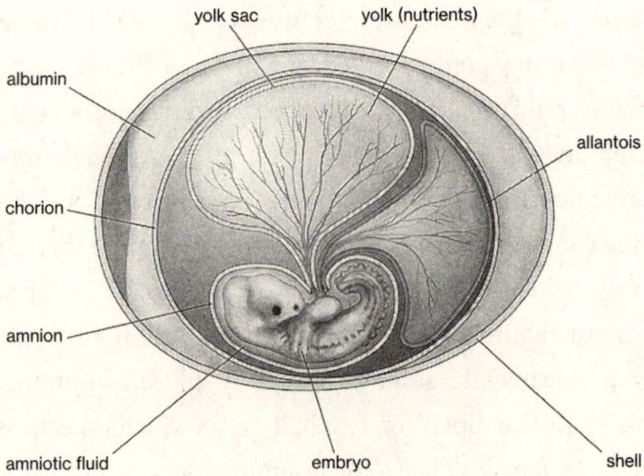

Amniotic egg

THE RISE OF THE COCK

There are a great many similarities between the sex habits of amphibians and reptiles in our ancestral line, but with a few significant developments. For one thing, our direct ancestors finally evolved the internal fertilisation that had already happened in evolutionary offshoots of a minority of fish and amphibians. The evolution of internal fertilisation happened very quickly in reptiles because their eggs were no longer laid in water. Spraying a fine mist of semen onto a bunch of eggs while on land certainly would not work the same way it did in water. Especially when one considers reptile eggs had hard shells.

In order to facilitate internal fertilisation, male reptiles grew protopenises. These small, tube-shaped organs were inserted into females during copulation, thrusting up the cloaca and getting as close to the eggs as possible, hitting them with a jet of sperm. While the eggs were developing inside the female reptile, their shells were still somewhat porous, allowing the sperm entry. Thereafter, the females would lay a fully hardened shell.

Our reptile ancestors housed their proto-penises inside a male cloaca, alongside their two testicles. It was as if both biological sexes had vaginas, but a penis popped out of one of them during sex. A proto-cock only usually made an appearance when the huffing and puffing reptile was on the verge of penetration. Arguably this is less fun, since it deprives one of other recreational uses of one's member. But having your genitals housed safely inside you rather than dangling dangerously below is perhaps more practical. Another significant difference is our reptile ancestors did not pee out of these penises like humans do. Meanwhile, some reptiles that split off from our family tree had a pair of hemipenises, two half-cocks which take turns being inserted into a female's cloaca for insemination, one per sex session. A tiny minority of reptile species did not evolve penises but got by squeezing sperm out of the male cloaca into a female's cloaca with a series of inverted muscles, in the same way one might squeeze toothpaste out of a tube. But for most reptiles in our lineage, the cock had arrived and was here to stay. So, yes, dear reader, if you either possess one of those dangling little tormentors between your legs, or if you have occasionally been the subject of visitations by one, it is intriguing to reflect that those obnoxiously throbbing appendages are roughly 330 million years in the making.

The economics of gametes remained much the same as with fish and amphibians. Because female reptiles invested more energy in producing eggs than males did in producing sperm, females were, generally speaking, the choosers and males were the chosen. Therefore males evolved several new methods for proving their worth as mates. Some species saw the skin of males turn vibrant, attention-getting colours in a display of virility. Other males performed a sort of courtly dance for females to get their attention. Still others used their front legs to affectionately stroke a female's face. Most reptiles also depended heavily on the use of pheromones to attract mates.

Reptiles in our main line of descent used internal fertilisation and then laid eggs externally. But there were evolutionary offshoots. A minority of reptiles evolved to have live births, and some reptiles evolved to become asexual again, inseminating themselves through a virgin birth, or parthenogenesis. But for the most part, penetration-giddy sex partners were the order of the day.

Initially, the earliest reptiles did not guard their eggs once they were laid. This resulted in predation, where carnivorous and omnivorous creatures would come along and eat them. Particularly with eggs laid by larger reptiles. So numerous species, including the ancestors of snakes, lizards and alligators, evolved to guard their eggs and care for their young. Those species which did not stick around after the eggs were laid generally tended to lay a tonne of them to increase the odds of some of them surviving and hatching. In those species, eggs were sometimes laid in their hundreds. Those larger species that laid fewer eggs tended to watch over them.

The care taken by genetic parents to look after their offspring became a growing trend, as parents began to go the extra mile to ensure the successful copying of their DNA. From an evolutionary perspective, it is no good having sex if the offspring of that carnal union die and end your genetic line. It is here, roughly 300 million years ago, that we begin to see the faintest glimmer of parental love, as nurturing instincts became more sophisticated.

LIZARDS WITH TITS

The Carboniferous gave way to the Permian era 298 million years ago. Earth's oxygen level shrank from 35 per cent to 23 per cent, just two points higher than it is today. As such, the giant bugs of the previous period shrank to sizes that were less terrifying. In their place, the reptiles flourished. Earth in the Permian period was extremely arid and filled with massive deserts, which suited reptilian species quite well. They began to diversify as they filled many new niches abandoned by the giant bugs.

Permian reptiles grew gradually larger and had split into two main groups: the synapsids and the sauropsids. The synapsids were the ancestors of mammals, the sauropsids the ancestors of dinosaurs. And although the synapsids were proto-mammals, they were initially quite reptilian in appearance. In a possible twist to your expectations, during the Permian era it was the synapsid ancestors of mammals, not the sauropsid ancestors of the dinosaurs, who were the larger, more numerous and more dominant life form on Earth. *Cotylorhynchus romeri*, one of the largest synapsid herbivores in the Permian, grew up to 6 metres long. One of the largest synapsid carnivores, *Inostrancevia alexandri*, could grow up to 3.5 metres long, and had 15-centimetre razor-sharp teeth.

While the earliest synapsids in the Permian period from 298 to 270 million years ago looked quite reptilian, there is good reason to believe that increasing numbers of synapsids began to look more proto-mammalian. For one thing, it is possible these later synapsids began to grow fur on their bodies, particularly those smaller species that were nocturnal and needed to stay warm at night. For another thing, they began to develop the trait that later gave the class of mammals their name – mammary glands.

The evolution of mammaries is somewhat convoluted, but allow me to get you abreast of the latest theories. As mentioned, smaller and more primitive reptiles just lay their eggs and leave them alone to hatch, compensating for this parental negligence by laying a great many of them. Conversely, larger reptile species slowly evolved to guard their eggs because they made a tastier, more substantial meal for predators and scavengers. Thus, many reptiles lay their eggs in protected nests. The problem with this from an evolutionary standpoint is it keeps one or both parents tied to the nest in order to guard it, preventing them from ranging further afield in search for food. In order to overcome this obstacle while still protecting their offspring, around 270 million years ago synapsids may have carried their eggs in a pouch, permitting them to travel across the Permian deserts untethered to a nest.

A pouch-bearing mammal

The problem with being a synapsid galloping around the desert with a bunch of eggs in your pouch is that the hard eggshells might crack from your more extreme movements. So it is distinctly possible that pouch-bearing synapsids evolved to lay eggs with shells that were softer and more flexible. Or perhaps this branch of reptiles never evolved the fully hard shells of most of their cousins. In either case, they still had the problem our amphibian ancestors had, of keeping those eggs from drying out and their offspring from dying. Within synapsid pouches, glands in their skin began to secrete a liquid to kept those soft eggs hydrated. By 260 million years ago, those glands began to produce a liquid that not only kept synapsid eggs moist but was actually a nutritious primitive milk, feeding the baby synapsids once they hatched in their mother's pouch.

As we shall soon see, those mammary glands grew more efficient, nutritious and specialised in our line of descent until we arrived at the stereotypical pair of knockers that are a source of fascination to many humans today. But more on those mammaries later.

A SEXUAL PLATEAU

The Permian period came to an end 252 million years ago with a mass extinction event called the Great Dying. It was caused by a volcanic super-eruption in what is today Siberia. Imagine a series of eruptions, each with the force of several nuclear bombs, throwing ash into the atmosphere and blocking out the sun. Then imagine this chain of eruptions goes on for a million years. The climate grew cold, killing off vegetation and starving the animals that thrived on it. Acid rain constantly pelted the planet, doing even more damage to that vegetation. Oxygen was ripped out of the atmosphere and oceans, killing off marine life. All told, 90 to 95 per cent of species died. It was the worst extinction event in natural history and nearly destroyed all life on Earth.

The Triassic era dawned with most ecological niches empty. The Great Dying obliterated synapsid dominance over the biosphere. Only a few dozen species survived. The most successful, and the only group to survive the subsequent Triassic era, was the cynodonts. These were our direct ancestors. Some were the size of dogs, others of wombats, and some (our direct ancestors) were smaller than rats. Female cynodonts were still laying eggs and male cynodonts still stored their penises and testicles inside their bodies like their reptilian ancestors in the Carboniferous and Permian periods. Thus, at the start of the Triassic, the fundamentals of the sex act for our direct ancestors had remained largely unchanged for 80 million years. That's longer than the period that separates us from the dinosaurs.

Meanwhile, dominance over nature passed to the synapsids' opposite numbers, from whom they had split 60 million years earlier – the sauropsids. These more reptilian-looking creatures also took a heavy beating from the Great Dying, but one group of them, the archosaurs, survived and thrived. Archosaurs had multiple lungs that allowed them to breathe better in an atmosphere that had been reduced to only 16 per cent oxygen. The archosaurs also benefited from the fact deserts got even bigger in the early Triassic than they had been in the Permian. The massive supercontinent we call Pangea had fully formed 250 million years ago, sucking in the remaining continents, and it was very difficult for moisture to penetrate its interior. This arid environment was prime breeding ground for the reptilian archosaurs, whose glandless skin allowed them to thrive in dry environments, and the number of different archosaur species quickly multiplied. The archosaurs are the ancestors of all dinosaurs, flying pterosaurs and crocodilians. Dinosaurs themselves formed only a small minority, roughly 5 per cent, of all archosaurs in the early Triassic. And just like the proto-mammalian cynodonts, most of the archosaurs also practised the 80-million-year-old routine of internal fertilisation, with a 'hidden' reptilian penis followed by egg-laying.

Then, roughly 234 million years ago, a period of heavy volcanic activity pumped carbon dioxide into the atmosphere, heating Earth and increasing the average humidity. This led to a period of heavy rain that lasted for 2 million years, devastating the desert-loving archosaurs. But dinosaurs, previously an obscure minority, benefited from the increased humidity. For the rest of the Triassic, the number of dinosaur species slowly increased.

Approximately 225 million years ago, our ancestors, the mammaliaformes, evolved. This group contained the ancestors of placental mammals (humans, lions, tigers and bears, etc), marsupials (kangaroos, etc) and monotremes (platypuses, echidnas), along with numerous extinct offshoots that don't belong in the classification of the above groups of 'crown mammals'. Mammaliaformes were furry, burrowing creatures that were likely warm-blooded and suckled their young with their mammary glands. They were quite small, averaging about 10 centimetres. They were also nocturnal to avoid crossing paths with large predatory archosaurs. And they too retained the now 105-million-year-old 'reptilian method' of sex.

The Triassic period ended 201 million years ago with yet another mass extinction. Its cause is still debated. Older theories postulate an asteroid impact. But the theory with most scientific consensus at the present is another round of super-volcanic eruptions like the Permian Great Dying, but wiping out a more modest 40 per cent of all species on Earth. Among the casualties were all the archosaurs except the dinosaurs, pterosaurs and crocodilians. Dinosaurs grew to be the dominant group, constituting approximately 90 per cent of all terrestrial vertebrates on Earth. They would remain so until the Cretaceous Extinction 135 million years later.

Our ancestors at the time, the mammaliaformes, remained nocturnal rat-like creatures that burrowed in the ground and stayed the hell out of the dinosaurs' way. However, as our ancestors quivered on the fringes for the next 135 million years, they must have gotten bored, because some of them started experimenting sexually. A series of revolutionary changes in our direct line of ancestry was at hand.

A JURASSIC BUN IN THE OVEN

The Jurassic period started 201 million years ago, as Earth's average humidity approached tropical levels. Pangea had begun cracking up, eliminating the dry desert interior that had previously been sheltered from wet weather. Rainfall hit more of the land, which sprouted thick forests that covered the newly forming continents. As a result of this increase in plant life, the oxygen level in the atmosphere increased to 25 per cent. Dinosaurs reigned supreme, with species such as *Supersaurus* clocking in at 35 metres long and super-predators such as *Allosaurus*, 10 metres tall, stalking the landscape.

Mammals remained around 10 centimetres long, largely hidden from view. But despite existing on the fringes of nature, they began to diversify intensely. Roughly 175 million years ago, the ancestors of monotremes split off from the ancestors of placental mammals and marsupials. Today, monotremes such as platypuses and echidnas are among the few mammals left who still lay eggs like our ancestors in the Triassic and Permian. It was soon to become an outmoded style of reproduction in most mammalian species.

By 165 million years ago, mammals had diversified in their habits as well. Some of them continued to live a rodent-like existence, skittering along the forest floor and burrowing into holes. Others climbed trees and evolved either jumping or gliding abilities that allowed them to move across forests without having to touch the ground. Still others went to the rivers, lakes and coastlines and developed semi-aquatic traits while quietly paddling in the shallows. Most of this diversification helped them to stay out of the way of dinosaurs.

By 160 million years ago, our direct branch of the mammalian family tree began to reject the antiquated, reptilian mode of birth of laying fertilised eggs. Instead, our female ancestors began giving live births to squirming little infants without the need for them to hatch out of an eggshell. This was not the first time live births had evolved in vertebrates, but it was the first time it had happened in our direct line of ancestry. The group of mammals who developed live births are called Theria, and they are the Jurassic ancestors of placental mammals (cats, dogs, humans) and marsupials (kangaroos, possums, bandicoots).

In previous iterations of reptilian and mammalian reproduction the unborn fetus had been kept alive by the nutrients contained within an egg. Now, 160 million years ago, mammals took nutrients directly from their mother. When she ate, a portion of what she consumed would sustain her offspring. The food was transmitted to the unborn offspring via a middleman – the placenta. This was a temporary organ that grew alongside the child in the initial stages of pregnancy. It connected the child to the mother's body. The placenta acted as a storage depot for all the nourishment the mother consumed when she was eating for two – or a brood of six to twelve, depending on the mammalian species in question.

Both the 'reptilian' eggshell and the 'mammalian' placenta are temporary and disposable devices. Prior to 160 million years ago, offspring would eventually cast off their shells. With our direct ancestors among the group called Theria, we would similarly cast off the placenta shortly after a live birth. Both designs merely kept the infant alive until it was hatched or born.

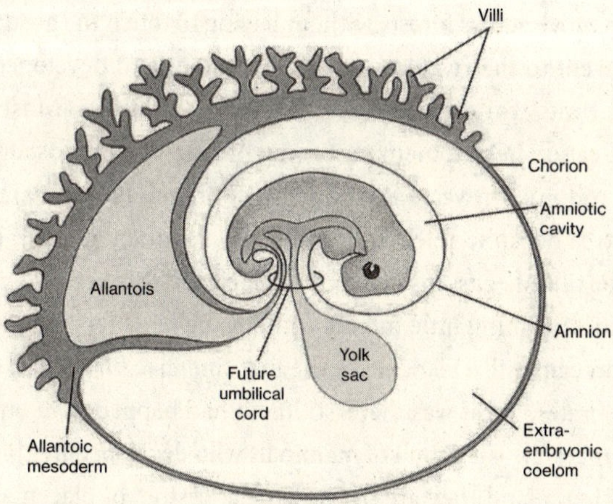

A mammalian embryo

Live births evolved in mammals 160 million years ago because the act of fully gestating in the safety of a mother's womb allowed offspring slightly more protection from the outside world than a thin eggshell. Not a bad move in a world where tiny mammals were constantly fleeing for their lives from dinosaurs. They could not always tote a bunch of eggs with them or stand around guarding a nest. Keeping the child inside its mother while the ten-centimetre-long mammal scurried across the forest floor, ran up a tree or burrowed into a hole made practical evolutionary sense. Offspring were no longer prematurely plopped out as an egg onto the ground, vulnerable to predation, a 'cracking' incident or slight changes in temperature. Even if a mammal quickly scooped up the egg and put it in her pouch a few minutes after laying it, there was still more risk than allowing the fetus to develop a little more behind the walls of the mother's own body.

One hundred and sixty million years ago, the common ancestor of both placental mammals (cats, dogs, us) and marsupials (koalas, kangaroos, possums) gave birth to offspring prematurely. That is, the babies were still not done gestating when they were born, because their wombs were too small to contain offspring at later stages of growth. As a result, they needed to cling to their mother's fur or sit inside a pouch while they continued to develop. The pouch was a sort of evolutionary halfway house between developing in an egg and developing in the womb. Since then, placental mammals have discarded the pouch. But the rudiments of what we would today consider a human birth were slowly taking shape.

Transformations were also taking place outside our family tree. The Late Jurassic is notable for the first flying avian dinosaurs (that is, the ancestors of birds). In the Triassic, a few dinosaurs had grown fuzz on themselves to keep warm. In the early and middle Jurassic, this fuzz evolved into feathers. And by the end of the period, the first few species took to the air. The ancestors of birds were the only dinosaurs to survive a looming disaster that would forever change the balance of power in the biosphere.

THE DINOSAURS GET FUCKED

The Cretaceous period began 145 million years ago as the world slowly began to look more contemporary. What do I mean? For a start, Pangea had fully broken up and the continents were taking a more modern shape and location at the rate of 4 centimetres per year. Grass evolved for the first time, carpeting large stretches of treeless plains with a myriad of successful variations. 140 million years ago, ants, a ubiquitous lifeform today, appeared for the first time. One hundred and twenty-five million years ago, flowering plants appeared and spread across Earth thanks to the concurrent appearance of bees. In short, some of the most common features we imagine when we think of nature began at this time.

In our direct line of ancestry, 125 million years ago, placental mammals split from marsupials. While marsupials continued to nurture newborns in pouches just like most Theria had done 35 million years earlier, placental mammals (lions, tigers and bears) dispensed with the pouch and got most of the gestation done inside a mother's womb. Again, in the Cretaceous we arrive at a more contemporary-looking arrangement – this time with mammalian reproduction. The only difference is that we still looked like tiny shrews or rats.

Meanwhile, dinosaurs such as *Tyrannosaurus rex* still employed the antiquated sexual and reproductive methods that had been around since 330 million years ago. T-Rex evolved 68 million years ago, not long before a disaster changed the world forever. A male T-Rex sported an internal penis contained within a cloaca. When this 12-metre-tall behemoth caught sight of a female T-Rex, he would clomp noisily over to her and, assuming he met her sexual standards, mount her doggy-style (as did most dinosaurs). The male's cloaca would meet the female's cloaca in what is known as a cloacal kiss.

Two tyrannosauruses enjoy an intimate moment

Thereupon, with blood pumping down through his massive frame, the male T-Rex's penis would emerge from hidden depths and enter his mate. Judging by most avian dinosaurs and crocodiles, a T-Rex's dick would have been rather small in proportion to his body: somewhere between 10 and 36 inches (25 and 91 centimetres). While that may sound hefty to human ears, on a 100-metre frame it was pitifully small. Some more charitable estimates use a duck's unusually long penis as a possible baseline for comparison, which would calculate the T-Rex penis at a whopping 30 metres, or over one-quarter the length of his body. However, it is unlikely there was an evolutionary reason for such a monstrous phallus to have evolved within a T-Rex's cloacal sack. While feverish speculation will doubtless continue (because some people are just built that way, I suppose) the odds are more likely that T-Rex had a small dick rather than a massive hog.

Regardless of the size of the boat, the 'motion of the ocean' took only a minute before the male T-Rex hopped off, with the female's eggs duly fertilised. But the world of T-Rexes, the ancien régime of dinosaurs, was coming to an end. Sure, reptiles still exist today, and they still fuck, but the reptilian act of copulation would never happen on such a massive scale again. Unless some particularly pervy CGI artists make the next *Jurassic Park* movie X-rated.

This was because 66 million years ago, an asteroid 10 kilometres wide hit Earth. The shockwave set off worldwide earthquakes and tsunamis. Forests burst into flames across entire continents. Acid rain pelted down on the planet, killing off scores of plant life upon which the dinosaurs depended. Dust flung up into the atmosphere by the asteroid impact blocked out the Sun and plunged the world into darkness. The lack of sunlight killed off even more plant life and starved even more dinosaurs. All told, the Cretaceous Extinction killed 70 per cent of life on Earth.

After the dust of the catastrophe settled, flies, worms, roaches and other corpse-eaters thrived amid the masses of dead and rotting animals. The tiny mammals that had evolved to eat insects managed to feed on them and survive. But the niches of the environment previously occupied by dinosaurs were ruthlessly emptied, and mammals strode forth to fill them, rapidly evolving into myriad new forms. And along with the emergence of strange new mammalian bodies came the evolution of mammalian sex.

After nearly 200 million years on the fringes of nature, mammals were about to have their moment in the evolutionary sun, heralded by a fanfare of fetishes and cheeringly accompanied by a crowd of newly evolved clitorises and a pulsing throng of external penises.

For lo, the Era of the Orgasm was at hand.

PART II

PRIMATE CLIMAX

66 MILLION TO 315,000 YEARS AGO

4

DAWN OF THE ORGASMIC EPOCH

66 to 55 million years ago

Wherein the placental mammals begin to orgasm • External penises sprang up • Clitorises grow in sophistication and sexual power • Masturbation takes hold on an unprecedented scale • Placental mammals diversify into a myriad of new forms • New erogenous zones emerge in mammalian bodies • Mammals start having anal sex.

The asteroid impact 66 million years ago killed off 90 per cent of terrestrial animals and 50 per cent of plant life on Earth. Large species were hit the worst. And that meant saying goodbye to most of the dinosaurs, except for the evolutionary ancestors of birds. The surviving mammals were extremely small – usually about 10 centimetres in length. None were longer than 50 centimetres and most of them weighed under a kilogram. For the first few years after the Cretaceous Extinction, they ate bugs and the surviving plant life. They scavenged on the fringes of nature as they had done for most of the previous 185 million years, since the start of the Triassic.

But since large non-avian dinosaurs no longer existed, there were plenty of empty ecological niches to fill – and mammals were uniquely positioned to do so. Mammals quickly diversified and grew in physical and neurological complexity. And this took sex in our ancestral line to new heights of physical and intellectual sophistication. As educated and 'sexually literate' as humans are in the modern age, there are still a few dark spots in our knowledge of sex that deserve to be illuminated – and it is these we turn to next.

DATE	EVENT
125 million years ago	Evolution of external genitalia
66 million years ago	Cretaceous Extinction, the placental orgasm, sophistication of the clitoris
60 million years ago	Last common ancestor with canines, felines, ursines
55 million years ago	Last common ancestor with ungulates, the first primates
40 million years ago	Last common ancestor with New World monkeys
25 million years ago	Last common ancestor with great apes

THE AGE OF THE ORGASM

Pleasure chemicals flooding the brain during sex was not new, in evolutionary terms. It had existed for as long as multicelled vertebrates had brains; going back some 530 million years, dopamine triggered a positive response in Cambrian fish after a successful sperm ejaculation or laying a clutch of eggs. It was nature's way of reinforcing that it was a good thing to replicate one's DNA. However, Cambrian fish didn't possess much consciousness and weren't aware of a sense of pleasure. They acted and reacted to stimuli mindlessly and mechanically.

Furthermore, similar injections of pleasure chemicals occurred in the brain when they ate, excreted waste or successfully evaded danger: all essential actions to keep reproducing and replicating DNA. So while there is a chemical reaction in their brains, there is no indication that fish, then or now, experience anything like an orgasm during external fertilisation.

When our ancestors crawled onto land and evolved into the first amphibians, their brains developed slightly. Not enough to manifest anything humans would associate with consciousness – amphibians were still largely ruled by instinct – but enough for them to learn from dangerous or pleasurable situations and modify their behaviour accordingly within a limited range of observation. So, 360 million years ago, our ancestors had developed a vague awareness that it was pleasurable and thus desirable to have sex. But perhaps no more than they deemed it pleasurable to eat insects or take a shit. Still no whisper of a full-blown orgasm.

When we evolved into reptiles around 330 million years ago and witnessed the rise of the cock in our direct ancestral line, a cluster of nerve endings developed in that internal proto-penis and afforded males some additional injections of dopamine during penetration. A flood of pleasure entered a male reptile's primitive brain upon a successful ejaculation. A collection of nerve endings also developed in a female reptile's reproductive tract, creating the potential for pleasure during penetration. But not all reptilian copulations were pleasurable for females by any stretch of the imagination. More on that later.

The same pattern existed after the split between synapsids and sauropsids around 300 million years ago. While some reptiles and birds stimulate the surface of their cloacas by rubbing them on various objects in a form of masturbation or dry-humping, indicating they find it pleasurable, there is no real evidence that reptiles or avian dinosaurs (birds) experience orgasms when either the sex or cloacal dry-humping reaches its conclusion. We also see no evidence of orgasms in monotremes, the egg-laying and internal-penis-holding mammals from whom we split 175 million years ago. So it is likely that during the Permian and Triassic periods the full-blown orgasm had not yet sprung into being.

But then we arrive at the Jurassic and Cretaceous periods and the last common ancestor of all placental and marsupial mammals that lived 125 million years ago. This is where we see the sexual landscape begin to change. The slow evolution of external genitalia in males and the 'open air' nub of the clitoris in females allowed for a lot more opportunities for pleasure. And once mammals learnt that their pulsing sex organs would give them no rest, they decided to return the favour. As the Cretaceous period ended 66 million years ago, with the wipe-out of the dinosaurs and the rise of mammals, the orgasm became increasingly intense in our ancestral line as it diversified more rapidly than at any point in the past 200 million years.

Between 66 million and 315,000 years ago, sexual stimulation became so intense and had such a profound effect on the physiology of the body that the mere word 'pleasure' doesn't even begin to describe it. Male mammals experienced throbbing muscular contractions in rapid succession, shuddering at lightning speed from the tip of their cocks, down their clenching shafts and as far deep as their prostate and even their anuses on the other side of their bodies. It was as though an earthquake had happened in their loins – or, more accurately, an eruption. Their entire bodies clenched as their minds went blank, their brain activity slowed down and their fear and anxiety evaporated.

Female mammals felt pulses that built in intensity over a longer duration, as shockwaves rippled through their entire pelvis, the mouth of their vagina, up their vaginal canals towards their uteruses and to the far-hidden depths of their swollen clitorises. Their skin heated up and, where visible, flushed all over their bodies, including the lips of the labia minora. Goosebumps rose across their skin and the tips of their nipples (those mammary glands that evolved several epochs ago) became more sensitive and erect. Female mammals experience an absence of fear and anxiety during orgasm that is more thorough and complete than the experience of a male, as the emotional slate is wiped and the mind enters a state of utter euphoria.

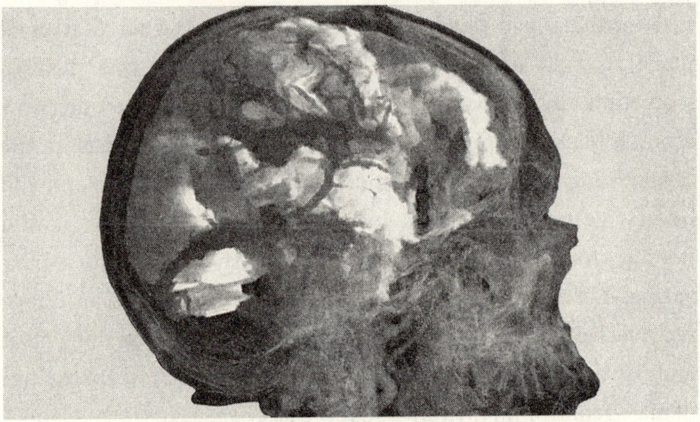

The brain during orgasm

The collapse of male and female mammalian bodies after this state, whether it lasts a few seconds or minutes, is designed to facilitate the passage of sperm, the fertilisation of eggs and that all-powerful command of nature to replicate DNA and carry on the blind chemical reaction that is nearly as old as Earth itself. It is what the French call *la petite mort*, or 'the little death'. And there is evidence that all placental mammals going back to a common ancestor 66 million years ago experienced this phenomenon to some degree, profoundly shaping the sexual practices and sexual psychology that followed as they diversified into all creatures great and small. With the Cretaceous asteroid impact, dear reader, the age of the orgasm was born.

THE EXTERNAL COCK

When the ancestor of placentals and marsupials split from egg-laying monotreme mammals 175 million years ago, we were still using internal penises which popped out of male cloacas during the sex act. It was the same hole they shat out of. Thus, the name monotreme is derived from the Greek for 'single hole'. By the time the ancestor of placental mammals split from marsupials 125 million years ago, the male genitalia had slowly evolved to become external. Marsupial males typically have their testicles dangling above their penises (sometimes by a considerable distance) rather than the other way around. Marsupial females typically have multiple vaginas. In the case of kangaroos, they have three: two for receiving the sperm and one for gestating offspring. In response, male kangaroos have a double-pronged penis to deliver the payload to the two sperm-vaginas. On the other hand, placental mammals, our direct ancestors, typically have the cock and bollocks in reverse order, something more familiar to humans, though the exact shape, colour and appearance of male genitalia vary wildly across species.

But the evolution of the external penis is still something of a mystery. If our direct ancestral line had got by with internal penises since around 330 million years ago, why change things now? Especially since it seems evolutionarily counterintuitive to have one's sex organs dangling in the open where they were more likely to be damaged. There are a few hypotheses as to why external genitalia appeared in our ancestral line between 125 and 66 million years ago. And no, contrary to popular belief, the idea that testicles outside the body keep sperm at the perfect temperature isn't among them. Sperm got along just fine for millions of years with the testicles inside the body.

The first hypothesis is they may have lent an advantage to internal fertilisation, not having to come out of a male cloaca first and instead having a head start on getting sperm as close to an unfertilised egg as possible. They'd potentially be able to penetrate further up a female's reproductive tract during sex and make sure that more rounds of copulation were successful in causing a pregnancy. Or at least you might think so. Not all mammals today have large penises relative to their body sizes. In fact, many mammalian penises are smaller proportionally to the bodies of their bearers than the average human in that respect (insecure readers are welcome to take comfort in this). As massive as its body is, a gorilla only has an average penis length of 1.8 inches. And plenty of species that still use internal penises can pop out surprisingly long phalluses relative to body size (duck penises, for instance, are nightmarish). So, in those cases, there isn't much of an evolutionary advantage for internal fertilisation compared to having an internal penis.

But consider the external cock in its proper historical context for a moment. Our ancestors in the Cretaceous were very small rodent-like creatures, only a few centimetres long. Yet they likely had penises that were just shy of a centimetre: pretty hefty relative to their body size. And when used for internal fertilisation of similarly sized females, these proportionally massive mammalian dongs may well have bestowed a significant edge to each round of sex leading to successful pregnancies. In that context, an external penis, once the mutation appeared, may have been selected for in the mammalian family tree.

The second hypothesis is a little less stark and mechanical. Sexual selection by mammalian females may have played a role. As previously mentioned, sexual selection is any trait that evolves that is not of immediate and obvious use to survival (fangs, claws, fast legs) but instead signals sexual worth to potential mates (for example, colourful plumes of feathers, seductive ribbits and croaks, impractically large antlers). In this case, the external penis may have evolved so that females could inspect the health and virility of a male before consenting to have sex with him.

This inspection is not as easily done when penises are internal. But if a tiny rodent-like placental had its cock and bollocks somewhat on display, females may have been able to have a quick peek and make better mate choices and avoid copulations that did not result in pregnancies – for instance, if the penis or testicles looked in any way deformed, mutated or injured. They could look for signs of robustness in the mammal's member, along with watching for erectile responses, the lack of which may imply impotence or some internal sexual health problem. Naturally, a small-brained mammal would not have sat and evaluated these traits like they were a doctor giving a physical, rather the attraction to (or revulsion from) male genitalia would have been instinctual and visceral, as it largely remains for humans to this day.

A third, related hypothesis has to do with the possible co-evolution of the clitoris and female sexual pleasure in mammals. An external penis may have increased the possibility of foreplay and a female becoming progressively more aroused during the initial stages of the sex act prior to penetration. Female arousal may have resulted in a greater likelihood of an orgasm, quasi-orgasm or ripples of sexual pleasure that left a female mammal relatively still and immobile after having sex. Not moving around after sex can increase the possibility that sperm can successfully reach their target and fertilise an egg. The orgasm may well have evolved to make her relative stillness happen more organically, instead of the female mammal immediately getting up and running off shortly after she pushed her grunting male mate off her, and he lit up the Cretaceous equivalent of a cigarette.

Whatever the evolutionary cause, the external penis had arisen triumphantly in natural history. Around the same time, ancestors in our direct lineage evolved a long, thin bone called a 'baculum' that helped to prop up the mammalian cock. The baculum was surrounded by the soft tissue that humans normally associate with a penis. The baculum's evolutionary purpose was to keep the penis pointed 'on target' during copulation in case a mammal should temporarily lose blood flow and their erection. This allowed the penis to stay inside the vagina in such dire circumstances until arousal could be revived and a male could achieve ejaculation. That way the mammal in question was not in danger of the proverbial 'playing a game of pool with a length of rope'.

The baculum penis bone may have evolved as a common trait in all placental mammals prior to 66 million years ago, or may have evolved multiple times in various lineages – perhaps evolving separately as many as ten times in placental mammals, which is testament to its usefulness in a world millions of years before Viagra. Either way, the penis bone was also dropped numerous times once it had outstayed its welcome in the ancestors of animals such as horses, elephants, rabbits and a smattering of underwater mammals. Apart from those species, most mammalian dicks still have bones inside of them. And while humans no longer have this penis bone, our direct ancestors certainly did.

Leaping ahead slightly in our story, our ancestors had penis bones when we evolved into the first primates 55 million years ago. We still had them when we split between the Old World monkeys in Afro-Eurasia and New World monkeys in the Americas 40 million years ago. And when the ancestor of all 'great apes' (gorillas, chimps, humans, etc) evolved in Africa 25 to 30 million years ago, the penis bone was still present.

Yet in the great apes it had greatly reduced in size relative to the fleshy part of the penis. There are several hypotheses for this change. Again, sexual selection may have led female great apes to only have sex with males who could maintain an erection, thus discriminating based on health and virility. This would have rendered bacula obsolete. Another hypothesis is during male–male conflict in great apes, the breaking of penis bones may have become a prime target to knock a rival out of the gene pool, making the penis bone an evolutionary liability. Another hypothesis is that a baculum inhibited an ape's ability to try different sex positions, thus potentially reducing female sexual pleasure. So, again, it is possible that the evolution of the human penis resulted almost entirely to accommodate female desires. It is refreshing to see evolution behave like a gentleman for once.

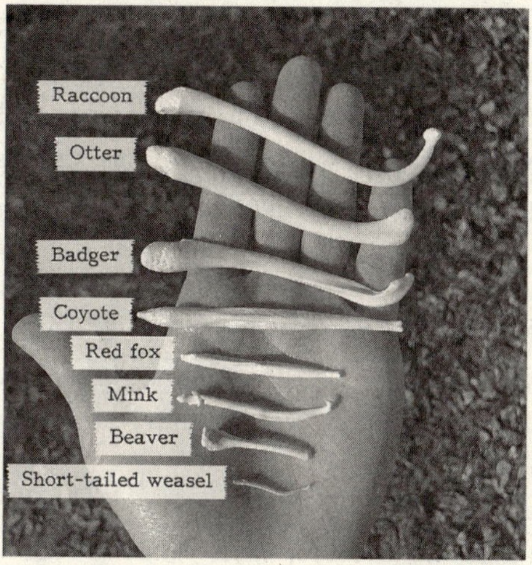

The penis bones of various species

THE CLITORIS CHRONICLES

The proto-clitoris evolved, at the earliest, 330 million years ago, as an evolutionary offshoot of the internal reptilian penis. The clitoris, just like the penis, is composed of erectile tissue that becomes swollen with blood during sexual arousal. The existence of the early clitoris is the result of the fact that an embryo in an egg or the womb does not gain gonochoristic sex characteristics until it is roughly 20 per cent of the way through gestation. In the case of humans, this amounts to eight or nine weeks in the womb. Until then, a small tube develops that can be the foundation for either a penis or a clitoris. While the penis goes on to facilitate penetration and fertilisation, and experiences pleasure stimuli while doing so, the clitoris confines itself to the realm of sexual pleasure. Yet if early clitorises had merely been 'vestigial penises' in previous epochs, they would not remain so forever. They later took on an evolutionary significance of their own as they grew in complexity and the raw sensual power they wielded.

In most reptilian and mammalian species, the clitoris is held internally (just like the internal penis) and therefore without any opportunity for external stimulation. Monotreme mammals (from whom we split 175 million years ago) keep their clitorises internally. But when external penises evolved in placental mammals between 125 and 66 million years ago, clitorises began to peek out as well, inviting the opportunity for external stimulation for the first time. The co-evolution of both dick and clit in our direct ancestral line also explains why both penises and clitorises have a bone in them (the baculum and baubellum, respectively). We've covered the many explanations of why the penis bone exists, but these do not apply to clitorises, which appear to have gained the bone before sex differentiation happened in the womb, and the proto-penis/clitoris was still just a fleshy tube.

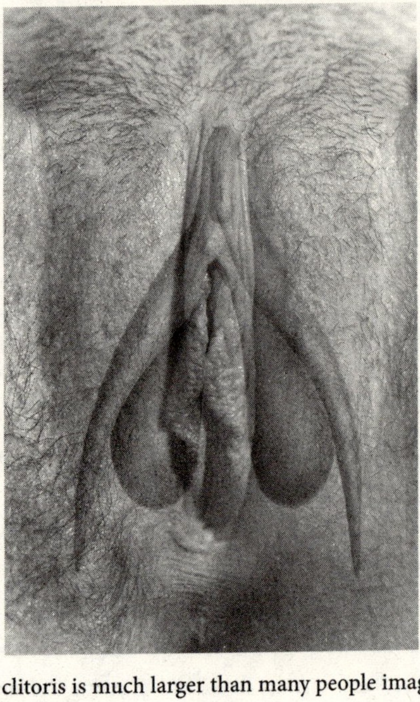

The clitoris is much larger than many people imagine.

Then, 66 million years ago, the clitoris undertook an evolutionary journey of its own. While the clitoris only presents as a small nub on the outside (that some unfortunate men have difficulty finding), the clitoris did grow internally to a massive degree. Ninety per cent of the clitoris resides inside the body, wrapping cosily around the vagina and connecting to both the vaginal canal and the labia with an intricate patchwork of nerve endings. There are approximately 8,000 or 9,000 such nerve endings in the clitoris, or roughly two to three times as many as in the penis. If female sexual pleasure were irrelevant to the act of reproduction, then it would make no sense that such nerve endings, outstripping those in the penis, evolved. And yet the clitoris continued to grow in complexity.

When the clitoris is stimulated, these nerve endings transmit to the rest of the female genitalia, causing similar states of arousal. First, it triggers the lubrication of the vaginal canal, which in turn facilitates penetration. So essential is the clitoris to the state of female arousal that an estimated 80 per cent of women cannot orgasm without clitoral stimulation. Given that clitoral stimulation is so crucial to female arousal, which in turn lubricates the act of copulation, it is no wonder that the clitoris stuck around, evolutionarily speaking.

When a female mammal experiences pleasure during sex with a welcome and desirable mate, she is more likely to stay in one place and not grow restless or attempt to flee. Furthermore, the existence of female sexual pleasure in mammals increases the odds that females will actively seek out sex, increasing the average number of copulations in any given species. Additionally, when a female mammal experiences intense surges of dopamine and other pleasure chemicals in the brain during sex, this may keep her in one place briefly after the sex act has ended, increasing the odds that the sperm will reach their target and fertilise her eggs. Also, when a female orgasms during sex, her vaginal muscles contract, squeezing the penis, prompting a quicker ejaculation from the male and drawing the semen upwards towards her eggs. In monogamous species, it is possible that orgasms reinforce female attachment to their mates, and in polyamorous species an orgasm can increase the likelihood she invites the same mate back for return sessions. And across many mammalian species the more attractive a mate, the more likely an orgasm is to occur, thus reinforcing a female's optimal mate choices. There is also the relatively new hypothesis that in ancestral mammalian species around 66 million years ago, female orgasms could trigger ovulations that were otherwise not on the individual mammal's calendar, thus increasing the odds of conception and reproduction. And although our direct line of ancestry leading up to humans has since lost the ability of orgasms to trigger spontaneous ovulations, the female orgasm may have remained as a vestige of this process, while the female orgasm itself found other evolutionary purposes.

Yet this throws up a few puzzles. First, female sexual arousal in mammals is not required to achieve pregnancy. Plenty of frustrated girlfriends and wives can tell you that. A 2015 survey found that women with regular partners only orgasmed 63 per cent of the time, and a 2017 survey of 1000 women found that 80 per cent of them could not orgasm during penetrative sex without some concurrent form of clitoral stimulation. In the more brutish corners of nature, where mammalian copulations can be brief and frequently coercive, the core components to insemination are penetration and male ejaculation. There are numerous copulations in many mammalian species where a female experiences little to no pleasure at all, to speak nothing of fear and pain during coerced or forced sex.

Yet if female sexual pleasure is not required for successful inseminations, why did it evolve at all? The answer seems to be that while female pleasure is not a prerequisite for mammalian pregnancies, it does increase the odds of reproductive success. In other words, if female pleasure increased the odds of a successful pregnancy in some copulations over the course of 66 million years of evolution, that was sufficient reason for it to stick around and perhaps even grow more elaborate. And there are no clear disadvantages that would lead it to recede from our mammalian family tree: no species has gone extinct because a female enjoyed sex too much. So, what may have started with the clitoris's co-evolution with the external penis proffered enough reproductive advantages to stick around, while at the same time not providing a single reason why it should go extinct.

The second puzzle is a bit more mechanical. Not all sexual positions afford clitoral stimulation, so why would the clitoris have continued to evolve its many sensitive nerve endings if it was seldom 'used' in many mammalian species? Sure, in humans and a few other primates, the missionary position allows for some clitoral stimulation from the grinding of pelvises during thrusting, as do many positions where the woman is on top – to speak nothing of the glories of cunnilingus. But the way most mammals copulate – the proverbial 'doggy-style' – on the surface affords little to no clitoral stimulation at all.

But, again, we have to consider the clitoris in its proper historical context. Sixty-six million years ago, our small rodent-like ancestors would likely have done it doggy-style, with the male mounting from behind for a brief copulation. Yet due to the physiology of the rodent-like female, with short legs and her torso close to the ground, there was high probability of clitoral contact with the ground during mounting with enough friction to promote a small ripple of stimulation. Copulation was brief, but that equally brief and mild bit of stimulation to an area as sensitive as the clitoris may have been enough for a female ancestral mammal to hold still until the sex act was completed. In fact, the heightened sensitivity of the clitoris compared to the penis may have developed because it needed to grab whatever chance it could for stimulation during the sex act. The other consideration is that while the clitoris is a primary pleasure centre, the G spot, which we discuss in a moment, is quite well stimulated during doggy-style.

As mammals evolved, the clitoris also took on other usages. In bonobos, for example, which split off from their common ancestor with chimpanzees roughly 3.5 million years ago, tribadism (or 'tribbing' or 'scissoring') became a useful way of forming social bonds between females. And it is done with insane frequency. This was particularly useful for bonobos because they live in female-dominated hierarchies. In hyenas, another female-dominant species from whom we split roughly 60 million years ago, female clitorises grew to be nearly as long as male penises. Female hyenas lick the clitorises of other females as a way of social-bonding and establishing a pecking order among them. Males, in an act of subservience, lick the clitorises of everyone regardless of rank, and may or may not be lucky enough to have their cock licked in return. And as a hyena's elongated clitoris also contains the vaginal canal and is in an awkward position high on their belly that males cannot mount without sliding beneath them, rape is almost impossible for hyenas, especially considering female hyenas are typically stronger, increasing the reproductive advantage they have over males.

Thus, while the clitoris may well have begun as a 'vestigial penis' hundreds of millions of years ago, the game changed once external genitalia arrived on the scene. Thereafter a number of good uses for clitorises and the female orgasm were likely selected for. And once the clitoris kicked into gear evolutionarily, it stuck around, with no good reason to disappear. Within our mammalian lineage since the Cretaceous Extinction 66 million years ago, the clit continued to find more uses in rapidly diversifying species. This remained the case all the way through history until we arrive at humans, where the clitoris not only continued to serve a useful reproductive function but also became a magnificent source of entertainment for everyone involved.

JACKING AND JILLING

By 60 million years ago the world had recuperated from the Cretaceous Extinction, and our cock- or clit-bearing mammalian ancestors were no longer tiny rat-like creatures. The ancestors of elephants, wolves, foxes, lions, tigers and bears (none of them any larger than dogs at the time) had split off from our direct lineage. And the lines between canine and feline further split 42 million years ago. By 55 million years ago, mammals the size of cats re-entered the oceans for the first time since the Devonian period and, over the next 15 million years, came to resemble ancestral whales and dolphins. Also around 55 million years ago, some small, quiet forest-dwellers split from our direct line to evolve into deer, elk, antelope and, after escaping the forest for the wide, open plains, the earliest species of horses. Finally, in our direct line 55 million years ago, the first primates emerged. They were tiny, no bigger than lemurs, dwelling in the trees with grasping hands and front-facing eyes. They had evolved to have stereoscopic 3D vision to jump successfully from branch to branch, and this ability required a slight boost in brain size.

Placental mammals spread across Earth, with the exception of the isolated landmass of Australia, where marsupials predominated. Inherent to all these wondrously diversifying species was the practice of jacking or jilling off. Our reptilian ancestors of various kinds were known to rub the surfaces of their cloacas on various objects, but thanks to the presence of external penises and the more discreetly positioned clitorises, mammalian access to their naughty bits became unprecedented. With the emergence of both male and female orgasms, the temptations of self-pleasure became overwhelming.

The ancestors of canines, felines, bears, goats, sheep, many types of rodents, some monkeys, otters and walruses all took up the practice of fellating themselves. Males would lick their penises in a state of erection, females would lick the broad opening of their vaginas. As thrilling as it no doubt felt, usually this practice was not pursued until after ejaculation or orgasm, and in many cases it arose naturally out of the practice of self-cleaning. A vast array of mammals also masturbated by dry-humping various objects. For canines this was an extremely frequent practice, but we also see it in the entire family of ungulates (horses, giraffes, boars, goats and rhinos). Lions and tigers are known to jack off with their front paws. Some species of monkeys pleasure themselves with their tails. Many types of rodents masturbate with their feet. One odd case from the order of Rodentia is the porcupine, which appears to enjoy simulating the prickly nature of its sex life by rubbing its genitals back and forth along rough objects such as tree bark, bush brambles and coarse stones. In another unusual case, elephants are known to wank each other off with their trunks. And finally, male chimpanzees and baboons are fans of ejaculating into their hands and hurling their semen at passers-by.

Generally speaking, masturbation serves the function of reducing stress, anxiety or aggression in mammalian species. Some forms of mutual masturbation between two mammals act as a form of social bonding. And in a minority of cases, male ejaculation is the objective, to clear and cleanse their reproductive tracts and potentially increase sperm production. As counterintuitive as it may sound to human ears, in many mammalian species the achievement of full-blown orgasm is not always the goal. Instead, the primary use of masturbation is as a momentary antidote to the fight-or-flight response triggered in a mammal by its adrenal glands. Unlike in humans, stopping halfway through does not appear to lead to much visible frustration in many species.

REPURPOSED FOR SEX

As mammals evolved from a tiny rodent-like size and their bodies became more complex, the erogenous zones on their bodies diversified too. Sex was not just a matter of caressing one's own genitalia or those belonging to someone else. Most of these erogenous zones were already highly sensitive to trigger a fear response should they be touched by an aggressive fellow member of their species, or a predator, or in case a small parasite like a tick or poisonous spider was crawling on them. The armpits are a great example of this, as this is precisely the sort of vulnerable spot a blood-sucking parasite might ideally take hold.

The origin of erogenous zones in places that are also sensitive enough to detect danger is why there is a thin line between erotic touching and uncomfortable, inappropriate touching that triggers instinctual alarm bells and makes people (and some other mammals) uncomfortable. The further sexualisation of erogenous zones in mammals is because an area is being touched that would normally only be visited by a fellow mammal during the act of sex. In most other circumstances – except for social bonding or carrying children – there are very few reasons why another mammal should get so close to those areas.

Many erogenous zones are adjacent to the genitals and possess sexual triggers because they imply that direct sexual contact is imminent. For instance, the inner thighs, the mammal's hindquarters, or the lower part of the belly. All seem to be tending in the direction of the centre of sexual gravity orbiting the genitalia. Other erogenous zones, such as fingers, toes, hands and feet, are stimulated in primates because they evolved to be highly sensitive in order to touch things. The high sensitivity merely lends itself to stimulation of a sexual nature through caressing, licking and sucking.

The nipples are an erogenous zone in most female mammals because since approximately 260 million years ago, their stimulation released powerful hormones. Sucking and fondling the mammary glands produced prolactin (secreting milk in the reproductive process) and oxytocin (a chemical used in the bonding of mother and child, as well as in stages of sexual attraction between males and females across most vertebrate species). Since stimulation triggers the vital release of these hormones, nipples tend to be extremely sensitive, producing sensations that often have such intensity that a sizeable minority of women can orgasm from nipple stimulation alone. In men, who also have nipples as a vestigial trait from early gestation in the womb (much like the sex differentiation between penis and clitoris) there is also a degree of sensitivity, but one that is much reduced and has only resulted in orgasms from stimulation in a smattering of recorded cases.

Touch to the neck and ears is erogenous, with either hands, paws or the gentle nibbling of teeth, since that is precisely what occurs during the mounting process in the vast majority of placental mammals. The ears and throat are also vital parts of the body that are highly sensitive in non-sexual situations to detect the threat of damage. Finally, the lips are an erogenous zone in a tiny minority of primates such as humans, chimps and bonobos, who are the rare few mammals who seem to have evolved to exchange sex pheromones while their lips are locked together.

In addition to the clitoris in female mammals, there are a great many nerve endings in the anterior wall in the front third of the vagina. This is where we find the G spot, a particularly sensitive cluster of nerves that can prompt orgasm when stimulated, the existence of which is still hotly debated among biologists. It is unclear whether the G spot is unique or whether it is more broadly an extension of the nervous system governed by the clitoris. Some biologists have speculated that the G spot is a 'vestigial prostate' (which produces the viscous liquid for male semen). But there appears to be only a weak connection between this area and the Skene's glands, which contributes to female ejaculation, perhaps itself a vestigial process, though not in squirting, which is mostly the result of clear liquid emanating from the bladder during sex.

A particular spot in the anterior wall of the vagina has yet to be found that can be classified as the standard G spot; anecdotally, it appears that some women have this sensitive area and others do not. Sexual sensitivity in the anterior wall appears to vary between individual women in the same way that some people's feet are ticklish and others are not. During penetrative sex, the penis does not easily reach the G spot in missionary position, but it is more effectively stimulated during doggy-style, the position in which most mammals copulate. So it is possible that varying degrees of sensitivity occur in the general vicinity of the first third of the vagina in order to facilitate female orgasm and all its potential reproductive advantages.

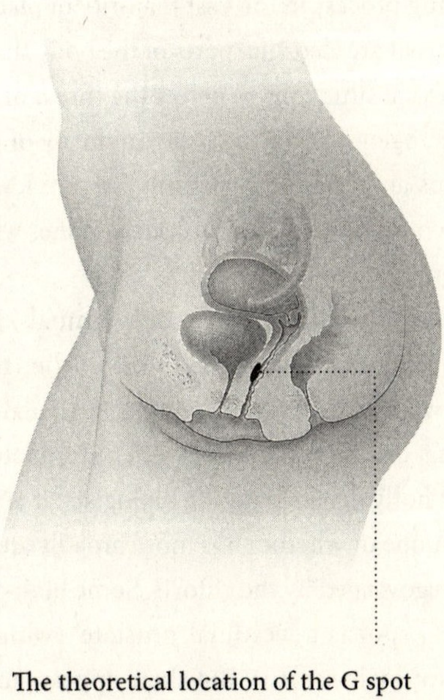

The theoretical location of the G spot

The sensitivity of the prostate is widely perceived to be the equivalent of the G spot in men, even if the prostate and G spot don't actually have any gonochoristic overlap. The prostate can be stimulated manually or by penetrative sex and massaged to the point that some men can achieve orgasm, though most require other sexual intervention, such as a reach-around, to achieve that happy state. Similarly, a number of nerve endings connected to the clitoris in the first two-thirds of the anus can be stimulated to the point of orgasm in a very small minority of women.

While bisexual and exclusively homosexual activity is hundreds of millions of years old, anal sex itself is something of a rarity in non-human mammals. It is known to occur mostly in the great apes but is also present in a few of the New and Old World monkeys. In the wider class of mammalia, some observers claim that anal sex is practised by some hooved animals such as giraffes and underwater mammals such as whale species. But by and large it is a rare thing.

POLYAMOROUS PRIMATES

As mammalian species continued to diversify, so did their particular soft spots and predilections. The primates, the biological order to which humans belong, first evolved 55 million years ago and their sexual habits became as diverse as the number of species that multiplied from them. Primates span the entire spectrum of mating behaviours, from polygyny (one male, many females), through polyandry (one female, many males), promiscuity (a chaotic festival of fucking) to pair-bonded monogamy (one male, one female).

Humans themselves have a mixture of many of these behaviours in our heritage. It has produced 'crossed wires' in terms of our evolutionary instincts, leading to some seriously conflicting sexual desires. And within that tangle of instincts, we begin to see the first glimmers of human love, infidelities, swingers' parties, and fetishes. It is by considering all those things within the context of our evolutionary history that we begin to understand why sex tends to make even the simplest of living situations turbulent. But at least it also has the virtue of sometimes making the sex amazing.

5

MONKEY BUSINESS

55 to 10 million years ago

Wherein primates split into the New and Old World monkeys 40 million years ago • The New World monkeys develop monogamy • The Old World monkeys develop polygyny and promiscuity • The great apes diverge from the Old World monkeys 25 million years ago • The gibbons live monogamously • The orangutans become quasi-polygynous serial rapists • The gorillas cockblock each other and live in harems.

The last common ancestor of all primates (monkeys, apes and humans – who taxonomically are just another type of ape) evolved in Africa approximately 55 million years ago. At first, they were tree-dwelling mammals, roughly 15 centimetres tall, resembling miniature monkeys. At the time, most were still nocturnal to avoid predators, much like our timid rat-like Cretaceous ancestors some 10 million years earlier. They were also likely insectivores, munching down on beetles and roaches, before subsequently branching out into eating roots, fruits and other plant matter.

A few of them headed north from Morocco into Spain and wider Europe before migrating down into Asia. By 30 million years ago, after plate tectonics had pulled Asia and Africa closer together, erasing vast stretches of ocean and raising the Arabian Peninsula from the depths of the seas, further species of primates headed from Africa to Asia directly. In both Africa and Asia, these were the ancestors of the Old World monkeys.

Meanwhile, another group of monkeys made their way into the Americas. How they got there is a *lot* more mysterious. Africa and South America had already split apart 120 million years ago, long before the dinosaurs went extinct, 65 million years before the first primates even evolved. The gulf between the two continents would only widen in the intervening years, creating the South Atlantic Ocean. By 55 million years ago, South America and Africa were separated by an ocean at least 1287 kilometres wide at the closest point between the two continents. And there's every indication that these primates began their journey at least 10 million years later, when plate tectonics had made the ocean even more vast.

This was not an easy body of water for primates to cross. Some would say the journey would have been impossible. We know that a land bridge did not exist between South America and Africa, because if it did a lot more African species would have made it across than just primates. The dominant hypothesis about how primates got to the Americas is that some of them floated across the ocean, set adrift upon large chunks of buoyant vegetation that acted as rafts. Perhaps there were a few tiny islands mercifully along the way which these primates could inhabit for a few generations before continuing along their journey. Not that these monkeys were consciously behaving like Christopher Columbus. The migration may have been quite inadvertent and accidental. But in modernity, primates have been observed floating on vegetation across large bodies of water in precisely this way, so the migration is distinctly possible.

If this hypothesis strains your credulity, know that the author may be in accordance with your views. Nevertheless, the 'monkey raft' idea is the prevailing scientific theory currently. But whether from

Africa to South America directly, or by a more circuitous route via northern Europe, Greenland and North America (for which there is no fossil evidence), by 40 million years ago primates were in South America and had split from our direct lineage to become the predictably named New World monkeys.

MONOGAMY IN THE NEW WORLD ...

You can tell the difference between New and Old World monkeys primarily by the shape of their noses. Old World monkeys have downward-facing nostrils more like humans. New World monkeys have noses that are flatter with nostrils that turn out to the sides. The difference must have emerged after the New World–Old World split 40 million years ago. Additionally, New World monkeys have grasping prehensile tails, much more functional than the tails of Old World monkeys, and slightly different sets of teeth. They can also see colour, an ability the descendants of Old World monkeys did not evolve until our genetic line was much closer to humans.

New World monkeys evolved various kinds of sexual habits. Some of them live in 'polyandrous' groups, where females have sex with more than one male and where only one female is sexually active in the monkey group at any one time. Offspring are then raised communally. Other New World monkeys operate in promiscuous groups, with a heavy dose of fierce male–male competition over females. Some species take this a step further, with a single dominant male monopolising the sexual services of all the females in a form of polygyny, while the rest of the males are out of luck.

But what is most intriguing about New World monkeys is the vast number of species that observe monogamous relationships. For instance, both titi monkeys and night monkeys pair-bond, with the male warding off others from mating with his girl. Only 3 to 5 per cent of mammalian species are monogamous, so the fact this practice evolved in so many species of New World monkey is quite remarkable.

Even more astounding is the fact that such monogamous monkeys see the males providing a lot of parental care for offspring by carrying the infants most of the time and providing them with food. Male parental care is another rarity in primates. Most other primate species are nurtured by the mother, and sometimes by a community of her female friends.

Titi monkeys in a monogamous pair-bond

… AND A CRAPSHOOT IN THE OLD

Returning to our direct line of ancestry, the Old World monkeys, we do not see monogamy to anywhere near the same degree. And with an increased sexual free-for-all came the increased need to ward against incest. This came in the form of 'mate dispersal', where one biological sex or another leaves the group in which they were born. Most non-monogamous New World monkeys do this, and the last common ancestor of all Old World monkeys (most assuredly *not* a monogamous creature) did this as well, passing it down to all descendant species.

A brief aside on boning your relatives: Mother Nature likes it when we have sex with newcomers, to increase genetic variation and speed along evolutionary change. She is not so fond of brother–sister, father–daughter or mother–son dalliances. First cousins are generally a bad idea too. This is because having two near-identical strands of DNA can increase the odds that a usually suppressed recessive gene gets further entrenched in your family line. These recessive genes are quite frequently harmful and can lead to severe physical deformities or intellectual maladies. The more frequently close relatives fuck, the greater the odds some of these problems will rear their ugly heads. As such, many species have in-built instincts against incest. That sense of revulsion you (hopefully) have when you contemplate the prospect of having sex with one of your siblings? That's evolution talking. And in the case of Old World monkeys, we had an advanced form of mate dispersal. Upon reaching sexual maturity, one biological sex or another consistently departed the natal group to prevent incest and inbreeding in a sex-crazed non-monogamous environment.

Accordingly, our last common ancestor 40 million years ago lived in 'matrilocal' groups, where females stayed with the group in which they were born while males instinctually set off in search of new groups where they could get laid. As a result, while female monkeys lived peacefully with their mothers and sisters, horny males were on the prowl. This tended to produce a lot of aggressive male–male competition for sex, with dominant males mating with multiple females rather than pairing up monogamously.

For instance, many baboon species live in mixed groups of

multiple males and females, with the males being new arrivals. Fierce competition between males and a rigid pecking order determine how often male baboons get to have sex with the females. The more dominant the baboon, the more often he gets to fuck. Sometimes, a beta male will try to circumvent the pecking order by cosying up to a female, grooming her and befriending her – provided he is not spotted by other males and driven off. But there is nothing monogamous about this 'simping' behaviour, since if the ingratiating male is successful he will move on and try the same tactics with multiple females rather than 'settling down'. Female baboons, for their part, can signal their interest to any individual male by shoving their swollen asses in a male's face to declare they are fertile and ready to have sex, in a distant evolutionary echo of twerking. Other Old World monkeys that live in multi-male, multi-female groups with a high degree of male competition are some colobus monkeys, vervet monkeys and mandrills.

The last of these, the mandrills, make for an interesting case. While most Old World monkeys live in communities of half a dozen to several dozen, mandrills live in 'hordes' of several *hundred*. Roughly 85 per cent of a mandrill horde is composed of females and their recent offspring. Adult males, who make up the remaining 15 per cent, are not a permanent part of the horde. Instead, they live rather solitary lives in the wilderness, until the mating season begins. Then they rush back to the horde and begin competing viciously with each other to determine which of them gets to have sex with the much larger number of females. Dominant mandrills are determined by their size; bigger, fatter flanks; redder faces and asses; and their bluer balls (literally blue, not figuratively). Out of a mandrill horde of, say, 700, roughly 300 of them will be adult females. And on average, only thirty-five males will be dominant and desirable enough to successfully mate with them. That's almost ten females per dominant male. The remaining, say, seventy males will be very much involuntarily celibate. Once the mating season is over, the males depart, leaving the females to raise the children on their own. Thus, our evolutionary history is littered with alpha-Chad douchebags who turn out to be deadbeat dads.

Other Old World monkeys don't just have male–male competition where multiple male 'victors' get to have sex but go the extra step into full-blown polygyny. This is where only *one* dominant alpha male arrives in a female natal group and mates with them, driving off all other male contenders, who watch jealously from the sidelines. Male geladas, for instance, leave their birth group upon attaining sexual maturity, and roam around in all-male groups of 'bachelors', vigilantly seeking harems of females to take over. Once such a gaggle of females appears, the males do not share space. Only one male gelada can take over a group of females. He then drives off all rival males. Thereupon the victorious male has sex with all the females in the group for a handful of years.

Even in the rare exceptions where two males reside in a breeding group, only one alpha male is allowed to have sex with the females while the other male largely remains celibate. Eventually that male either leaves in frustration or quietly tries to tempt away a couple of females to start a group of his own. Meanwhile, if a more potent male rival shows up, the original alpha can be overthrown, banished and replaced. The alpha male must also maintain good relations with the females in his group or they might refuse to have sex and overthrow him themselves – and then eagerly await a more suitable alpha-Chad to take his place.

In baboons, mandrills and geladas, females sexually compete with other females in quite a vigorous fashion. They will try to monopolise the sexual attentions of the most attractive alpha males for themselves, being quite aggressive with their sisters in an attempt to keep them away. Intimidation and even violence between females can occur. Given that the male Old World monkeys don't stick around and that they provide little to no parental care for offspring, it's clear this female competition isn't driven by romantic jealousy or a monogamous quest for a strong male provider. Female competition among Old World monkeys is purely to keep the hottest beefcakes and their presumably superior genes all to themselves. Otherwise, the male's copulations might be too thinly spread across a group of females, with some of the sisters running the risk of missing out.

But nature always likes an exception to the rule. An unusual group of Old World monkeys are the macaques. They live in female-led societies where females do not hesitate to be very aggressive towards males. This is augmented by the fact that female macaques stay in their natal sorority for life and form strong social bonds with each other – much firmer alliances than many other matrilocal primates. Also, the females tend to be quite choosey when selecting a male for sex; they tend to reject a larger proportion of potential suitors. As in all Old World monkeys, the male macaques split off in adulthood from their birth groups and try to ingratiate themselves with a new group of females. But, unlike other Old World monkeys, male sexual success is mostly down to female acceptance and 'primate politics' rather than male–male gatekeeping and competition. If the male is accepted into a new group, however, they get to mate with multiple females. If not, the male macaque gets to remain in the forest, lonely, unloved and unfucked, until death. So, for males the end result is the same as for other Old World monkeys: they either get to have a lot of sex or none at all.

LEAVE ME AND MY GIRLFRIEND ALONE

Meanwhile, 25 to 30 million years ago, the great apes split off from their last common ancestor with the Old World monkeys. Apes are distinguishable from monkeys by the fact they lost their tails. They also tend to be bigger and have broader chests and larger brains relative to their body sizes. The earliest great apes appear to be rather solitary creatures rather than highly social animals like many Old World monkeys. No troops of dozens or hordes of hundreds. Just apes tarrying alone in the woods and occasionally coming across a potential mate or a rival.

The first living evolutionary cousin of ours to split from our direct lineage was the gibbon, approximately 17 million years ago. They share roughly 96 per cent of their DNA with humans. Gibbons are tree-dwelling creatures that feed on fruits, leaves, flowers and sometimes insects. They inhabit South and Southeast Asia (their ancestors having migrated there from Africa). They are often referred to as 'lesser apes' due to their smaller size compared with gorillas, chimps, humans, etc. Gibbons are fairly solitary and extremely territorial, discouraging other gibbons from entering their foraging territory by a series of fierce shouts and intimidating 'power' stances.

As a result of this solitary nature, male and female gibbons attract mates by shouting to each other from a kilometre away. Sort of like how an increasingly solitary humanity conducts most of their courtships via phone apps like Tinder. Once the gibbons meet, if they both like what they see, gibbons usually pair-bond for life. That is to say, unlike the Old World monkeys, *gibbons are monogamous*. Aside from humans and gibbons, no living apes practise monogamy.

The evolutionary reason for monogamous behaviour in gibbons is that, due to their social organisation, heavy male–male competition associated with polygyny and promiscuity would be disastrous – particularly if rival males committed infanticide. In many other primate species, a male would kill the offspring of a rival male and then mate with the grieving mother, in order to ensure *his* code of DNA was replicated into the future rather than the rival's. Infanticide of this kind is an ugly instinct that evolved through DNA's quest to blindly replicate itself, regardless of the suffering inflicted on individual creatures.

The problem is, gibbons are non-gregarious and a little sex-starved, and even when they manage to find a mate and pair-bond, they don't have sex very often. Gibbons only fuck in oestrus periods, when a female gibbon is fertile – which you can tell visually from the swelling of her hindquarters. Ovulation is not concealed. The rest of the time, the gibbon couples stay together, cosying up but not having sex, largely isolated from the rest of their species. Gibbons can simply not afford to have a lot of male–male competition and infanticide, or the species would probably have died out.

Instead, gibbons pair-bond in monogamous relationships, and both of them protect their offspring. Gibbon fathers will drive off rival males who might pose a danger to his children. And he cannot do this if he is crossing a kilometre of forest to track down the calls of another female. Accordingly, gibbon mothers recognise that attracting two or more males and having sex with both increases the risk that one of them will jealously kill some of her children. So, instead, monogamous gibbon couples look out for each other, living quietly and peacefully, building their own little bubble in a rather wicked world.

However, the evolutionary wiring of the promiscuous or polygynous Old World monkeys from whom the gibbons split 25 million years ago was not erased overnight. As such, gibbons are known to commit the occasional infidelity, copulating outside the relationship. But this is rare and punished with the gibbon equivalent of sexual jealousy from the other spouse. Also, on rare occasions, gibbon couples may experience such a rash of aggression towards each other that they split up for good (aka 'divorce') and go off and try to find another mate in a form of serial monogamy. However, due to the evolutionary pressures on gibbons to reproduce, 'divorces' are relatively rare; most stay together for life, and the gibbon divorce rate is considerably lower than the one in humans. But we can certainly see the parallels in gibbons to those humans who get hitched, have affairs and/or split up because of irreconcilable differences.

THE VIOLENT SEX LIVES OF ORANGUTANS

The next evolutionary cousin to split from our direct ancestry were the orangutans, approximately 15 million years ago. Humans share roughly 97 per cent of their DNA with them. Orangutans inhabit the jungles of the islands of Borneo and Sumatra in Southeast Asia (again, with their ancestors migrating there from Africa). They also previously used to exist on the South Asian mainland prior to 60,000 years ago, but have since been driven to extinction by either climate or, more likely, human hunter-gatherers. Like gibbons, orangutans are primarily tree-dwellers eating fruits, leaves and the odd insect. And like gibbons, orangutans are quite solitary creatures.

Where the differences begin is that orangutans are *not* monogamous. They practise a sort of quasi-polygyny, where a male will seek to have sex with multiple females at the expense of other males. It would be full-blown polygyny if orangutans weren't so solitary. As a result, there is a great deal of male–male competition as they try to monopolise access to sex in their surrounding kilometre of forest. Dominant males signal their virility by growing massive (and slightly ridiculous-looking) flaps of skin on the sides of their faces, called flanges. These flanged males have specific calls that attract interested females, who prefer gentlemen with these fleshy protuberances. The flanged male calls can be so powerful that it can arrest the growth of flanges in younger males who hear them and feel intimidated. It would be like a human adolescent boy chatting up a girl, only to have his balls refuse to drop, facial hair refuse to sprout, muscles refuse to gain definition and his penis refuse to grow any bigger because a hotter guy on the football team started hitting on her. Once the flanged male orangutan grows too old and loses his virility, he will lose the skin flaps and be supplanted by a freshly flanged newcomer.

As a result of the quasi-polygyny and the vigorous male–male competition, orangutans have a significant amount of sexual dimorphism (that is, evolved physical differences between biological males and females). Male orangutans are two times heavier than female orangutans. Females tend to be attracted to flanged males and are ready and willing to have sex with them. Females also tend to be decidedly *less* receptive to the overtures of unflanged beta males.

The flanges on this male orangutan's face render him very attractive to females.

One of the darkest traits of the orangutans arises because females have concealed ovulation: that is, they give no clear sign to males when they are fertile and when they are not. Which means male orangutans try it on with them all the time, while only the females instinctually know if they are sexually in earnest. And because female orangutans are not very receptive to the sexual advances of unflanged males, rape is horrifically common. If the female is not ovulating, she generally does not resist the sexual assault of an unflanged male, because the risk of pregnancy is non-existent. But if she knows she is fertile, the female orangutan vigorously resists the prospect of getting impregnated by a non-virile male – and this is where things can turn violent. Because orangutan copulations take an average of 15 minutes, these rapes are harrowing and can result in injury to a resisting female. This is also one of the reasons why female orangutans tend to orbit the general vicinity of dominant flanged males, who will protect them from the predatory beta male rapists. And this is how a dominant male orangutan will form a polygynous, dispersed harem of surrounding females.

Orangutan sexual violence is not just an evolutionary echo of the vile behaviours we sometimes see in humans. The rates of sexual violence among orangutans are astounding. Adjusting for population sizes, sexual violence is 25,000 to 200,000 times more frequent in orangutans than in any modern or pre-modern human society. A separate estimate is that one-third to one-half of all orangutan copulations are rapes.

Orangutan quasi-polygyny with high male–male competition has a few other consequences. First, females evolved to counter the threat of male infanticide of their children by having long periods of infertility after giving birth. They are not fertile again for an average of eight years, and they tend to nurse their offspring for a similar amount of time – longer than any other mammal. Thus, male orangutans cannot simply arrive, kill off their rival's children and immediately impregnate a female again. Second, since there is no evolutionary incentive, we do not see infanticide in orangutans, despite male–male competition being high.

Another common feature of polygynous primates is a high frequency of male bisexuality and homosexuality. As we saw in Chapter 2, bisexuality evolved in vertebrate species around the same time gonochorism (sex differences) did, 510 to 525 million years ago, and the earliest evidence of exclusively homosexual individuals stems from 330 million years ago (though this trait could also have arisen much earlier). Such behaviours exist in an overwhelming majority of vertebrate species. But in polygynous species, where a minority of alpha males have sex with most of the females, with a great many other males left sexless on the sidelines, male–male homosexual behaviour is statistically more common. This evolved in orangutans to relieve the sexual frustrations of the unflanged males, who might go years (if not their entire lives) in the reproductive doldrums. As a result, male orangutans are known to have consensual anal sex with each other. They also blow each other. However, with the characteristic sexual violence of orangutans, males also rape each other anally.

GORILLA 'WARFARE'

Gorillas split off from humans between 10 and 12 million years ago. We share roughly 98 per cent of their DNA. Whereas orangutan polygyny was indirectly caused by the female sexual preference for flanged males, gorilla polygyny became instinctually entrenched into gorilla mate-guarding behaviours. A typical gorilla group consists of one silverback male and a harem of females. Other male gorillas who are not able to compete with a silverback dwell in the forest, with only other males for company. As a result, these beta males have the option of either being celibate or engaging in a great deal of gay sex. This is a general trend in primate species. Where there is polygyny, there is a greater frequency of gay sex. Although that is not to say it is absent elsewhere. Gay sex happens virtually everywhere in primates, just with lower frequency when the species is not polygynous.

Prior to gorillas, our family tree was 'matrilocal': Old World monkey females stay with their family groups their entire lives, whereas males strike out towards unknown frontiers. Even in orangutans, who are reasonably solitary, mothers spend many years with their offspring before the children head off for a more lonesome existence in the wild. And even then, adult offspring retain a social link with their mother for as long as she is alive. With gorillas, we begin to see a transition away from matrilocal mate dispersal. Female gorillas do not stay with their kin and instead wander off from their relatives once they reach a mature age. And when gorilla females join the harem of a silverback male, the female newcomers are all strangers to each other.

In that sense, gorillas are a transitional branch in our family tree, between the matrilocal and patrilocal primates. The latter is where males stay with their kin groups their whole lives and females are the newbies. However, given that a gorilla male generally wants to be the only fella present in a harem of females, the rest of the males tend to get the punt as well. But, as we shall see, things were tending in the patrilocal direction ...

Male–male competition for control of a harem resulted in a large degree of sexual dimorphism in gorillas. A male gorilla is two or three times the size of a female. However, while male gorillas may look physically imposing, most of their aggression towards rival males is intimidation rather than violence. They strike power stances and chase other males off. By and large, it is warfare by bravado. Though be under no illusions: a gorilla can very easily kill another male if he needs to.

There is a significant difference in size between these female (left) and male (right) gorillas.

Because usually only one male gorilla exists in a group at any one time, there is less emphasis on being able to have sex quickly and often than in apes, who have multiple males in a group. As a result, gorilla testicles are roughly 40 per cent smaller than human testicles, despite a gorilla's much larger size. And gorillas have penises that range between 2.5 and 7.5 centimetres in length, with an average of 4.5 centimetres. In keeping with these unimpressive stats (at least to human ears) gorilla copulations last only 1 minute on average. This is much faster than orangutan sex sessions, but slow compared with other great apes, who, as we shall soon see, have multiple males in a group and operate in an atmosphere of greater sexual frenzy.

Unlike orangutans, gorillas are firm believers in the evolutionary benefits of infanticide. When a rival male steals a silverback's harem, one of his first objectives is to kill all the offspring fathered by his predecessor. That way it is the new alpha's DNA that gets passed on, rather than the old one's. The ever-present threat of infanticide from rival males causes silverbacks to jealously guard their harems and protect their children. And while male gorillas do not usually supply their offspring with food, this protection is more parental care than a lot of primates get from their fathers. Accordingly, female gorillas can reject their silverback if he fails to protect their children from infanticide. A silverback's harem can also be stolen if he is defeated in dominance displays by a rival male. Alternatively, if a female finds the male interloper more attractive, she will quietly slip away and join him in a newly formed group.

The non-related females tend to bond more with their silverback than they do with each other. Female–female bonds in gorillas are quite weak. Such is the impact of the transition to patrilocal mate dispersal. As a result, gorilla groups are strongly male-led, with the silverback the centre of social gravity. And despite their rivalries, other male gorillas show slightly stronger bonds with each other. The beta males out in the wild are companionable, socialising and sometimes dabbling in anal sex, until a group of females is in the offing. And occasionally a silverback will permit his son to stay in the harem after he has reached adolescence. But this comes with some conditions.

The silverback usually insists on doing most of the fucking in the harem; the son runs the risk of getting thrown out if he dallies with any of the females.

Gorilla females, meanwhile, compete quite vigorously for the attention of the silverback, since his goodwill (not support from other females) is the key to a female gorilla having her offspring protected, thus preserving her 'genetic investment' and passing on her DNA. As a result, the ladies compete in a rigid hierarchy of alpha and beta females, forging alliances to keep others in subordinate positions and using intimidation tactics. Imagine a high-school clique of 'popular girls', add slightly more body hair, and you won't be too far from the truth. The silverback seems to take notice of this female hierarchy, as he has sex with females on the basis of rank rather than prioritising those that are fertile.

Gorilla females will solicit sex from a silverback even when they are already pregnant, to maintain social bonds with him and keep him sweet. If the silverback has sex with one female in the harem, they all scramble to have sex with him, so as not to lose out in the competition for his affections. Conversely, on days when the silverback doesn't have sex with anyone, none of the females in the harem seem to bother. In short, gorilla sex seems to serve a strategic purpose attached to group politics, as well as the obvious reproductive one. This is not so distant from how sex is sometimes dispassionately and strategically used in human societies – whether in ancient and medieval dynastic marriages, 'honeytraps' in international espionage, the oft-reviled 'golddiggers' or the worst kind of quid pro quo in business, entertainment and politics.

As for pleasure, while gorilla females can enjoy clitoral stimulation and are capable of orgasm, most copulations proceed without anything of the sort. In a gorilla harem, the male 'comes first' both figuratively and literally. If, dear reader, you feel that arrangement is unfair to the females, buckle up, because things are about to get considerably worse. And with every step we take through our lineage, the shadow of these engrained instincts in our ancestry looms larger over our own conflicted sexual natures.

EVENT	DATE
First primates	55 million years ago
Split of New and Old World monkeys	40 million years ago
First great apes	25 million years ago
Split with gibbons	17 million years ago
Split with orangutans	15 million years ago
Split with gorillas	10 million years ago

6

CHIMPS FROM MARS, BONOBOS FROM VENUS

10 to 4 million years ago

Wherein the chimps split from our last common ancestor 6 to 8 million years ago • Gorilla polygyny evolves into multi-male, multi-female promiscuity • Chimps live in large patrilocal groups where male competition is rife • They provide a prelude to our slowly evolving impulses towards war • Chimp females live wretched, submissive lives in brutal male-dominated societies • Bonobos split off from chimps 2 million years ago • They suppress male aggression with female alliances and copious sex • A strict matriarchy supported by cunnilingus and female competition emerges • Bonobo mothers coddle their sons and occasionally kill the children of their female rivals.

Chimpanzees split off from the direct lineage of humans 6 to 8 million years ago. We share roughly 98.7 per cent of our DNA with them. Due to the extinction of all other forerunners of *Homo sapiens*, such as *Homo erectus* (extinct 110,000 years ago) and *Australopithecus afarensis* (extinct 2.9 million years ago), chimpanzees are our closest surviving evolutionary cousins. Accordingly, there are a great many similarities in our instincts and behaviours, along with some notable differences. The challenge is to not overstate or understate these things. A lot can change in 6 to 8 million years, but, due to the slow march of natural selection, a troubling amount can remain eerily the same.

The evolution towards greater social organisation, seen with gorillas in comparison to gibbons and orangutans, continued with chimpanzees 6 to 8 million years ago. Chimpanzee groups typically number between twenty and fifty individuals. Even, on rare occasions, a maximum of 150 individuals in a wider and loosely associated confederation. Smaller foraging groups of four to twelve males frequently splinter off from the main group, search for food or patrol their territory, before rejoining their wider community. Thus, the social complexity of our ancestral line steadily increased, and this directly affected how our ever-narrowing branch of the genetic family tree approached the issue of sex.

A VERY HAIRY PATRIARCHY

Unlike most gorilla harems, chimpanzee groups consist of multiple males *and* females, co-existing in a sophisticated patchwork of hierarchies and alliances. As such, chimpanzees transitioned away from the polygyny (one male–multiple females) that we see in many primates to promiscuity (non-monogamous couplings of males and females). As male chimps tolerate the presence of many other males within the same group, there is slightly lower male–male competition than in gorillas, where a single male drives off all other males and tries to dominate a harem. As a result, there is slightly less sexual dimorphism among chimpanzees than there is among gorillas. Male chimps are generally 25 per cent larger than females, in contrast to gorillas being two to three times larger. That said, chimps have to be made of sturdy stuff due to continued violence and intimidation over access to sex in the group. The average chimp male is two to four times stronger than an adult human male, despite the difference in height and weight between the two species, because of intense chimp male–male competition. Stories of people having their faces ripped off by an angry male chimp are testament to this difference in strength.

Within a group of chimp males, a clear dominance hierarchy exists and their social bonds can quickly sour into aggression. The male hierarchy is built around the higher-ups having greater access to food and mates. The alpha-Chads tend to get laid a lot, and the beta-Bobs tend to take what they can get when they can get it. Sexual jealousy abounds among male chimpanzees. They frequently use infanticide to eliminate their rival's genes, and higher-ranking males have a better chance of warding off potential child-killers, while nevertheless committing a few child-murders of their own.

Dominant chimp males are not always the biggest bruisers – though strength is certainly a factor in violent confrontations. Due to the increased social complexity of chimpanzees, dominant males must strike up and maintain careful alliances with other males. A dominant male must be a savvy, manipulative politician. A chimp Machiavelli. As a result, low-ranking males tend to have higher levels of testosterone and aggression. They *need* it to climb the social ladder. But once a male reaches the top of the hierarchy, his testosterone levels actually *decline*, since raw aggression is less useful in preserving a careful patchwork of alliances. Other males can be equally conniving. They have been known to gang up and overthrow a dominant male in the chimp version of a political coup. The ultimate aims of such contests for power are food and females. If you see in this behaviour an echo of primitive human politics and social organisation, you aren't completely wrong.

These within-group rivalries and hostilities are only suspended when chimp males are defending their foraging territory from 'outsider' males who clearly represent a much greater threat to the gene pool than internal rivalries, due to their potential to steal mates and foraging territory. This is also a clear echo of humans placing aside internal hostilities when they are called to war with another tribe or nation.

Of course, chimpanzees do not have wars in the modern sense. They are too few in number and disorganised. But they do have a microcosm or evolutionary precursor of war reminiscent of conflicts between human foraging bands. Male chimps will typically go out foraging in groups of four to twelve individuals. They look for plants and insects and sometimes even hunt and eat colobus monkeys, which they devour raw. Yet sometimes these male gangs do not forage at all. They wander the edges of their territory, 'on patrol' for any chimp males from outside their group. If a strange male has wandered into their territory, the chimp patrol will lynch him, kicking and slapping him, tearing off his ears or bits of his face, and ripping off his penis or testicles to eliminate him from the gene pool. The chimp gang then leaves their victim in the forest to die of his wounds. These patrols also make raids into the foraging territory of enemy chimp groups. When two opposing chimp patrols meet each other in the wild, they will often attack each other. If eight or more chimps are in such a patrol group, they will even risk a full-on charge at the enemy. There have been a few rare observations of

Chimp patrols can be extremely violent.

one chimpanzee group gradually wiping out all the individuals in another chimp group and seizing their foraging territory. When this behaviour is displayed by humans, we call it a genocide.

SEX AMONG PSYCHOPATHS

Chimpanzees are firmly patrilocal, meaning male kin stay together their entire lives, and the transient females who leave their natal groups once they reach sexual maturity are the newcomers. Because chimpanzee females are not related to each other, they tend to have weak social bonds compared with the related males. Female chimps also isolate themselves more when foraging rather than travelling in groups of female friends. Due to the lack of strong female alliances, female chimps are generally dominated by all adult males in the group. When a young male chimp grows up, he typically works his way through all the females, intimidating them and exerting his dominance, before he attempts to challenge the rank of any of his fellow males.

When a female stranger tries to join an existing chimpanzee group, the other resident females tend to be hostile towards her, because she represents sexual competition. So she has to start at the bottom rung of the female hierarchy. For their part, male chimpanzees will not accept any new female unless she is oestrus (a female chimp's hindquarters swell up like a balloon and turn red when she is fertile). If the chimpanzee female is immediately ready for sex and reproduction, the males welcome her in – much to the displeasure of the existing females. But if the female newcomer is not fertile and tries to join a chimpanzee group, the males will chase her away and even beat her up. On rare occasions, this discouragement can turn lethal. Males do this because non-fertile females are a potential drain on food resources within the group's foraging territory. As far as the male chimps are concerned, there is no point accepting another mouth to feed if she is not fertile at the time or, even worse, barren. Again, these evolutionary instincts derive from maximising the chances that a species will replicate their DNA. Less food without compensating with more sex jeopardises such a prospect.

Female chimps have their own pecking order and alliances, with older arrivals generally dominating more submissive newcomers. Female chimps practise nepotism, where the offspring of a high-ranking female will enjoy the same alliances and protections of the mother. A low-ranking female cannot bully the young daughter of a high-ranking female with impunity. Males also practise nepotism, sharing food with their brothers and mothers, along with giving food to unrelated females in exchange for sex (prostitution – the 'world's oldest profession'). Males will not share food with rival males and tend to snub members of their own family if they are more distantly related. Why? Because in a world where copying your DNA matters most, kindness and altruism can sometimes fade the further you move from your own bloodline. This phenomenon is known as kin-selection, where animals will sacrifice a little (like food) in exchange for helping an individual relative that is almost an exact copy of their own DNA code. All this is an evolutionary whisper of the hereditary principle that exists in pre-modern human societies (tribal chieftains, pharaohs, emperors, kings, dukes and marquises, etc) and, let's face it, the nepotism that still rears its head among the rich and powerful today.

Despite the chimp females' relative isolation from each other and subordination to chimp males, they do have strong sexual preferences. Females prefer to mate with dominant males of high rank. This affords their offspring greater protection from infanticide and greater access to shared food. Approximately 35 per cent of chimp sexual encounters are initiated by the female. When a chimp female has sex with a dominant male, she can increase the odds she will rise in the female hierarchy (especially useful if she is a newcomer) and, after having sex, the male tends to grow possessive of her, chasing off any other hopeful males. Thus, female chimp sexual preference tends towards hypergamy, where she prioritises liaisons with males of higher status to the benefit of her offspring, and where she is more reluctant to have sex with males of lower social status. This mating strategy is not entirely absent from *Homo sapiens* either.

The other 65 per cent of the time, sex is initiated by chimp males. While they tend to try to have sex with all females in the group, male chimps prioritise females who have already given birth, thus proving they are fertile and capable of having children. So chimp males prefer a gal with a few notches on her belt – provided she is not too old, of course. This stands in stark contrast to the tendency of many pre-modern human cultures, which valued virginity and a lack of sexual experience in women; women with too much experience or willingness to have sex were 'slut-shamed'. Chimpanzees, on the other hand, tend to hold females with a proven sexual track record in high esteem. In a species that is highly sexed, promiscuous and frequently uses infanticide to eliminate rival offspring (and even kids whose paternity is in doubt), female chastity is *way* down the list of priorities.

Chimps only have sex when females are oestrus. Which means a lot of fucking is crammed into one part of the calendar. During an 'oestrus cluster', females are penetrated up to eight times a day. And in that period, male chimps must move quickly lest they be beaten to impregnating a female by a rival male in the group. As a result of all this local 'sperm competition', chimps evolved to have larger testicles, carrying a greater volume of sperm than gorillas. Their penises also evolved to be larger, averaging 5.5 inches when erect, with a range of 3 to 7 inches. A cock approaching a human average is impressive considering chimps stand at only 3 to 4 feet tall (90 to 120 centimetres). Also, while polygynous gorilla copulations average only 1 minute, chimpanzees got that average time down to *7 seconds*. Again, the presence of other males in the primate group and a limited window for sex meant that chimp males had to be quick. Their efforts could be interrupted by a rival at any point.

You would think with a brief copulation time there would be little in the way of female sexual pleasure. And to a certain extent you are right. Female chimp orgasms are rare to come by. But they do occur, usually if coupled with other forms of stimulation prior to penetration (not an entirely foreign concept to humans either). But more than that, chimp female orgasms serve a social purpose rather than merely being reflective of pleasure. Chimp females 'vocalise' their orgasms more loudly and frequently when they are having sex with a high-ranking male. Arousal may well be a part of it, since it is a high-ranking male, but these vocalisations are also used to announce her sex session to nearby females, trumpeting to the female hierarchy that a dominant male has accepted them.

EVOLUTION'S DARK PASSENGER

Rape is commonplace among chimpanzees; they are a promiscuous, aggressive society. Females resist mating with males who have low social status, or if the male is too old or physically unhealthy, or if the female is simply too busy foraging for food. Chimp males whose advances are not accepted immediately resort to sexual coercion. At first it takes the form of intimidation and harassment. Chimp males will shout, shake tree branches, throw objects, charge at a female and even chase her. If this does not force the female into submission, the male will quickly resort to outright sexual assault.

Chimp females are generally attacked from behind, sustaining most cranial injuries to the back of the skull, due to the male chimp tendency to mount from that direction. Males will hit females with their hands (they are incapable of punching), bite them, kick them and drag them across the ground by their heads, fur and limbs. Once the female is held in position, the male will physically discourage all attempts to flee. However, serious injuries are rare during these rapes because female chimp resistance is seldom prolonged. Unlike orangutan sex, chimp copulations are brief, and the strength difference between male and female chimps renders more strenuous resistance risky with low likelihood of escape. To avoid inflammation, tearing and other injuries to the vaginal tract, the standard physiological response is for the vagina to become lubricated, despite the female chimp's mental and emotional distress about an unwelcome partner. This physiology is entirely divorced from any notion of consent or attraction, let alone pleasure. Unsurprisingly, chimp orgasm vocalisations during these rapes by lower-ranking males are rare to non-existent.

Perhaps more disturbing than the act itself is the aftermath. A female chimp raped by a low-ranking male can be punished with aggression by high-ranking males who sought to have sex with her instead. If an offspring results from the rape, there is a high likelihood these high-ranking males will kill it. Perhaps most disturbing of all, sometimes a female victim will begin to stick close to her rapist within the chimp group, since having the protection of a low-ranking male for her offspring is better than having no protection at all.

Female chimps tend to stay away from the borders of a group's foraging territory, remaining within the centre of the group, surrounded by male patrols. This is because if there is even a whiff of suspicion that a female has mated with an outsider, the inevitable result is infanticide. Conversely, if an outsider male manages to slip through the dragnet of chimp patrols and approaches the females, they offer less resistance and may even vocalise during sex like they do with high-ranking males of their own group. They are acknowledging that the outsider male is demonstrating immense skill and dominance to barge his way deep into rival territory, or signalling that a chimp takeover of that territory is in progress. Female chimps appear to strategise that it is best to seek terms with the invading forces. Given what they often endure, one can hardly blame them for having limited loyalty to the resident males.

BONOBO SEX BONANZA

Approximately 2 million years ago, while our ancestor *Homo erectus* was evolving in the wide-open savannas of east Africa, two groups of ancestral chimpanzees to the west got separated by a widening Congo River. The chimps to the south evolved into bonobos, who have radically different habits from chimpanzees. They are more peaceful and are a female-led species. Instead of using violence to resolve conflicts, they often use sex.

As bonobos split from chimpanzees rather than directly from us, if chimpanzees are our closest evolutionary cousins, bonobos are our 'second cousins'. Humans share an estimated 98.4 per cent of our DNA with them, only slightly less than with chimps. We also share with them many sexual behaviours that are rather unique for great apes. These behaviours evolved 'convergently' in the past 2 million years: that is, they evolved separately, often for different reasons, rather than being inherited from the same last common ancestor.

The sexual behaviours bonobos share with humans are: missionary sex (though to a lesser degree than humans, happening only 15 per

Bonobos and humans share many sexual practices.

cent of the time – most of the time it is still doggy-style); kisses with an exchange of tongues; a greater emphasis on foreplay than in the other primates we've covered; cuddling after sex; high frequencies of fellatio and the eating of ejaculate; mutual masturbation; 69ing; lesbian 'scissoring'; and heaps and heaps of cunnilingus by both male and female tongues. On average, bonobos masturbate every 1 to 2 hours and initiate sexual contact with a partner every 90 minutes, though much of this sexual contact does not involve penetration and is not done to ejaculation or orgasm. When penetration does happen, bonobo copulations last an average of 15 seconds, roughly twice the average of chimps. Although male sperm competition is significantly reduced in bonobos compared with chimps, 2 million years is not enough time to significantly increase bonobo sexual stamina back up to the polygynous orangutan levels of 15 minutes.

Unlike chimpanzees, but like orangutans and humans, bonobos have concealed ovulation: males do not know when a female is fertile. Bonobos are specifically evolved to use concealed ovulation to confuse paternity of their offspring. Females have sex with different males, at different times, so none of the males know whether it was their sperm that impregnated her. This prevents male infanticide of rival offspring. Indeed, infanticide perpetrated by males has not been observed in wild bonobo groups.

Both bonobos and chimps have sex sixty times more frequently than orangutans, due to living in social groups rather than being largely solitary. They have sex roughly twenty times more frequently than gorillas, as they live in multi-male and multi-female promiscuous groups. Bonobos and chimpanzees have roughly the same amount of sex. However, because chimp females show when they are fertile, all that sex is clustered into an aggressive male frenzy roughly 25 per cent of the time. The equivalent amount of bonobo sex is more spread out, which keeps bonobo males from getting frustrated by long dry spells. This reduces violence and tension.

Bonobos typically live in groups of twenty to fifty promiscuous individuals, much like chimpanzees. A common greeting during social interactions is for one bonobo to touch another bonobo's genitals in a 'bonobo handshake'. A bonobo will thrust their erect penis or engorged clitoris outwards until this action is performed. The act itself reduces tension. The greeting may then be followed up by cunnilingus or grooming each other's hair, both forms of social bonding.

Male bonobos do *not* patrol their foraging territory like chimps. In fact, all bonobo foraging parties are mixed groups of males and females, rather than male-only squads. As such, when two different bonobo 'tribes' meet in the forest, the bonobo males may get a little tense at first at the sight of strange males (the chimp instincts die hard) but instead of aggression or violence erupting, the females from each tribe will cross over and start having sex with each other and the males on either side. Imagine if the UN Security Council conducted its meetings via orgy. The sex diffuses all tension. The old cliché that rears its head at this point in narratives about bonobos is 'make love, not war'.

It is important to note, however, that the diplomatic sex does not create friendly relations between male bonobos of different groups. They stay sequestered from each other on either side while the female bonobos cross and have sex with them. The whole idea is to have the tense males avoid any interactions whatsoever. So even in bonobos, it would appear that 'peace and love' have their limits. Nevertheless, lethal aggression is practically unheard of between male bonobos.

Due to their relatively recent split from chimpanzees, bonobo males are still bigger and somewhat stronger on average than females. But on the rare occasions where a bonobo male is aggressive towards a female, an alliance of female bonobos lynches him. The females will chase the male off, shout and hoot at him, and sometimes even slap him, kick him or break a few bones – like a finger or two. However, such actions are not frequently necessary. The males know their place. Bonobo males do not form strong bonds or alliances with each other and tend to stay in quiet isolation when foraging, completely flipping the script on the behaviour we see in chimps.

Most intriguingly, bonobos are patrilocal, much like chimpanzees. Male kin tend to stay together their entire lives, whereas females depart their natal groups and join new ones. So bonobo females who form strong alliances with each other are entirely unrelated. This is intriguing in the sense that one would think that kin would have an easier time forming such alliances than total strangers. Especially when one considers that in chimps and gorillas, unrelated females tend to have relatively weak social bonds and be competitive and hostile to each other. Not so in bonobos.

When a new bonobo female seeks to enter a community, she appeals to the female hierarchy to accept her. She achieves this by grooming her new hosts and performing cunnilingus and scissoring with the bonobo females already in residence. She does *not* require the approval of the local males to join the group. This is quite unlike chimpanzees, where a chimp female will appeal directly to the chimp males, who will accept her regardless of the reaction of the females (usually they are unenthused). In bonobos, a new arrival is entirely dependent on forming strong female social bonds.

AN IMPERFECT MATRIARCHY

Nevertheless, bonobo females are not egalitarian in the slightest. They have a rigid hierarchy of dominance and submission. And while bonobo males do not generate much conflict, social tension is common between bonobo females. The female hierarchy revolves mostly around priority access to food. Low-ranking females must perform sex acts on high-ranking females to gain closer access to food and potentially form alliances against other females in the group. As such, females use sex to curry favour and counter their lower status. Higher-ranking females are less into sex than lower-ranking females, and sex between two high-ranking females is very rare indeed.

And while bisexuality is common in both male and female bonobos, exclusively gay or lesbian individuals are relatively rare. The female-led promiscuity of bonobos does not seem to breed the inverse trend of more frequent exclusive homosexuality that we see in male-led polygynous primates such as gorillas and orangutans.

The other aim of female bonobo hierarchies is reproductive success. But unlike male hierarchies in chimps, which govern priority access to mates, female bonobos are a little more circumspect. They achieve reproductive success through micromanaging the sex lives of their sons. Because bonobos are patrilocal, sons are closely bonded with their mothers. Conversely, mothers do not seem to give much of a shit about their daughters, since they'll be taking off as soon as they reach sexual maturity. Contrary to popular belief, sex within a bonobo group is not always a free-for-all. Sure, the non-orgasming bonobo handshakes, lesbianism and other tension-reducing acts can be. But when it comes to actual reproduction and impregnation, a mother's rank determines how often her little momma's boy has sex. If a bonobo male has penetrative sex with a lower-ranking female, a high-ranking mother may interrupt the copulations of her son, mid-thrust, and chase off the lowly female. The mother will then prod her son towards a higher-ranking female instead. And you thought *your* mother-in-law was difficult ...

When it comes to sex itself, despite it being a female-dominated society, approximately 95 per cent of all heterosexual encounters are initiated by the males. So even in bonobos, the onus is usually on the guys to make the first move. In fact, bonobo females actively solicit sex even less often than chimpanzees, where they take the initiative 35 per cent of the time. They also reject male advances quite a lot, picking and choosing what sort of male impregnates them, since it could impact their offspring and their place within the female hierarchy. And, unlike chimpanzees, female rejection does not run the risk of rape. Indeed, there is largely no rape or sexual intimidation in bonobos because the female coalition shuts down that sort of aggression quickly.

Bonobo females have more frequent orgasms than other apes we've covered. They vocalise their orgasms more often with males than with females, partly because male–female penetrative sex more frequently results in orgasm than the social-climbing sex acts between females. Additionally, only low-ranking females tend to vocalise in sex with either males or females. High-ranking females do not seem to bother. As with chimpanzees, vocalisations are socially useful. A low-ranking female will announce to the group she is having sex with a male or female of consequence to bolster her position in the female hierarchy. At some point in the last 6 million years since we split with chimpanzees, human women lost this social-climbing aspect of sex vocalisations. Those ecstatic screams and moans have become more the result of pure sexual pleasure. And also, according to some theories, possibly an instinct towards increasing their bonds with a mate – indeed, the act of faking an orgasm seems to serve this purpose in the absence of sufficient sexual pleasure.

Lest we run away with the idea that bonobo communities are some sort of utopian 1960s hippy communes, there are a few other considerations. The highly sexual bonobos sometimes practise incest and paedophilia. Before they leave the natal group, sisters scissor sisters. Brothers jack off brothers. Mothers occasionally feel up their sons' genitals or even wank them off or blow them. These actions are done to reduce tensions, so the usual evolutionary prohibitions against incest don't seem to apply. Incest resulting in pregnancy between mother and son does not often occur.

Another consideration is that while lethal violence in bonobos is rare, and male violence against females uncommon, the same cannot be said of female violence against males, or female violence against females. In service of the matriarchy, females have been known to bite, slap, kick, push, drag, pin down and charge at each other. The female-led societal structure is unique among the great apes, but it is no less rigorously enforced than male-led structures. Even in circumstances that seem more idyllic to human eyes, Darwinian evolution rarely plays nice.

And while male infanticide of offspring has not been observed, females have been known to practise it. Higher-ranking female bonobos will sometimes steal babies from the lower ranks, take them away into the forest, dump them, chase off the mother's attempts to retrieve them, and let the babies starve to death. All in the service of eliminating the genes of a rival female who has mated with a high-quality male. Thus, bonobos are *not* the utopian society they are sometimes depicted as being. In some senses, the power struggles of the chimpanzees just shifted to a different arena. Same sins, different pile.

PLAYING WITH THE WRONG TOOL

There is another, more evolutionary, consideration that had long-term consequences for *Homo sapiens.* Chimpanzees, for all their horrific faults and psychopathic levels of masculine aggression, use tools proficiently. They fashion sticks to fish termites out of the ground for food. They use rocks as hammers to smash open nuts. They use leaves as sponges to soak up rainwater for drinking. They use pointed sticks as stabbing implements. They use tree branches as levers. They fashion banana leaf umbrellas. And chimps even have an element of culture; adults teach children these things. All subsequent ancestors in our direct lineage from 6 million years ago to today used tools. For instance, 3.5 million years ago *Australopithecus afarensis* used tools much like chimps do. Tool use intensified with *Homo habilis* 2.3 million years ago, and this trend got more and more powerful down our family tree until the emergence of the extremely inventive and adaptive *Homo sapiens.*

In contrast, bonobos don't often use tools outside captivity. In sanctuaries and labs, they are often prodded to do so, but it is an entirely different story in the wild. While bonobos certainly have the mental capacity to use tools (they aren't far removed from chimps, after all) somewhere in the last 2 million years of evolution bonobos lost the instinctual inclination to use them for food acquisition in the wild. For one thing, competition over food among bonobos is, in general, less fierce. The environments in which they dwell generally have abundant food. And male bonobos don't use food to purchase sex like male chimps sometimes do. Why? Because sex is also abundant. What scanty bonobo tool use there is generally is deployed for social bonding: using sticks to help groom hair or even as crude sexual aides.

Termite fishing

As such, tool use has a limited evolutionary benefit for bonobos in terms of either sheer survival or competition for mates. Bonobos don't need to waste valuable energy on them and can spend their days socially bonding and having sex. As such, if our last common ancestor 6 million years ago was more like the bonobo than the chimpanzee, it is highly unlikely the intensified use of tools would have reason to evolve in subsequent ancestral species. And without those evolutionary forerunners, a species as inventive as *Homo sapiens* probably would not have evolved at all. And whatever existed in our place would likely still be rutting maniacally in the forests of Western and Central Africa.

Instead, for better or worse, our ancestors 6 million years ago were much more like chimpanzees than bonobos. And, as a direct result of that somewhat unfortunate reality, fate had a series of much more dramatic changes in store.

EVENT	DATE
First primates	55 million years ago
Split of New and Old World monkeys	40 million years ago
First great apes	25 million years ago
Split with gibbons	17 million years ago
Split with orangutans	15 million years ago
Split with gorillas	10 million years ago
Split with chimpanzees	6 million years ago
Split between chimps and bonobos	2 million years ago

7

GETTING ERECTUS

4 million to 315,000 years ago

Wherein our ancestors become bipedal • The bendy penis facilitates more sex positions • Breasts and other aspects of the female form take shape • Our ancestors begin flirting • Monogamy sends shockwaves through our sex lives • Cocks and balls ebb and flow in size • Evolutionary baggage keeps infidelity and non-monogamous arrangements alive • Love evolves • Our species becomes more adept at tinkering, inventing and creating culture.

Our last common ancestors with gibbons and orangutans spent most of their lives in the trees. Our last common ancestors with gorillas and chimps spent relatively more time on solid ground, but still dwelt in African forests, with physiology better suited to climbing than walking long distances. Approximately 6 million years ago, we walked bow-legged and used our long arms on the ground for balance. Then, approximately 4 million years ago, the global climate shifted into a dry phase. The forests receded and our ancestors found themselves in sparse woodlands and wide-open African savanna. There was less of an evolutionary incentive for these apes to climb trees and a much greater incentive for them to be able to cover long distances in search of food. They did this by walking upright on two legs, without needing their arms for locomotion. This practice is known as bipedalism. The trailblazers of bipedalism were our ancestors in the genus *Australopithecus*, with most species of that genus living between 4 and 2 million years ago.

EVENT	DATE
Split with chimpanzees	6 million years ago
Bipedalism, bigger breasts, bendier penises	4 million years ago
Homo habilis and verbal bonding	2.3 million years ago
Homo erectus and monogamy	1.9 million years ago
Homo sapiens	315,000 years ago

Australopithecines were about 1 to 1.2 metres tall. They looked a lot like chimpanzees, having split off from them only 2 million years earlier. Australopithecine brain size wasn't much bigger than chimps and their capacity for tool use was about the same. They were largely vegetarian, but occasionally scavenged raw meat from animal corpses (they had no controlled use of fire for cooking). Australopithecines were still patrilocal, with male kin sticking together and females being transient, much like chimpanzees.

Where Australopithecines differ from chimps is their degree of sexual dimorphism. While male chimps are 25 per cent larger than females on average, Australopithecine males were an estimated 50 per cent larger than females, though precise rates of dimorphism varied from species to species. A higher rate of sexual dimorphism implies an even greater degree of male–male competition than in chimps. Even if sexual dimorphism remained roughly the same, it is a fairly safe bet that the aggressive sexual practices shown by chimpanzees also prevailed in bipedal Australopithecines.

In fact, there's good reason to believe that male–male competition was even *worse* than in chimpanzees, with genetic analysis indicating most female Australopithecines were impregnated by a tiny minority of males. In the African savanna, we transitioned back to the game of alpha-Chads and mostly sexless betas to the extent that Australopithecines weren't so much promiscuous as they were bordering on gorilla-like polygyny again. The only thing that seems to have prevented the return of full-blown polygyny was the fact that Australopithecines still lived in large multi-male, multi-female groups, averaging twenty to fifty individuals in size, rather than single-male harems. Tribes of Australopithecines contained a multitude of females being aggressively guarded by a small number of males, with tensions and jealousies running high. With that came the characteristic sexual violence of chimpanzees, rivalries between males within the group, and outright hostility to males beyond it. The promiscuity of Australopithecines was definitely not of the 'free love' variety.

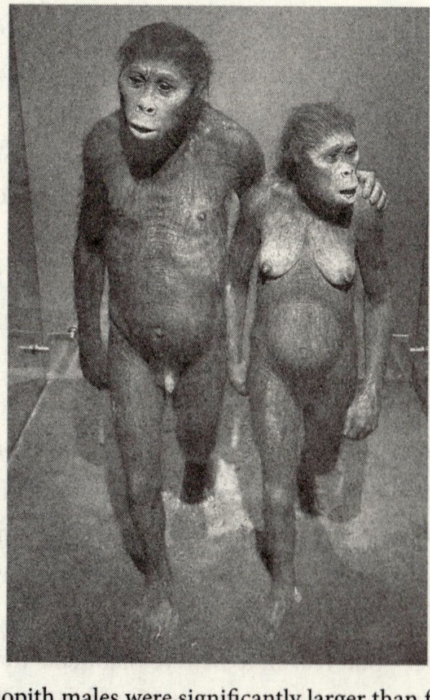

Australopith males were significantly larger than females.

SAVANNA SEX AND BIPEDAL BREASTS

Meanwhile, the transition to bipedalism in female Australopithecines pushed the vagina and cervix to a further forward position between their loins than the more 'ass-ward' location of the vagina in quadrupedal chimpanzees. Physiologically, this made missionary-style sex more common. Chimpanzees generally don't use missionary, and even bonobos only use it 15 per cent of the time. From this point forward, missionary took an increasing share of total copulations, with the added benefit that the frontal rubbing afforded an increased chance of clitoral stimulation. So that's one silver lining, at least.

The movement of the vagina closer to the front provoked corresponding changes in the penis. The baculum (the penis bone that props up the dick in primates and many other mammals) shrank further, allowing the penis greater flexibility should doggy-style still be employed. This also opened the door to a wider number of sex positions. Physiologically, the bipedal penis could comfortably engage in cowgirl, sitting and kneeling positions, and – indispensable to a bipedal species travelling across endless miles of African savanna – sex standing up. So while the group dynamics of sex remained toxic, at least the diversity of the sex was improving. Sadly, due to the continued high competition between males, average copulation times were still likely a matter of seconds rather than minutes. Though given how much sexual coercion was likely going on, this was probably a boon rather than a bane.

Bipedalism also increased the average size of female breasts. Prior to this, primate mammary glands were modest in size and mostly for the purposes of nursing children rather than sexual attraction. Chimpanzee tits, for instance, are usually rather flat and saggy, containing considerably less fat than human female breasts. When it comes to sexual attraction, male chimps are almost universally what we might call 'ass men', looking for the tell-tale swelling on a female's posterior that shows she is oestrus.

A myth has grown up, sometimes still perpetuated in academia today, that men are attracted to women's breasts because their cleavage resembles buttocks, thus evoking a chimp-like lust. This is nonsense. On the African savanna 4 million years ago, cleavage was hard to come by. Australopithecines did not wear push-up bras. And if you've ever peeked inside a *National Geographic*, you'll know loose, floppy boobs are very rarely packed so tightly together that they bear much resemblance to ass cheeks. Also, naked in the savanna, one could still see everything on both sides. There was no need to evolve a replica set of hindquarters on the front.

Instead, the most likely explanation for larger breasts was that bipedalism increased the need for females to carry larger fat reserves as they covered long distances across East Africa in search of food. These fat reserves would be used when nursing babies as they travelled. If no food was forthcoming for several days, female foragers would simply burn through their fat stores to keep feeding their newborns while the mothers went hungry for a brief period. Those fat reserves would be stored primarily in the breasts, hips, ass and thighs.

As a result, larger breasts with more fat deposits became sexually selected for. The average size and roundness of breasts grew accordingly. Males got aroused by females who seemed like they'd be able to nurse young across long distances. That did not mean that obesity (fat all over the body) was sexually selected for. Strategic storage of fat in breasts, hips, ass and thighs still allowed for decent locomotion across long distances. But too much fat on the body and corresponding heart and respiratory limitations meant a female would struggle to keep up in a nomadic lifestyle. And falling behind endangered not only her survival but that of her offspring (especially in a promiscuous Australopithecine species without much fatherly childcare).

Thus, a relatively slender frame and narrow waist, ample breasts and a posterior with some fat deposits in it was the ideal stature to endure a tough life of travelling daily on foot while nursing and child-carrying. These proportions directly contributed to the odds of a child's survival. These 'slim and stacked' proportions also signalled youth, which implied greater fertility. And although humans are no longer nomadic, and the ideal ratio of body frame to mammaries and glutes has varied across human cultures through the years, these rough proportions still command instinctual sexual power over most males today – with all the accompanying body insecurities, psychological conditions and harmful dietary problems.

However, as we shall soon see, given that male primates tended to mate with the widest possible range of females (or else risk losing out genetically and *never* having offspring) it doesn't help to overstate the importance of these precise proportions in the past 4 million years of sexual selection. It was just a general trend that prompted the evolution of typically larger breasts than chimps. Relatively flat-chested waifs, muscular and athletic women and more Rubenesque figures were all found sexually attractive to varying degrees. Sometimes immensely so. Male primates tended to want to copulate with a wide range of shapes and sizes. What was most important beyond specific body types was an indication of good health, fertility and the ability to survive (pregnant or with children) in the gruelling route-march across many kilometres of territory in search of the next meal. If the Darwinian system of natural selection sounds a bit harsh regarding female body-image here, rest assured, dear reader, that the deeply rooted insecurities of the fellas, from height to baldness to flabby man-boobs to wrinkly little dicks, are going to get their turn in due course . . .

SEDUCED BY THE HANDYMAN

We have at last arrived at our own genus. Approximately 2.3 million years ago, *Homo habilis* (Latin for 'handy man') evolved in East Africa. They were not much taller than chimpanzees and Australopithecines, again standing between 1 and 1.2 metres tall. Their brain size was only slightly bigger. But *Homo habilis* is notable for an increase in intelligence and inventiveness. They were much more efficient crafters of tools. They were among the first species to regularly hit flakes off stones to use their sharp edges for cutting. This is not an easy thing to manufacture, and even modern humans have difficulty with it. However, no tinkering or improvement in technology is detected in *Homo habilis* in the 700,000 years the species existed. Its repertoire remained frozen in time, much like the tool use of chimpanzees. Tinkering and improvement of technology over multiple generations of a species – a process called collective learning, or technological accumulation – was to appear only subsequently.

Homo habilis lived in groups slightly larger than chimps and Australopithecines, roughly thirty to eighty on average, and also sometimes in bigger, loosely associated confederations. They were also likely promiscuous and patrilocal, much like their chimp and Australopith forebears, with high rates of male–male competition, bordering on polygyny. This was soon to change.

Homo habilis's talent for tool making led to their evolutionary success, setting off a population boom in East Africa. Combined with a larger group size, the increased number of group interactions put pressure on *habilis* to socialise, form bonds and navigate alliances more adeptly than their primate ancestors. In previous species, the great apes and Old World monkeys would achieve this primarily by grooming each other's fur. But as group sizes became more cumbersome, they had to find another method of bonding. And that was by conversation and gossip. *Homo habilis* had a larynx placed much higher in the throat than ours, which left it with a very restricted range of sounds. But combined with a system of grunts, yells and gestures, the human method of relating to others via a fireside chat was taking shape. And given the importance of navigating a competitive primate alliance to gain access to food and mates, there was clear selection pressure for these conversational abilities to continue to grow.

Sexual selection also played a pivotal role in spurring along our ancestor's skills at communication. Female members of *Homo habilis* began to choose mates who were able to charm them with a little bit of conversation. The rudiments of pick-up lines and pillow talk had evolved at last – though to human ears the first pick-up line was likely little more than a series of grunts and some lewd pointing.

The sexual selection of smooth talkers is not so unthinkable. For millions of years the great apes had established their place in a hierarchy based on their ability to form alliances. Once we arrive at *Homo habilis*, primitive conversation would have played a vital role in that. And, as a male, the higher you were in the hierarchy, the better the prospects for your offspring. So, unsurprisingly, the male 'gift of the gab' became crucial to many seductions – and remains so to this day. Female conversation skills were even more important, since she had to maintain good relations with a high-ranking mate to protect her offspring from infanticide, and maintain alliances within the female hierarchy. Conversation was so important it kicked off a major cognitive revolution in our direct lineage 400,000 years later. Without a little bit of primordial flirtation, *Homo sapiens* probably would never have existed.

I'VE ALREADY USED MY 'ERECTUS' JOKE

At this point in our story, we are on the verge of something amazing. Around 1.9 million years ago, *Homo erectus* emerged. The evolutionary changes are so numerous that it represents a veritable explosion in the fossil record. For starters, *Homo erectus* was much taller than chimps, Australopithecines or *Homo habilis*, ranging between 1.52 and 1.82 metres. Just shy of the range of human heights. By this time, our ancestors had mastered the art of bipedalism, able to cover long distances with long, powerful legs, considerable stamina and significant speed to escape predators in the savanna.

There is some indication that the increase in height was sexually selected for by females. Of course long legs helped when crossing vast distances in the never-ending search for food, but height also correlated with weight and therefore average strength. This was useful in male–male competition, intergroup conflicts over foraging territory, and dealing with various dangers imposed by predators and other natural hazards. Average height in various populations was also governed by diet, and in periods of starvation and malnutrition this average dropped considerably. The diversity of male heights in *Homo erectus* also implies this was not the only factor in maintaining a decent rank in the male hierarchy or being considered a good female mate choice (alliances, communication skills and parental care were also factors). A tall and muscular fool, pariah or coward was no good. So the short gentlemen of the world can breathe a feverish sigh of relief. In a sense, height is like breast size in terms of reproductive success. The major difference being, in modern times, that it is not as socially acceptable to list minimum cup-size requirements on your Tinder profile as minimum height requirements seem to be.

Homo erectus had also lost the thick coats of body hair that protected against chilly nights in the damp forests of Western and Central Africa. Hair was less useful in the intense heat of the savanna in East Africa. So, we lost most of the body hair and gained a few more sweat glands and a fair amount of melanin in our skin to protect us from the sun (a trait that only faded as some *Homo sapiens* moved into colder climates between 64,000 and 12,000 years ago). A patch of hair remained on the top of our heads that protected the tops of our bipedal bodies from the sun's glare. This mop of hair also clung onto some of the pheromones emitted from the body that were useful for sexual attraction. Similarly, we retained thicker clumps of hair in the armpits and around the genitals. The rest of the body retained only a light dusting of hair, though precise amounts differ genetically and hormonally from person to person.

Homo erectus

Male facial hair remained, and actually grew bushier, since it was sexually selected for as a sign of virility. And unfortunately, a convoluted tangle of genetics, metabolism, testosterone levels and age produced baldness in a large cross-section of males and a few females. When it came to sexual selection, our instincts rashly judged a book by its cover and considered baldness to be a sign of ageing or ill-health, thus implying reduced virility in males and reduced fertility in females, leading to a rash of insecurities that haunt us to this day. To be more precise, it is the sight of thinning, uneven and scraggly hair that prompts this instinctual reaction, rather than the bald scalp itself. Hence why many people opt to shave it all off. Moreover, the impact of baldness on male and female mate choices is often overstated. In terms of genetics, baldness is still a common thing after 2 million years precisely *because* humanity's cue-balls get laid just fine.

Homo erectus lived in groups that averaged between 50 and 150 people, with wider confederations numbering in several hundred or even thousand. To cope with this increased social complexity, *Homo erectus*'s brain is considerably larger – roughly twice the size of *Homo habilis*. A tremendous increase in brain size in just 400,000 years shows that natural selection favoured intelligence. Female mate choice likely also played a role in this continued evolution, with intelligent and resourceful males capable of navigating social alliances being sexually selected for. Sexual selection also applied to the evolution of speech, with *Homo erectus* able to emit a wider range of sounds and possessing all the traits necessary for proto-language, rudimentary grammar and the exchanging of thoughts in spoken sentences. Palaeolithic 'pick-up lines' thus grew more elaborate but probably no less douchey.

Brain size also seems to have been sustained by *Homo erectus* consuming more meat than any of their forebears, with the remains of large African fauna such as elephants and rhinos being found at their campsites. We do not yet know if *Homo erectus* cooked this meat, since their use of fire appears to be sporadic rather than controlled. But the high concentration of calories in meat provided a burst of energy to the large hungry brains of *Homo erectus*. To get the same amount of energy from eating plants, they'd have to eat a far larger amount and spend many more hours foraging to get them.

The increase in brain size (in which sex had a pivotal and powerful role) created a highly adaptable and inventive species. *Homo erectus* was the first of our genus to spread out of Africa and settle in Western Europe, the Mediterranean, the Middle East, South Asia and far-flung regions in East Asia. But even more astounding, for our purposes, is what they were doing sexually.

BIG-BRAINED ROMANCE

With the evolution of *Homo erectus* 1.9 million years ago, the entire sexual landscape was rocked to its very core – as were the wider foundations of what it meant to be human. This is the part in our long story, the grand narrative of sex (or the 'chronicle of fuck', as my colleagues and I jokingly call it) where a key element of human sexuality finally falls into place. Monogamy had returned to our direct evolutionary lineage.

Due to the remarkable increase in the brain size of *Homo erectus* in just a few hundred thousand years, the head size of newborns increased dramatically without a sufficiently corresponding evolution of the width of the female birth canal. In fact, the heads of infants grew so large that giving birth became much more dangerous and gruelling, with female members of *Homo erectus* becoming more dependent on outside help. And that included assistance from the male who had impregnated her.

Male mates had a role in providing food and protection after childbirth to ensure the survival of their offspring. Without this increase in male parental care, very few offspring would have survived, endangering the entire species. As such, male parental care began to be offered on a scale rarely seen before in primates. Many primates protect their offspring, but it is rare for males to consistently bring infants food.

Additionally, once born, babies took longer to reach maturity. They couldn't lift their heads, could barely move around and were more dependent on their mother for a longer period. Even after offspring could move around on their own, considerably more years were required before they were able to fend for themselves in the wild. Again, male mates had to compensate with paternal care to maximise the chances of reproductive success, and both mothers and fathers needed to work more closely in concert to feed and protect their young.

As a result, *Homo erectus* evolved monogamy in order to give their large-headed offspring a fighting chance. This was the first time monogamy had happened in our family tree since gibbons some 17 million years earlier. Since then, male–male competition in a polygynous or promiscuous environment usually resulted in a small number of males managing to breed. Now most individuals within *Homo erectus,* male and female, pair-bonded to maximise the chances they would pass on their DNA.

The evolution of monogamy in *Homo erectus* had some immediate knock-on effects. Male–male competition within a group became less vicious and unrelenting than in promiscuous or polygynous communities. This reduced average sexual dimorphism. Unlike gorillas, chimps and Australopithecines, *Homo erectus* males were only 15 per cent larger than females on average.

To be sure, male–male competition for mates still existed, with high rates of aggression, especially when a male was defending an existing monogamous relationship. But pair-bonding meant that *all* males were not constantly vying for sexual access to almost *all* females, with the most dominant males (in either strength or alliances) winning most frequently and yet constantly having to watch their backs to defend their positions from usurpers. Instead, male sexual jealousy was mostly confined to the creation and preservation of monogamous relationships (with a hell of a lot of infidelity, as we shall cover later). And once males were pair-bonded they usually underwent a drop in testosterone levels, because while aggression is useful for landing a mate, the lack of aggression is a boon to retaining social bonds with females and to providing paternal care to offspring. It's a useful quirk of body chemistry that transforms men from horny fuckbois into wholesome dads, rather than wife-beaters and child abusers.

Meanwhile, female sexual jealousy evolved from being mere competition with other females for the periodic attention of a few attractive dominant males in the polygynous gorilla and promiscuous chimp species, to mate-guarding the sexual activity of her pair-bonded mate, irrespective of his rank in the dominance hierarchy. Males did not need to rise as aggressively in the hierarchy to secure reproductive success with a female, again reducing aggression. A lower-ranking male could get by just fine because they already 'belonged' to someone.

In a sense, female jealousy also bestowed on our female ancestors a great deal more sexual agency than they had possessed in the previous 12 million years. Instead of mate-guarding being a largely male domain, where groups of females were treated as passive prizes to be competed over by a few aggressive male douchebags, female jealousy spread the burden of that aggression more evenly across the species. If a strange female approached someone's fella, she was chased off. If a male's eyes strayed to another girl, he was met with anger and aggression. Unusually for primates, *Homo erectus* females likely endeavoured to keep their pair-bonded males in check. And by shouldering the burden of jealousy, females not only reduced the necessity for aggression in males but also turned down the volume of aggression in a *Homo erectus* group. This in turn probably allowed for more social bonding between group members, more communication and more sophisticated alliances. All of which was good news for our intellectual evolution.

The sexual selection of both intelligence and communication skills, combined with the evolutionary value of skilled tool use, made the sexual selection of pure brawn less necessary. Huge male body sizes relative to females and unrelenting displays of chimp-like aggression within the group were simply no longer as required for reproductive success when there were other desirable traits. All of this lowered tensions within a group.

However, inter-group hostilities remained quite high. External *Homo erectus* groups threatening to usurp foraging territory (the limited supply of food in the savanna) also threatened to steal away females in the event of a violent conflict over that territory in which the defending males were killed or driven off, along with any infants being murdered by the invaders. So, for very practical evolutionary reasons, inter-group hostilities were as intense as they had been for our last common ancestor with chimps 6 million years ago. In fact, due to the increase in our intelligence and capacity for using tools, these skirmishes on the borders of foraging territory were likely even more bloodthirsty and vicious.

This inter-group hostility was only ameliorated by deliberate pair-bonding of two individuals from two different *Homo erectus* groups. With a linking of DNA between two communities, a primitive 'diplomatic marriage' provided a good reason to interact more peaceably. According to genetic analysis, it appears that a female most commonly moved to a new *Homo erectus* group with her mate, while most males stayed in the group where they were born, retaining the patrilocal tendency of chimpanzees. But as we move closer to modern humans, this no longer remains a hard-and-fast rule like it was in chimps.

Homo erectus also evolved concealed ovulation, where males had a limited idea of when females were fertile. The promiscuous bonobos evolved this to confuse paternity so the males would not kill the children of their rivals. In *Homo erectus* and its descendants, concealed ovulation was used to increase the frequency of sex in order to encourage bonding between monogamous mates. Essentially sex drew two people together and made them more likely to stick together. Although no longer embarking on a promiscuous sexual frenzy to the same degree as chimpanzees or bonobos, *Homo erectus* couples had sex just about as frequently as them.

Accordingly, the average copulation time increased from a matter of seconds to an average of 8 minutes from penetration to orgasm. The longer monogamous couples spent in each other's arms, the more their attachment to each other was reinforced. And while females still moaned loudly when they orgasmed, they lost the social utility of signalling to the rest of the group that she was fucking a specific male. If she was pair-bonded, others already knew who she was hooked up with, in addition to *Homo erectus* having spoken ways of communicating this information. Sex had become more of an intimate matter between two individuals (perhaps even spawning the desire for privacy). Instead of primarily being a device to flaunt social status like in promiscuous chimps, the orgasm was adapted to increase the attachment of her male mate while they were in the throes of mutual sex pleasure. Or one-sided pleasure, in the case of fake orgasms; a 2011 US study revealed that approximately 60 per cent of women have faked a vocalisation at some point in their lives, and alarmingly, 15 per cent of women fake with their partners on a regular basis.

As a direct result of the pair-bonding utility of sexual pleasure, monogamous couples also began to engage in a wider variety of sex acts beyond penetration – much like the bonobos before them, but for different reasons. Kisses on the mouth exchanged pheromones to increase attachments to mates, foreplay of various kinds increased, cuddling after sex became common, and fellatio and cunnilingus played the role of further forging two people more firmly together. This was a far cry from the uninventive 7-second mountings from behind being conducted by chimpanzees.

Meanwhile, thanks to monogamy, lower-ranking and unattractive males were now having more sex than they had ever had in the 40 million years since the evolution of the Old World monkeys – perhaps even the last 55 million years since the evolution of primates. They were no longer as likely to remain sexless on the sidelines. Incels still existed but were a much smaller portion of the population. Dominant males may have had slightly less sex than their promiscuous and polygynous forebears, but (as we shall see) they were frequently the beneficiaries of most breaches of monogamy. Thus, with the rise of pair-bonding, alpha-Chads lost comparatively little. Meanwhile, healthy and fertile females were having pretty much the same amount of sex they had always partaken in – the only difference was some of them were now doing it with slightly less attractive males. I will leave it to the reader to decide which is preferable: a lacklustre monogamous existence with a '6' or a life in the harem of an '8', '9' or '10'.

ERECTILE MONOGAMY

The evolution of monogamy in *Homo erectus* also had a profound and lasting effect on the male genitals – in some respects for the better, in some for the worse. In chimps (and likely Australopithecines), the frenzy around mating meant that copulation times were short and testicles held quite a lot of sperm. The goal was to fuck as many mates as possible in the shortest possible time. As a result, chimp testicles are sizeable, averaging 100 to 150 grams. With the advent of monogamy, average testicle size shrank by a factor of three, to between 35 and 50 grams. Our direct lineage has never recovered from this relative shrivelling. In fact, by *Homo sapiens*, the average had dropped to 20 grams.

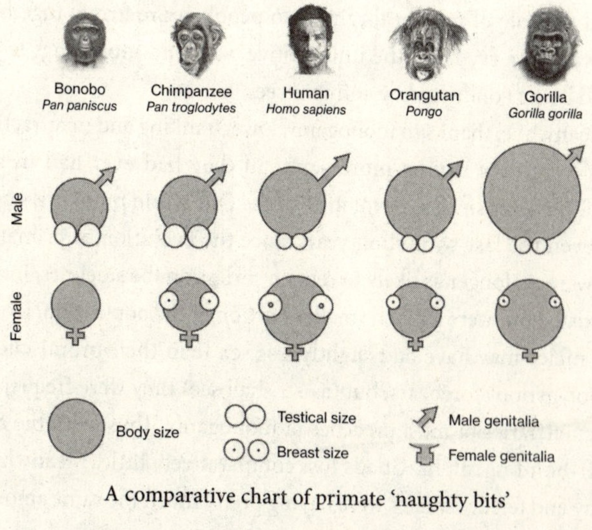

A comparative chart of primate 'naughty bits'

Balls may have shrunk but penis sizes did not. Our last common ancestor with chimpanzees (and likely Australopithecines and *Homo habilis*) had fairly long penises despite their short stature. The average erect chimp penis is 5.5 inches long, with a range of 3 to 7 inches. When our height shot up to 5 or 6 feet (150 to 180 centimetres) and our balls shrank, the average penis length remained stable – likely due to sexual selection. Bipedal apes such as *Homo erectus* had their dicks more firmly on display than quadrupeds. A good-looking dick capable of sustaining an erection was a sign of male health and virility. Also, one facet of female sexual pleasure was penetration of a vaginal tract that had remained comparable in size to the chimp-like penis for the past 6 million years. And monogamy made female sexual pleasure more important since it facilitated strong bonds with a long-term mate. Thus, while *Homo erectus* shot up in height, his dick length did not recede.

And, since we are here, *Homo sapiens*, much like chimpanzees, have an average erect penis length somewhere between 5.1 and 5.5 inches. Only 0.25 per cent of men are smaller than 3 inches, 1.5 per cent of men are between 3 and 4 inches, 10 per cent of men are between 4 and 4.5 inches, and 15 per cent are between 4.5 and 5 inches. In other words, roughly 26.75 per cent have measurements that most men would be sheepish about admitting in modern culture. Meanwhile, approximately 25 per cent of men are 5 to 5.5 inches, 30 per cent are 5.5 to 6 inches, with a total 55 per cent of men packing the 'standard equipment'. Beyond that, we begin to see diminishing returns: 15 per cent of men are 6 to 6.5 inches, 1.5 per cent are 6.5 to 7 inches, 1.5 per cent are 7 to 7.5 inches, and 0.25 per cent are 7.5 inches and above, with 7-inchers, 8-inchers and 9-inchers being the most common on display in porn. The world record for penis size is around 13.5 inches naturally, or else 19 inches after some rather painful stretching modifications, possibly motivated by dysmorphia or some other mental disorder.

In other words, 70 per cent of men have what the internet has dubbed 'husband dick' (5 to 6.5 inches), implying a penis a woman would be happy with in a long-term relationship. However, a 2015 UCLA study determined that the average female preferred penis size for sex is between 6 to 6.5 inches, leaving 85 per cent of men (larger or smaller) out of luck. Furthermore, the average preferred size for penetrative sex toys is between 7 and 8 inches, a tiny portion of the flesh and blood population. And given that over 80 per cent of males fall below 6 inches, it is no wonder that anxiety among men regarding penis size is as common as negative thoughts about weight, breast size and body proportions are for women.

However, another consequence of big brains was the greater role of psychology in males *and* females achieving sexual pleasure and climax. In fact, what you've got going on in your head during sex is nine-tenths of the law. In that regard, the excitement a new partner feels at being with you or the compelling sexual scenarios regular partners paint for each other will make or break good sex between men and women, regardless of what size peckers or what body shapes are at play. So stop worrying about the size of your dick and let your freak-flag fly.

As a minor point, contrary to popular perceptions, numerous studies have found limited to no correlation between average penis size and either height or ethnicity, with averages between groups differing only by a fraction of an inch, if at all. In other words, racist porn stereotypes have little or no foundation in the real world. And, regarding height, if you intended to take home a tall, dark stranger in the hope he was packing, statistically speaking you are overwhelmingly likely to be disappointed.

Meanwhile, in *Homo erectus* 1.9 million years ago, the increased brain size of infants expanded the average width of the vagina compared with previous species. The male penis thickened correspondingly, again driven by sexual selection favouring female sexual pleasure to facilitate pair-bonding. The result was humans having much thicker, meatier cocks than other primates. Chimpanzee penises (although similar in length) are extremely thin by comparison, tapering from an already thin base to an extremely narrow tip. Average chimp girth is 5 centimetres in circumference. Average human girth is 11.7 centimetres. Roughly 65 per cent of men have a girth between 10.2 and 12.7 centimetres, 15 per cent between 6 and 10.2 centimetres, and 20 per cent between 12.7 and 15.2 centimetres. Statistically negligible percentages fall on either side. Female sexual preferences average between 12.2 and 12.76 centimetres, with most of those surveyed claiming girth was more important than length. The relatively larger percentage of men who 'pass muster' or 'almost pass muster' in thickness might explain why most male penis dysmorphia fixates on length rather than girth.

THE SEXUAL BAGGAGE OF MOTHER NATURE

Our direct evolutionary lineage may have transitioned to monogamy 1.9 million years ago, but one needs only to look around at modern humans to realise the transformation was not that cut and dried. Our last common ancestor with chimpanzees 6 million years ago, our Australopithecine ancestors 4 million years ago and our *Homo habilis* relatives 2.3 million years ago were all promiscuous and highly sexed. As a result, we are host to conflicting sexual instincts, with newer monogamous impulses at odds with the deeply buried promiscuous ones. Humans are more often hypersexual, more prone to infidelity and more frequently inclined to non-monogamous arrangements than more reliably monogamous species such as gibbons or titi monkeys. Monogamy has become the rule, but a rule with a thousand loopholes and exceptions.

For starters, genetic analysis of our evolutionary lineage shows there is a deficit of Y-chromosome diversity in our family tree. There is approximately 30 per cent more diversity of mothers between

1.9 million and 315,000 years ago than fathers, whereas undiluted monogamy would have put the split closer to 50/50. This means that although we started pair-bonding 1.9 million years ago, the population of fertile females was still getting impregnated by a smaller proportion of males – just not to the dramatic degree we see in promiscuous chimps or polygynous gorillas.

This implies either: 1) a significant amount of cuckolding was going on outside the pair-bonded relationship, with pair-bonded males unknowingly raising the offspring of 'hotter guys'; 2) a minority of males were impregnating females without pair-bonding, via either one-night stands or sexual coercion; 3) some polygyny was still going on, where multiple females either chose or were coerced to become the mates of a solitary male – indeed, we sometimes see polygyny in modern human societies, so it is not unthinkable it would have persisted as a minority arrangement in *Homo erectus* and its other descendants. The most likely answer is a combination of all three. The bottom line is that perfect monogamy did not completely replace other sexual behaviours overnight. In fact, it never did. It seems our promiscuous evolutionary past dies hard.

Even in a strictly monogamous primate group, females will often cluster around the most attractive males at first, in hopes of pair-bonding, to the exclusion of the less attractive males. It would be foolish to think that such a cluster does not sometimes involve sex as an initial enticement. It is only when an attractive male (a 'Chad') pair-bonds with a female (a 'Stacy') to the exclusion of other female hopefuls, that the rest of the females will disperse among the wider population of less appealing males.

Monogamy did not increase the average desirability of males relative to females, despite the more even distribution of mates. Sorry, fellas, but that's Darwinism for you. While men – instinctually eager to have sex with most shapes and sizes – will rate a wider swathe of women as average or above average in attractiveness, women tend to rate 70 to 85 per cent of men as having 'below average' attractiveness, despite that contradiction of terms and numbers. This is because for the last several million years, high male–male competition blessed only the top of the pile with high reproductive success. Those Adonises tend to stand out from a rather lacklustre crowd, and for at least the last 15 million years female sexual preference developed a keen eye for such rakishly handsome traits. The silver lining of this rather cruel biological reality is that 1.9 million years ago, with the evolution of monogamy, females began sexually selecting other traits beyond physical attractiveness or hierarchical status. They marked males out as good life partners and nurturing and protective fathers to their offspring. In a nutshell, despite nearly 2 million years of monogamy, women still think most men are ugly, but fortunately women can come to love their hairier, smellier and sweatier counterparts for a multitude of other reasons.

Meanwhile, when it comes to infidelity, both monogamous males and females can be the loser in evolutionary terms, which is why intense sexual jealousy on both sides is used to compensate. When a female is sexually unfaithful, it obscures paternity and disinclines the pair-bonded male to look after offspring, just in case it turns out not to be his kid (DNA tests weren't exactly an option in the savanna). After all, why would a male invest energy in something that isn't going to replicate his own DNA? Conversely, when a male is sexually unfaithful, it potentially splits his parental care between the offspring of two different mothers, thus endangering the survival of both. A female will be less than pleased to see the fatherly care of her DNA halved.

When infidelity turns violent, a cuckolded male will often kill the 'illegitimate' child, the rival male and sometimes even the mother, before moving on to a new pair-bond. In chimps, a male would simply commit infanticide before having sex with the grieving mother. Conversely, a 'cuckqueaned' female will often kill the 'illegitimate' child and, if possible, the rival female and her cheating partner before moving on to a new pair-bond. Among promiscuous chimps, a female would do nothing of the sort. Males provide limited parental care anyway, so a chimp female loses next to nothing when the deadbeat father of her child has sex with another lady.

However, when sexual jealousy is either suppressed or absent in individuals, non-monogamous arrangements become possible, facilitated by the much longer evolutionary past where we were *not* monogamous. These arrangements are in the minority, though it is difficult to arrive at precise percentages about people's private sex lives, especially when many non-monogamous arrangements eventually gravitate towards monogamy in later life anyway. In order of frequency from most common to most rare we see:

1. Promiscuous males and females refusing to pair-bond, with males sometimes initiating pair-bonding but leaving after sex, or females avoiding both pair-bonding and pregnancy (the latter of which would hold immense evolutionary penalties in the savanna 1.9 million years before birth control). The fact that promiscuity is common in humanity is hardly surprising, given it is removed from us by only 2 million years and has been around for at least the past 6 million.
2. Pair-bonded couples permitting each other to have sex outside the relationship (that is, 'swingers'), who will suffer no great evolutionary penalty *provided* their own offspring are cared for (the evolutionary loser appears to be those side pieces outside the relationship). When it comes to inviting a third person into a relationship, this third party is more commonly a female since with a third-party male there is the risk (again, in the savanna) of the pair-bonded female becoming pregnant with his child. As with promiscuity, a flexible pair-bond is hardly surprising, given how recently monogamy has evolved.
3. 'Friendzoning', where a female will pair-bond with one male but enjoy the utility and, if there is offspring, 'parental' care of other unbonded

males without having sex with them. This is a recent evolutionary invention thanks to monogamy, but with chimp-like precursors. Whereas 6 million years ago such male attention (grooming, sharing food) would probably have resulted in sex, monogamy restricts sex to one male, with the 'chimp tactics' of the others falling flat. Due to the tendency of the other male 'hopefuls' to eventually pair-bond with other women who actually have sex with them, such arrangements are not long-lasting. And given chimps usually transition to coercion when such bonding tactics fail, the evolutionarily residual male anger in *Homo sapiens* that ends most friendzoned relationships is hardly surprising.

4. Voluntary polygyny, where multiple females will consent to a (usually higher-status) male having sex with all of them. Provided all offspring are properly cared for, this holds no great evolutionary penalty. And polygyny is only removed from us by 10 million years and – or probably much less, considering that our Australopithecine ancestors likely practised it between 4 million and 2.3 million years ago. Coerced polygyny became more common with the introduction of culture, religions and states, as we cover in Chapter 8 and 9.
5. Voluntary polyandry, where multiple males will share one female while suppressing their sexual jealousies. It is extremely rare because there is no clear evolutionary precursor in 55 million years of our direct ancestry. However, promiscuous primates such as chimps technically share one female, and the only difference in polyandry is there is scarce male–male competition. As such it can arise in circumstances where low-ranking males do not risk competing because most of them are likely to lose in such a contest and have difficulty finding another mate. Alternately it arises in scenarios where the males are all related (with similar DNA) thus making the reproductive success of their kin less of a travesty for their own genetic line and sexual instincts.
6. Voluntary polyfidelity (multiple men and women in a closed sexual group) differs from promiscuity in the sense that sexual jealousy is suppressed within the group of males and females, while keeping

> jealousy alive to keep outsiders away. This balancing act of deeply held instincts makes it extremely rare and entirely unseen in any primate species prior to *Homo sapiens*, who have the mental capacity to sustain such a precarious balance. And, of course, even in humans it is extremely rare.

From *Homo erectus* to *Homo sapiens*, the lines between monogamy and other arrangements were incredibly blurred and much more fluid. Once *Homo sapiens* began socially enforcing monogamy through tribal marriage traditions, and especially when these traditions were etched into laws with the rise of agrarian states about 5500 years ago, the lines became much more distinct. And where non-monogamous relationships occurred, they were often the products of cultural ideas rather than biological instincts. A lot more thought, ideological justifications and discussion went into them, and these rationalisations were vital to sustaining them.

LOVE

In our direct line of evolutionary ancestry, female parental care for offspring has existed (to one degree or another) for roughly 300 million years. At the very least, female parental care has existed in our direct lineage since synapsid proto-mammals began suckling their young approximately 260 million years ago. Commensurate with this long lineage, the existence of maternal love is easy to understand. When mothers began investing huge amounts of their energy and lifespan into ensuring their offspring survived, their instinctual attachments grew correspondingly. The love of a mother is the product of a quarter of a billion years of evolution, and it shows. Through countless species, and through numerous mass-extinction events, without a mother's care and attention we would not have survived. (I speak in biological generalities, of course. I hope those people who grew up with unloving or abusive mothers will understand this is a wide-lens view.)

Conversely, levels of paternal care varied down our lineage from species to species, most often with males in the past 260 million years providing little to no fatherly care at all. That is quite true of most of our history since the evolution of Old World monkeys 40 million years ago. Then there was a slow increase. Male gorillas provide some degree of protection for their young from infanticide by their male rivals. Chimpanzees live in patrilocal groups with their male relatives (including their fathers) and sometimes shared food with females (and by extension their offspring). But all this male parental care is somewhat limited in scope. However, with the evolution of monogamy 1.9 million years ago, fatherly love rapidly intensified; otherwise our branch of the family tree would have withered and disappeared from Earth.

When *Homo erectus* evolved and a big-brained child was helpless for a much longer time, with mothers struggling with more severe childbirth and a rigorous nursing period, the male genetic investment went far beyond just sex in order to achieve 'reproductive success'. He needed to care for his young for at least half a dozen years (especially with the high pre-modern mortality rate of mothers giving birth) or there were harrowing odds the child would not survive. And so around the same time *Homo erectus* males were developing emotionally intense pair-bonds with females, they were doing the same with their children. (Though, again, I speak in biological generalities. Looking back at our recent evolutionary baggage, the existence of deadbeat dads, bigamists with twenty-five children whose names they don't remember, and modern baby-daddies who have no intention of committing to the women they impregnate, is quite easy to comprehend.)

In general, the evolution of love for one's children because they are the literal manifestation of the replication of our DNA is fairly straightforward. DNA replication is a simple chemical reaction that has been ongoing for 3.8 billion years, creating all sorts of complex natural phenomena. This includes powerful instincts and emotions, as well as fangs and feathers. We feel strongly for our children because it is one of the most deeply encoded aspects of our being.

The same goes for the evolutionary phenomenon of 'kin-selection', where, as we have seen, an individual is more likely to sacrifice their own survival chances to benefit someone who shares almost all their DNA (brothers, sisters, first cousins, aunts, uncles, etc). This tendency towards altruism fades the further away from your immediate family you proceed. And while it would be highly inaccurate to say that all immediate family members love each other, even cases of conflict between family members tend to be more emotionally tumultuous for us than if those disagreements had arisen with people to whom we are unrelated.

When it comes to the strong friendships we strike up with people who are *not* family, this also has a fairly straightforward evolutionary explanation. Within primate groups such as chimpanzees, social bonding and alliances are vital to survival. Our status within a group hierarchy and the number of people we have 'backing us up' often determines how quickly we get access to food and also our mating prospects. This was a fact of life for our last common ancestor with chimpanzees 6 million years ago, and remained so throughout Australopithecines, *Homo habilis* and *Homo erectus*. Some of the friendships we strike up are superficial and transient, and some of them are powerful friendships for life. Both augment survival and even reproductive success. So the affection we feel for our friends has its roots in evolution as well. Yet because these friendships are not *directly* important to the replication of our DNA like child-rearing or pair-bonding, they are generally less keenly felt than parental or romantic ones.

Which brings us to the evolution of love between an unrelated male and unrelated female in a monogamous species from 1.9 million years ago onwards. There is no shared DNA, thus no kin-selection. Yet the love between a couple is usually many times more intense than the affection we feel for our relatives and friends. At first glance, the existence of romantic love may seem a bit baffling. We certainly do not *need* to feel love for our mate to have sex with them or experience the instinctual love we have for any resulting children. So why does romantic love, the kind poets and musicians never seem to shut up about, exist?

Currently, the most widely accepted evolutionary theory for the existence of romantic love is, somewhat predictably, that it enhances the pair-bond, keeps couples together and thus increases the odds of our children surviving (certainly more of a risky proposition in the East African savanna 1.9 million years ago than it is today). This strong emotional bond goes far beyond just ape-like sexual jealousy and male and female mate-guarding. It is such an intense experience, physically and mentally, that it can unleash torrents of dopamine in the brain and severely impact an individual's health should a romantic couple be forever parted.

The most potent form of romantic love appears to prevail between humans in a monogamous relationship for an average of eight to twelve years, or roughly the same amount of time it would take to rear a child to not be so defenceless in the wild. This makes biological sense, because romantic love is definitely not vital to the survival of a mother or father individually (in fact, the idiotic things romantic love sometimes makes us do can *endanger* that survival). Instead, the focus of romantic love is on offspring. The business of replicating one's DNA. The only thing more important than keeping your belly full, your lungs full of air and your head attached to your shoulders. It is possibly not a coincidence that, on average, modern marriages and de facto relationships in Western societies (where social, religious and legal enforcement of monogamy has been heavily diminished) experience a breakdown around the eight- to twelve-year mark.

Yet love is not a monolith and the phenomenon changes in nature the longer it endures. Should love between a pair-bonded couple survive beyond the minimum period necessary to ensure a child can fend for itself in the wild, it tends to evolve beyond strong, passionate romantic attachment into something cosier and more mundane. And before we get too cynical, remember roughly 55 per cent of modern marriages *do* endure beyond this point. What remains when passion fades is a partnership where a couple's fundamental life logistics, goals and personal interests are intertwined. So much so that it is difficult to imagine life without the other person. This state of being is common, albeit not universal. This part of a loving relationship appears to be more learnt than instinctual. Nurture instead of nature, where one gains a psychological dependence on another person. This is quite different from the intensely felt biological instinct that draws two people towards monogamy in the first place.

Whether a couple deigns to have a child or not, that biological imperative is where the intense feelings of love come from. A romantic affair where the prospect of children never pops into either person's head is the rough equivalent of watching a scary movie to trigger the flight-or-fight response of one's adrenal glands. It may not be the originally intended purpose, but it evokes a response all the same. Love is a DNA-driven mechanism that can be deployed in a plethora of ways.

The existence of love as a pair-bonding device for the purposes of nurturing offspring occurs independently of whether offspring are actually born. Childless couples (voluntary and involuntary) pass through the same intense period of romantic emotions and potential maturing into a more stable partnership as those with children. Gay and lesbian couples (with or without children) experience all the same manifestations of romantic love, just with an obvious difference in whom they feel sexually attracted to and choose to pair-bond with. So, while romantic love may have first emerged in *Homo erectus* for rather practical evolutionary purposes 1.9 million years ago, it is a phenomenon that has taken on a life of its own. And that is why neither William Shakespeare nor the Backstreet Boys shut up about it.

THE BIRTH OF CULTURE

As the first species of our genus to spread out across the Old World, it goes without saying that *Homo erectus* was pretty good at using tools. But between 1.9 million and 1.78 million years ago, we see very little evidence of tinkering or technological improvement within that same species. Like chimpanzees, they seemed to adopt a range of tool uses and then stop progressing. Millions of years later, chimps are still fishing termites out of the ground with sticks, not working in skyscrapers as CEOs of giant termite farming corporations. It appeared the same would be the case with *Homo erectus*. However, 1.78 million years ago, *Homo erectus* invented a new type of hand axe. Over the next 250,000 years, they began tinkering with these hand axes, improving them in quality and converting them into multipurpose picks, cleavers and other implements. Two hundred and fifty thousand years is a rather slow pace of research and development, but here at last was a glimmer of something new under the sun ...

The ability of a species to accumulate more innovation with each generation than is lost/forgotten by the next is known as collective learning. This allows a species to continue to evolve their tool kits, ideas and adaptiveness, even when their brains and intellectual capacities evolve much more slowly. The first glimmer of collective learning was seen in *Homo erectus* by 1.5 million years ago. Subsequent species intensified this skill, and where technological innovation began with a trickle, it soon became a flood.

Homo antecessor evolved 1.2 million years ago, *Homo heidelbergensis* evolved 700,000 years ago and Neanderthals evolved 400,000 years ago. These species presided over the first controlled use of fire, the first blade tools, the earliest wooden spears and the earliest use of composite tools, where stone was fastened to wood. *Homo heidelbergensis* became the first of our genus to colonise all of Eurasia. Neanderthals adapted to climes that made clothing necessary for insulation and warmth. They used complex tool manufacture, with prepared stone cores, producing a variety of implements, sharp points, scrapers, hand axes, wood handles, with deliberate use of good stone materials, and countless variations and improvements over time.

By the time we arrive at the first *Homo sapiens* evolving in Africa approximately 315,000 years ago, collective learning had reached its apogee. We are fairly intellectually and anatomically similar to those *Homo sapiens* who lived those many hundreds of millennia ago. Yet we have moved from stone tools to skyscrapers within a blink of an eye in evolutionary time. Three hundred and fifteen thousand years ago, we were capable of the same tinkering and innovation that modern humans are, we were capable of complex language and we were capable of abstract thought.

Additionally, we had the ability to devise traditions, rituals, laws and ideals that shaped our behaviour even while our evolutionary instincts remained the same. In a word, we developed culture – something that can dramatically alter human behaviour within the space of just a few decades or centuries, despite the more glacial pace of our instinctual and biological changes. And it was the intervention of culture that profoundly impacted our approach to sex, as we moved from hunting and gathering, to agrarian states, to modernity. Nature and nurture were about to begin their courtship dance.

PART III

CULTURAL AFTERGLOW

315,000 YEARS AGO TO THE PRESENT

8

FETISHES OF THE FOREST

315,000 to 12,000 years ago

Wherein Homo sapiens *stop being strictly patrilocal to avoid committing incest • We start having ritualistic tribal marriages at scandalously young ages • Despite monogamy, we continue to be pervy cheating dirtbags • Our own evolutionary instincts ruin our chances of prehistoric utopia • Abstract thinking produces dirty thoughts • Sadomasochism rears its head in most of the adult population • The pedestal effect plays off our evolutionary self-interest to give us increasingly weird fetishes.*

By the emergence of *Homo sapiens* roughly 315,000 years ago, after a long evolutionary march of 2 billion years, our sexual instincts were hardwired into our systems. From the basic desire to reproduce to the periodic compulsion to masturbate and the general tendency to pair-bond, our instincts formed the bedrock for sexual changes that would now take place in the realm of ideas, traditions and culture. Culture changed human behaviour more rapidly than the evolution of our instincts ever could. But often the traditions, concepts and romantic ideals that humans devised for themselves crumbled before the powerful throbbing impulses of our evolutionary wiring – as they still often do today. 'Nurture' had to constantly operate within the realistic bounds of 'Nature' and vice versa. And so, the dance began.

Collective learning, the ability to accumulate more knowledge with each generation and pass it on to the next, fuelled complex and rapidly changing culture. Over decades, centuries and millennia, ideas and technologies were tinkered with, improved, altered or discarded. This is most abundantly clear in the field of technology. The computers of the 2020s are much more advanced than the giant, primitive computers of the 1960s. Your smartphone has greater computing power than NASA did during the *Apollo* Moon missions. We also see it in the evolution of language, from Old English, to Middle English, to Modern English. Words are tinkered with, improved, discarded. Every year we add to our lexicon new words such as 'simp' and concepts like 'big dick energy'.

Collective learning extends to human ideas around sex, romance, marriage and children. Ideas about sex can vary drastically between societies and across centuries. In an Amazonian foraging tribe, extramarital sex may be culturally tolerated, while it is regarded as betrayal and disgrace in a Judeo-Christian society. The cutting of an infant's foreskin or clitoris may be encouraged in some cultures for religious or 'hygienic' purposes, and regarded as mutilation and child abuse in others. And while the delivery of a pig or cow in exchange for a woman's hand in marriage may have been standard practice in a Neolithic farming community 11,000 years ago, it is hardly the sort of romantic gift a guy would consider bringing his Tinder date today.

Humans were pretty much the same physically and mentally 315,000 years ago as they are today. Just as emotionally capable, just as sexually inclined, just as intelligent. But they became experts at hunting, gathering and surviving in harsh conditions rather than experts at spreadsheets, fixing cars or building a following on OnlyFans. And they lived in nomadic foraging bands composed of a few dozen men and women with whom they spent their entire lives, rather than in cities populated by millions of strangers. Although *Homo sapiens* had already evolved its smorgasbord of sexual instincts, the hunter-gatherer lifestyle had a profound impact on how those instincts played out culturally. Some of these behaviours will be familiar, and some foreign. All of them are ancestors of our own sexual practices, and that heritage informs our perspective of how we date, wank and fuck in modern times.

EVENT	DATE
The evolution of *Homo sapiens*	315,000 years ago
Mass migration of humans out of Africa	64,000 years ago
First humans in India, East Asia and Australia	60,000 years ago
First humans in Europe	40,000 years ago
First humans in the Americas	12,000 years ago

ROCK HARD IN THE OLD STONE AGE

From 315,000 to 12,000 years ago, we lived as hunter-gatherers in the Palaeolithic (Old Stone Age). That is 96 per cent of all human history. And between the origin of our species 315,000 years ago and the start of agriculture 12,000 years ago, an estimated 20 to 25 billion foraging humans lived, had sex, raised children and died on the surface of the Earth. Due to the nature of foraging – not growing any food but merely consuming wild flora and fauna before the nomads moved on while the area replenished itself – the entire surface of Earth could support no more than 8 million of us at any given time. Usually a lot fewer.

From 315,000 to 64,000 years ago, most of us dwelt in Africa, with a few spilling over into the Middle East; Eurasia, the Americas and Oceania remained largely uninhabited. During that period there were between 10,000 and 500,000 of us in Africa. The low watermark of the human population was 74,000 years ago, when the genetic record shows our numbers shrank to just 10,000 people, from whom all 8 billion people now alive are descended. Given that 74,000 years is an incredibly short time in evolutionary terms, it is no wonder that humans are the most closely related of all mammalian species on the planet today (just not to the point of being completely inbred). There is more genetic diversity between two different groups of chimpanzees separated by a few dozen kilometres than there is in the entire human race.

After 64,000 years ago, we gradually spread across Eurasia, headed down towards Australia, and even crossed the Bering Strait to the Americas, until we inhabited almost every corner of Earth by 12,000 years ago. Only then could our numbers swell to the 8 million-forager maximum Earth could support.

Hunter-gatherer groups at their smallest scale centred around the immediate family unit (mum and dad looking after their children) before extending out to the wider kin-group (relatives), which formed the core of the forager body politic. In many ways, kin-based foraging societies operated like Italian mafia families do in modernity, because there was no 'state' authority to speak of. Justice was dispensed by the family, loyalties were accorded mostly to the family, and intermarriages and blood feuds with other groups were handled, again, as a family. Given our evolutionary history, this prioritising of first our offspring, our DNA, and then our wider kin who share pretty much all our DNA, is hardly surprising.

The wider tribal group of people who were *not* related consisted of other families numbering a few dozen to a few hundred at a maximum. The wider tribe may have been governed by a chief (the equivalent of the pre-1931 Mafia 'boss of all bosses') or a council of elders (similar in

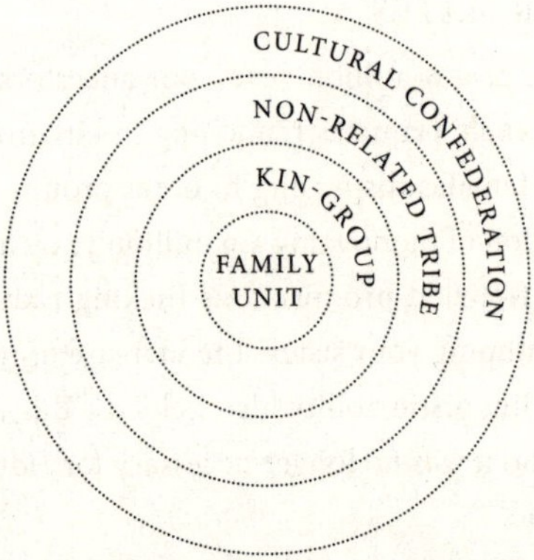

operation to 'The Commission' founded by Lucky Luciano in 1931, which consisted of the heads of all the major crime families). In the surrounding area of many kilometres of foraging territory, a wider confederation of the same tribal culture might number into the thousands (provided there was enough food for everyone in the region). Thus, from the relatively small group sizes of chimpanzees and Australopithecines came the larger group sizes and higher social complexity of *Homo sapiens*.

Large tribal confederations might be grouped under a single leader or council, before splintering into much smaller pieces again with some regularity. Due to the vast distances separating people, and the fact that all traditions were passed on orally, and due to general 'cultural drift' over generations, no tribal culture remained the same for more than 200 or 300 years. There was also the menace of tribal warfare, conquest of foraging territory by another culture, and the genocide or absorption of one cultural group by another. A tribal culture in any region would look foreign to one that existed 1000 years later, perhaps even having a different name, different gods and creation myths and a strongly altered language dialect. No tribal culture remains in stasis for multiple millennia. Not even close. The gene pool of a foraging region might remain relatively the same, but culturally the tribe is ever-changing.

MAIL-ORDER MATES

For most of the past 6 million years, our ancestors had been fully patrilocal, with male primates remaining in kin groups where they were born and females dispersing to other groups to avoid incest. Then the evolution of monogamy 1.9 million years ago and the relative decline of frenzied promiscuous fucking reduced the risk of accidentally schtuping your sister. The increase of intelligence, self-awareness and linguistic ability also helped ('Billy, stop staring at your cousin!'). So it was no longer necessary for *Homo sapiens* to be strictly patrilocal.

Instead, families remained together for longer, often until formal tribal marriages could be arranged. Furthermore, men sometimes *did* leave their natal groups in search of mates, settling down in new communities. But it was still mostly women who were sent off to neighbours – usually after a monogamous mate or husband had been found, rather than the girls taking off into the wild once they reached sexual maturity as in chimps or bonobos. Regardless of whether it was a man or woman departing the family group, in *Homo sapiens* these departures frequently took the form of highly ritualised tribal marriages, designed to strike up alliances and reduce hostilities. Budding diplomacy to either prevent or end territorial wars. While chimps and bonobo males do not associate much beyond their birth groups, in humans this was not so, with men frequently interacting with non-relatives in non-violent contexts. And, whether the foragers were aware of it or not, the constant movement of monogamous mates to and from the group promoted both genetic diversity *and* the exchange of cultural knowledge.

In foraging societies, girls got married and had sex soon after they reached puberty around the age of thirteen (or earlier) – something that would seem unusual in modernity, when the age of consent in developed nations is between sixteen and eighteen and the average age a woman has her first child is between twenty-seven and twenty-nine.

Forager girls would be pregnant with their first child long before they reached the end of their teens. By the age of twenty a woman would likely have two or three children at varying stages of development. But usually the number was not any higher. A nomadic foraging woman could only nurse and carry one newborn infant at a time, as the tribe moved across many kilometres in search of food. Communal child-raising could help, but generally pregnancies were spaced out. Unexpected or unwanted pregnancies, where infants were born too closely together, were dealt with after birth by infanticide, usually by abandoning the child to die from exposure. It was quite common, in the order of 10 to 25 per cent of all births. Aborting a pregnancy while offspring was still in the womb would have almost certainly resulted in the death of the mother.

Boys, meanwhile, got married slightly later, usually in their late teens. On average this might place a young man three or four years older than his bride: for example, a 17-year-old boy marrying a 13-year-old girl. Boys could only marry once they had 'proven themselves a man' (worthy and capable of providing for a wife and children) by some rite of passage or tribal ritual. As one hell of a 'for instance', the Etoro people of modern Papua New Guinea are among several Pacific foraging peoples who believe boys must ingest the semen of older men in order to attain such masculine status. As you can see, the influence of culture on the sexual practices of *Homo sapiens* can be profound. Removing culture, it is highly unlikely your typical young man would instinctually gravitate toward eating the jism of older men (including relatives) to prove his masculinity.

Additionally, in human foraging groups, older men of high status often took second wives (or multiple wives) well into their thirties, forties and, if they were still alive, their fifties and sixties. (The average life expectancy of foragers was twenty-five – not because nobody survived beyond their twenties but because so many foragers died young from violence, illness and infant mortality. The survivors could live for a substantial lifespan provided they were not murdered and did not get sick.) While the marital age of women centred around the years they were fertile (thirteen to forty, and the earlier the better), the emphasis on men as providers extended marriage to ages when they were more skilled, knowledgeable and had perhaps achieved higher social status. Hence the general tendency of women to date men of equivalent age or higher (sometimes much higher), with the inverse trend of women dating significantly younger men being decidedly more uncommon (but not unheard of and usually after a previous marriage and/or kids).

This analysis of forager couplings may sound cold and utilitarian, involving a great deal of family and tribal formality in arranging marriages. Indeed, many forager marriages would have been loveless (and even coerced). But we cannot discount the evolutionary impulse towards love that was doubtless present in some of these matches. These human beings had the same emotional range and proclivities as us, after all. And many forager marriages *were between* teenagers. At that stage of life, infatuation is most intense and love requires minimal knowledge of the other person, minimal critical thought and minimal consideration of the practicalities of the future.

Naturally, as with modern teenage infatuations, these feelings might be shortlived as the young husband and wife got to know each other. However, there was much more holding a marriage in place after puppy-love had faded than in modern times: obligations between families, the ritual and religious significance of the match, and the blunt realities of a young man and woman relying on each other to survive and raise offspring in a harsh, nomadic foraging world. When social ostracism, religious violation, starvation, death and the death of your children draw near, there is much more incentive for a couple to keep a marriage alive, even after passions have disappeared.

FORAGING BEYOND CIS-HET

Of course, not all Palaeolithic foragers were straight. Approximately 8.5 per cent of the human population are bisexual (15 per cent of women, 2 per cent of men), 1.5 per cent of the population are gay (or roughly 3 per cent of men), 0.75 per cent are lesbian (or roughly 1.5 per cent of women), 0.5 per cent of the population are asexual (0.8 per cent of women, 0.2 per cent of men), with the remaining 88.75 per cent of the human population being straight (though doubtless with some significant wiggle room if the above statistics are slightly off). The frequency of bisexuality and homosexuality tends to fluctuate slightly between different species in our family tree. The slightly greater prevalence of exclusively gay men (as opposed to women) may be due our recent polygynous past (orangutans, gorillas and possibly Australopiths), and the larger number of bisexual women may be the result of the evolution of stronger female bonds in the past 1.9 million years than existed in our last common ancestor with chimpanzees 6 million years ago. Just like how bisexuality and strong female bonds evolved in bonobos 2 million years ago. So if nearly one-sixth of the population is something other than straight, how did these people conduct their love lives in foraging societies for the past 315,000 years?

Direct evidence from the Palaeolithic of bisexual and exclusively homosexual individuals is thin on the ground, confined mostly to a few possible depictions of gay sex in engravings and cave paintings. Some foraging cultures in North America and Oceania assigned a wide swathe of non-hetero and nonbinary activity to a third gender, or its equivalent. However, a substantial number of other foraging cultures, such as the Aka and Ngandu of Central Africa, report 'no homosexual activity' at all. This is probably not a homophobic denial by these tribes. Foragers do not typically regard homosexuality with hostility and it is not outlawed like incest; rather, there is just limited awareness of it as an occurrence or a concept. This might be due to low population sizes in clans and tribal groups. If your widest social network as a forager is 150 people (Dunbar's number: the proposed maximum number of people with whom one can sustain an ongoing interpersonal relationship) then maybe two of them will be gay, one of them lesbian, eleven bisexual women and one of them a bisexual man. Of course, the regular day-to-day social networks of most foragers don't come anywhere near *half* that number. You'd spend your entire life with a few dozen people, many of them family members, and unless you were particularly nosy it is unlikely you'd become aware of everyone's inner thoughts and sexual desires.

Thus, exclusively homosexual individuals were relatively rare in foraging communities, and not visible to many members of a tribe. Some gay or lesbian individuals might find lovers who were bisexual. And those bisexual individuals would likely have been married from a young age, like everybody else, keeping their gay or lesbian lover officially as a very close 'friend'. In fact, due to the formal, familial and ritualistic nature of tribal marriage, an exclusively gay or lesbian individual would very likely *also* find themselves with an opposite-sex spouse, perhaps marrying in their early teens, before they'd had an opportunity to fully explore their sexual orientation. Thus, the visibility of exclusively gay or lesbian individuals would be low for the average forager being questioned on the subject by a visiting anthropologist. Gay and lesbian sex occurring in foraging societies (and it certainly did occur) would have been private and conceptually detached from familial and symbolic notions of marriage between foraging clans.

That said, there is a lot of cultural variation between foraging groups. More warlike foraging groups, such as the Amazonian Waorani, sometimes display homophobia when it comes to gay male sex (less so with lesbian sex) but usually in the context of either demanding men display a warrior-type masculinity or in preventing marital infidelity. On the flipside, some Pacific foraging cultures have ritual homosexual activities in which even straight tribal members take part, though these rituals are not defined in the dichotomy of 'gay' versus 'straight'.

When it comes to trans, nonbinary and intersex individuals, the odds of them appearing in a foraging group of a few dozen people are even lower. For starters, an estimated 0.02 per cent of people are visibly intersex at birth (via direct observation of the genitalia), with more individuals showing some form of intersex trait via hormonal development by the time they enter puberty. Nevertheless, a sizeable minority of current and former foraging cultures have a term for a third gender. However, there is usually some grey area: these third-gender concepts commonly act as an umbrella term for approximately 5 to 10 per cent of the population who may be intersex, exclusively homosexual, bisexual, nonbinary or gender dysphoric, in addition to feminine heterosexual men, masculine heterosexual women and anyone androgynous in physical appearance or behaviour. Due to low population numbers, the use of third-gender for 5 to 10 per cent of people in some North American and Pacific foraging groups was much more frequent than identifying people by more specific categories. However, after the population explosions following agriculture 12,000 years ago and industry 250 years ago, with the world containing hundreds of millions then billions of people, these concepts and communities became increasingly well defined.

Regarding trans and nonbinary people, it is difficult to discern when in our long evolutionary story this emerged. We have no way of finding out if other species in our family tree, such as primates or even more distant evolutionary cousins, experience gender dysphoria. It raises interesting questions since sex differentiation goes back over 500 million years. But by the time we arrive at 315,000 years ago, *Homo sapiens* was pretty much the same animal as it is today, so it is likely that trans (or trans-adjacent) and nonbinary people existed in Palaeolithic forager populations. It is also a safe bet that dysphoria has an evolutionary heritage, though how far back it goes in our lineage no one can currently say. Statistically, a highly variable estimate of 0.04 per cent to 0.6 per cent of people have gender dysphoria, with up to a further 1 per cent of the population in modernity now identifying as trans or nonbinary for personal, cultural or ideological reasons. In Palaeolithic foraging cultures, lack of surgical technology would have prevented physical transitioning, but cultural signifiers might have placed them within tribal notions of the masculine, feminine or third-gender. And like gay and lesbian individuals, it is highly likely that trans and nonbinary people would still have found themselves swept up in formal, ritualistic and heteronormative tribal marriages.

PROMISCUITY AND POLYGYNY 2: ELECTRIC BOOGALOO

The instinct towards monogamy in *Homo sapiens* did not come without the considerable baggage of 40 to 55 million years of evolution. Promiscuity and infidelity, as you might expect, were still common in human foraging bands. Even today in the developed world, a large University of Chicago survey conducted in 2000–2016 found that approximately 20 per cent of men and 15 per cent of women cheat on their partners. While most modern foraging groups frown on promiscuity (particularly marital infidelity), some foraging cultures *permit* a degree of promiscuity – though the picture is far from the modern notion of free love or hook-up culture. The Curripaco of the Amazon allow extramarital sex, but illegitimate pregnancies and couplings without the husband's consent are often punished. The Kayapo allow promiscuous sex in exchange for gifts, but men who have sex with women without offering something in return are considered 'thieves' and women too reluctant to have sex for payment are shamed as prudish and sometimes subjected to punitive rape. The Matis allow brothers and fathers to share the same woman, keeping DNA within the bounds of kin-selection.

One of the most extreme examples of this patriarchal form of promiscuity is the Canela tribe. They consider girls sexually mature at eleven to thirteen, and the first boy a girl sleeps with is automatically considered her husband. However, the marriage is not finalised until pregnancy occurs. So the girl can have sex with numerous men, each becoming her husband in turn, until one impregnates her. Once the girl is pregnant, there is a ritual dinner where she must have sex with up to twenty men in the tribe, one at a time. One of the stated purposes of this ritual is to allow less attractive men who have not found a wife a chance to have sex, to stop them from becoming embittered and endangering tribal cohesion. Another is for the sex to renew their 'masculine vigour'. Girls who refuse to partake in the ritual of sequential sex with up to twenty men in one evening are sometimes gang-raped all at once as a punishment. Once she has given birth, the girl is frequently deprived of sex with her husband (who turns his sexual attentions elsewhere) so she may focus on motherhood. Masturbation is forbidden for both men and women, and due to the fact that the sex positions used by the Canela avoid clitoral stimulation, female orgasm is rare.

We are not talking about a modern notion of promiscuity for recreation, where men and women head down to 'da club' for an evening of loud music, overpriced drinks, illicit drug use and a sloppy intoxicated fuck in a toilet cubicle. We are not even talking about chimpanzee males violently forcing themselves onto a random assortment of females for 7 seconds. While promiscuity is socially tolerated in a minority of foraging cultures, it comes with strings – most of them unfavourable to women. And they are invariably set up in a cultural environment where pair-bonding/marriage already exists. And there are many foraging groups where no form of promiscuity is tolerated at all.

Polygyny is much more common in human foraging groups than socially tolerated promiscuity. While monogamous marriage is almost universal among foragers, many foraging cultures permit one man to take many wives. Wide-ranging anthropological studies have found that approximately 85 per cent of all human cultures that have existed permit non-monogamous relationships, and the chosen practice is almost invariably polygyny (usually in a small minority, 1 to 5 per cent, but sometimes more widely in the case of religiously compelled polygamist societies). Usually, a man with multiple wives in a foraging group is of high-status, a tribal leader or religious shaman. Meanwhile, most of the tribe remain socially monogamous, because otherwise the roughly 50/50 population split between men and women would mean having too many men frustrated and alone. That sort of widespread sexual jealousy destroys tribal cohesion. So, you don't usually see men with multiple wives as the dominant practice in any culture (foraging or otherwise) unless there is a pretty hefty religious justification for it.

Yet it appears there was some disparity in reproductive success among men during the Palaeolithic. Y-chromosome analysis indicates that prior to the advent of agriculture 12,000 years ago, a minority of men were responsible for the lion's share of impregnations: the same phenomenon that arose in *Homo erectus*, only slightly diminished in scale. There are various possibilities:

- a lot of cuckolding was going on
- women were gravitating towards a small pool of highly attractive men in illicit pre-marriage promiscuous couplings
- polygyny among the highest-ranking males was co-opting such large numbers of wives that it reverberated down our family tree
- warfare, male mortality and the abduction and sexual enslavement of women by opposing tribes were frequent.

Or a combination of all the above.

The result was that a lot of forager men got squeezed out of the gene pool, despite many attempts to socially enforce monogamy and keep an eye on the paternity of children. For example, the Curripaco, who permit some promiscuity, have on occasion been observed by anthropologists committing infanticide when children are not sired by the husband. Some Ye'kwana husbands abandon their children and wives if the latter are discovered to be sleeping with other men. Some Piaroa will either kill or abandon children whose paternity is in doubt. The Secoya cloister women to prevent them from having sex, and men who sleep around promiscuously are socially ostracised or exiled. Some Warao fathers will immediately refuse to look after children who do not physically resemble them. And although the Aché believe that pregnancy is caused by multiple inseminations by two or three men (essentially 'filling up the tank' till a baby pops out), some husbands have been observed by anthropologists beating their wives if they get too emotionally attached to the secondary or tertiary male inseminator. In cases of outright infidelity (sex and pregnancy where the husband is *not* involved) the cuckolded Aché husband will sometimes kill his rival and even bury an illegitimate child alive with the corpse of its father. Meanwhile, Aché women who have children but no husband to partake in group hunts will not receive any food from the tribe and must fend for themselves. Among the Hadza of East Africa, 80 per cent of marriages end in divorce, mostly due to extramarital affairs. Thirty-five per cent of these divorces end with one man killing another, 25 per cent with the woman attacking the husband's sidepiece and only 40 per cent without violence. In Central Africa, the Aka people are arguably one of the most egalitarian foraging cultures in the world today; both men and women hunt, and fathers provide a lot of care for their children, carrying infants 45 per cent of the time and splitting childcare with the mother relatively equally. But divorce is exceedingly common, with two-thirds of all cases being from infidelity. Men often kill rivals over this, and both men and women are sometimes known to kill the illegitimate children of their spouse.

Aka fathers and their children

For perspective, a 2005 Liverpool John Moores University study found that approximately 4 per cent of men in post-industrial twenty-first-century society are unknowingly raising children that aren't genetically theirs. A range of 2 to 5 per cent has been found by several other modern studies. Conversely, according to Y-chromosome analysis and observation of modern foraging groups, the rate of paternity fraud in the Palaeolithic foraging societies was likely considerably higher: 15 to 30 per cent (depending on how much of the Y-chromosome shortage we attribute to other causes). Consequently, after agrarian societies arose 12,000 years ago and especially after the first states formed 5,500 years ago, attempts to prevent infidelity and police paternity only intensified, with all the sexual taboos and sexual repression that accompanied it. Thereafter, Y-chromosome analysis reveals that the number of men raising their own children gradually increased as agriculture and state societies spread across the world.

FOOD AND EQUALITY

Palaeolithic foraging societies had a simple division of labour, with everyone engaged in food production. Sexual dimorphism had receded significantly since the evolution of monogamy 1.9 million years ago, with men being roughly 15 per cent larger than women on average. Nevertheless, the difference in strength meant that most men hunted and most women gathered. But we know from studying modern foraging groups over the past two centuries that there was overlap. Some women were athletic and/or had specialised knowledge that made them proficient hunters. Some males were extremely knowledgeable about local plants, were not athletic or were too old to track game. And either sex could be particularly talented in or personally predisposed towards either pursuit. Still, exceptions do not make the average, and generally speaking, women gathered and men hunted. Often this was reinforced by cultural and religious norms.

Men, whether hunter or gatherer, would share food with their mate and offspring, continuing the 1.9-million-year tradition of fatherly parental care. Foragers also tended to share food across the group (it would be suicidal for a group to fight over every berry, nut or scrap of cooked flesh when there was enough for everybody). But the communal nature of food sharing in forager groups is often overstated. This was not Stone Age communism. By observing modern foraging groups, we know that men and women prioritised sharing food with their offspring and immediate kin over sharing it with non-relatives. And men tended to keep more meat for themselves than they gave to women or children. Tribal hierarchy gave the higher-ranking members priority access to recently caught high-calorie game, with status determining access to food in either quality or quantity. Food sharing tended to break down in times of starvation, leading to sharp divisions along family lines in the resulting conflict. And if you didn't pull your weight with food-gathering, you might be cut out of sharing altogether. In modern foraging groups, sometimes a wife or husband (and their children) will be cut out of food-sharing because one spouse isn't pulling their weight – in some cold-hearted cases this is even when the spouse is sick or injured rather than merely lazy.

There was much less wealth disparity than in agricultural or modern societies. But it would be ludicrous to assert that there was no concept of property/territory or disparity of wealth. On the one hand, nomadic individuals or families did not claim to own a particular patch of land. They were not sedentary, they did not farm. And they only had wealth and possessions they could carry with them. On the other hand, foragers *did* lay claim to food-gathering territory and skirmished bitterly with other tribes for it. Given how much land was needed to feed a relatively small number of people, such territorial claims were often a matter of life and death.

The idea that in the Palaeolithic there was never any shortage of food is also false. Sure, a nomadic band might spend a generation or two in an underpopulated region where food was relatively plentiful. But as the local population grew (frequent infanticides notwithstanding) those local resources would be depleted faster than they could naturally replenish themselves. It is why human foragers caused multiple extinctions of megafauna in every new continent they entered after leaving Africa 64,000 years ago. A nomadic band had to move on or it would starve. If the neighbouring regions were barren or overpopulated, this led to food shortage – and conflict.

Moreover, forager burials sometimes vary in the kinds of jewels and trinkets and the quality of tools interred with the body, denoting disparity of social status. When it came to good tools and 'shiny things', there was always something to be jealous of, even though the possessions nomadic humans carried with them were few. There were also romantic jealousies. Observation of modern foragers indicates these are responsible for a huge proportion of interpersonal violence. But far and away the most valuable capital in foraging bands was social status. People competed for a good reputation and a respected place in the tribal hierarchy (and to avoid becoming an outcast), with disputes, alliances and political manoeuvres. Just as we see in our many primate cousins, only with greater intensity, complexity and social sophistication.

Which brings us to men and women. Hunting was boom-and-bust. When the (mostly male) hunters were successful, the group could eat for days. And meat was much more calorie-rich than the plants that could be gathered. Many more plants had to be consumed to get the same amount of energy. But when hunters came back with empty hands, a tribe might go weeks on little or no meat. As a result, an estimated 60 per cent of all food for foraging groups came from gathering. The fact that the (mostly female) gatherers were more consistently bringing in food did *not* translate to equal political power for women. In most historical foraging groups which had literate observers, and in most modern foraging groups, it was high-ranking men (and neither women nor low-ranking men) who at least nominally held the ability to issue orders to the group, dispense justice, make war and forge inter-group alliances. But women still had significant influence on the politics and traditions of the group, given the interpersonal nature of politics in small foraging bands. Individual women also frequently wielded immense influence over their family units and kin-groups, if their personalities were so disposed. Especially if they ranked higher in the female hierarchy or were attached to a high-ranking male – in both cases a low-ranking man would be foolish to disrespect them, unless he wanted his head bashed in with a rock.

Generally, female political capital came in the form of soft power, rather than direct commands. However, even in foraging cultures where individual women were highly respected, culturally women in general were viewed as subservient to men, in a way more reminiscent of nineteenth-century Western male chauvinism than any egalitarian society to be found in the twenty-first century. Moreover, as a very solid trend in modern and historical foraging groups, the more hostile, warlike, barren and unforgiving an environment in which a tribal culture existed, the more male-dominated and even misogynistic cultural attitudes tended to be.

These sex-based dynamics among foragers likely arose for two reasons. First, because of continued sexual dimorphism; men could regularly resort to physical coercion should disagreements arise in a group (whereas women generally could not). Second, because of the continued high levels of male aggression and competition in *Homo sapiens,* which drove men to chase power and social status. Conversely, dimorphism and competition over women led to an instinct of male expendability, with men (particularly low-ranking men) more likely to be given dangerous, painful, violent and potentially deadly tasks such as fending off predators and engaging in warfare. 'Women and children first' as a notion did not emerge spontaneously in modern times; it is present in spirit in historically observed and present-day foraging groups.

Meanwhile, *both* men and women had hierarchies, with some individuals more popular and respected than others in the group. These hierarchies functioned in a web of popularity, gossip, reputation, alliances and pettiness that is vaguely reminiscent of the self-organisation of teenage cliques in modern high schools. The human forager 'apple' had not fallen far from the *Homo erectus, Australopithecus* and chimpanzee 'tree'.

DAYCARE COMMUNISM

Infants were often raised communally. Women would look after each other's children while they engaged in daily food-gathering. Men would also pitch in after the hunt, instructing children that were not their offspring in various skills and the traditions of the tribe. But the communal raising of children in foraging groups can be overstated. Mothers prioritised care of their own newborns. When another woman helping a mother had a child of her own, she peeled off – her priorities skewed towards her own DNA. And while men raised and protected other people's children, most of the time this was done within their kin group (their nephews and cousins, etc), with the instruction and protection of non-relatives a secondary priority. As a general principle, the closer a child was related to you, the more care you gave that kid. In this respect, communal childcare in foragers is not so different from childcare in pre-modern farming communities (hence the old aphorism 'it takes a village to raise a child') and even modernity, where relatives and friends (to speak nothing of paid babysitters and educators) pitch in. Again, these people living in the Paleolithic were mentally and physically just like us. Just in different circumstances.

Human foragers were not like bonobos, who raise children communally because random and copious sex has obscured paternity (and, even then, bonobo females are very much prejudiced towards their own male offspring). Even in human tribes where some measure of promiscuity is permitted, it is highly unusual for people to not have a fairly good idea of the paternity of a kid. In such cultures, extra-marital couplings often come with a great deal of ceremony and public knowledge of who's sleeping with whom. Some researchers have mistakenly concluded that modern forager use of the words 'mother' and 'father' for multiple people implies clouded paternity and/or communal raising. In fact, these titles are often bestowed as a mark of respect, in the same way we might call a priest 'father' or a senior-ranking nun 'mother'.

Even in semi-promiscuous modern foraging bands, if a child has no clear paternity, the potential fathers tend to show disinterest in raising it, providing limited parental care – or none. As the saying in many modern foraging groups goes, 'the child of everyone is the child of no one'. Meanwhile, in monogamous arrangements, foraging male parental care is just as capricious and unpredictable as females providing access to sex in the first place. The general tendency of women to be the gatekeepers of sex and men the gatekeepers of committed relationships prevails (with many context-dependent exceptions) to the modern day. And in cases of human forager polygyny, generally the more women a man had access to, the greater the likelihood he would be a negligent father.

THE CHIMP ENDURES

Warfare, in terms of several hundred or thousand men taking to the field and fighting pitched battles, was not a fixture of the Palaeolithic. Forager numbers were too small and thinly spread across a vast territory. What existed instead was a jacked-up version of what is seen in chimpanzees – turf wars over foraging territory (the source of food). These wars most often took the form of raids and small skirmishes of a few dozen men. Camps might be attacked, the men killed and the women carted off into sexual slavery. Eventually the victorious side would harass a rival tribe until they withdrew from the foraging territory, or else a peace was negotiated (often capped off with a symbolic marriage). However, sometimes a war could end in genocide, with all the enemy killed and any survivors absorbed into the rival culture.

As deadly as tribal warfare was, interpersonal violence within a tribe was far worse. Take the Waorani of Ecuador, for example. Although they are an extremely warlike culture, frequently engaged in conflicts, only 8 per cent of Waorani deaths are from skirmishes and raids conducted by neighbouring cultures. A staggering 42 per cent of all deaths are from interpersonal violence.

Studies of Palaeolithic skeletons that show signs of dying from deliberately inflicted violence establish a murder rate of approximately 10 per cent averaged out across both peaceful and warlike foraging cultures. That is roughly 3000 times higher than any modern First World nation.

The Palaeolithic world had a real problem with interpersonal violence. And the root of much of that violence was sex. Fights between men over mates, spouses killing spouses, the killing of illegitimate children – this is how many of these Palaeolithic skeletons met their end. Such crimes still rank high among all modern murders, with roughly 30 per cent of all murders being carried out by a romantic or sexual partner, and approximately 60 per cent of all child murders being committed by one or both parents. Jockeying for high-status, petty rivalries, blood feuds and quarrelling among relatives were other likely causes for murder. And a major incentive for competing within a tribal hierarchy was increased odds of reproductive success.

A complicating factor is the massive variation of empathy and reciprocal altruism among humans. Approximately one in 100 people display all the traits that denote psychopathy, as applied by modern criminologists, and up to one in twenty people showing at least some of symptoms associated with the wider psychiatric diagnosis of anti-social personality disorder (ASPD). While most humans have some degree of empathy (the ability to see things from someone else's perspective) and reciprocal altruism (self-sacrificing behaviour that ultimately has an evolutionary benefit), some people in any given human population are incapable of empathy and/or are less likely to do self-sacrificing acts. Evolutionarily speaking, psychopathy versus altruism balances out like a bell curve. At one end are those who are extremely psychopathic and Machiavellian, and at the other those who are extremely kind and empathetic. Most people are clustered towards the centre. If you are too much of a psychopath, you risk being exiled or killed before you pass on your genes. If you are altruistic to the point of being a doormat, you also run the risk of not passing on your genes.

In the foraging era, being a psychopath held some reproductive benefits if you were able to ruthlessly pursue what you wanted, either as a lone wolf or acting as a dominant manipulator of a group (hence why many modern professions that have power or prestige, such as politics and business, attract psychopaths). The blunt fact is that psychopathic, sociopathic or anti-social behaviour often led to reproductive success. In the Palaeolithic, murder and sexual coercion were certainly not off the table. Meanwhile, hybristophilia is sexual attraction to people who show violent and/or criminal behaviour; intriguingly, the approximate rate of hybristophiles is also one in 100 people. While most do not go beyond the realm of fantasising, some hybristophiles even have children with their love interest – making hybristophilia a viable evolutionary strategy just like psychopathy.

This does not mean that one in 100 people are sexual sadists or deranged serial killers. Sexual sadists are closer to one in 10,000 people and sex-based serial killers are one in 1.2 million. These are harrowing statistics when you consider the population of modern cities and countries, but serial killers were less of an existential threat in the Paleolithic world, due to low population numbers. On the other hand, sexual sadism, unfortunately, very likely *did* result in offspring during the hundreds of millions (or even billions) of coercive sexual encounters that occurred in our evolutionary history.

We have already covered how nomadism meant people could not have children too close together, resulting in utilitarian infanticide being committed in approximately 10 to 25 per cent of all births. The same constraints of nomadism often applied to the elderly and infirm. Geronticide and euthanasia were practised among foragers, particularly during periods of food shortage, with the aged and infirm being abandoned by their foraging groups and left to perish in the wild. Some foraging cultures developed ritualised ways of killing the sick and elderly, such as the ancient Germanic practice of stabbing them to death on an altar and then lighting their bodies on fire, rather than leaving them to struggle and die more gradually.

In short, the foraging world was not the utopia it is sometimes depicted as being. Our lifeways and evolutionary baggage made sure of it. These foraging humans were the same creatures as us, with the same capacity for murder, deception and other forms of criminality, brutality and sadism. And it doesn't take a cynic or true-crime buff to acknowledge that the average human is no saint. All the sexual and hierarchical murders are strains of behaviour that go back 6 million years to our last common ancestor with chimpanzees. The more negative and violent aspects of our Palaeolithic existence and evolutionary ancestry sometimes contributed to our darkest sexual fantasies and fetishes.

CUMMING TO ABSTRACTIONS

An essential element of sexual fantasies and fetishes is abstract thought: the ability to contemplate things that are not there and circumstances that do not exist. Our last common ancestor with chimpanzees 6 million years ago could consider cause and effect in their immediate environments but was not capable of more abstract thinking. A chimp can reason about what might happen if they acted on something around them. For instance, they can consider that by inserting a stick into a termite mound or cracking open a nut with a rock, they will get food. Or by challenging the authority of a dominant male in the group, there is going to be a fight they will likely lose. However, chimps do not seem to have much capacity for thinking about things that are *not actually there*. Namely, abstract thinking, which allows humans to create architectural designs, draw blueprints for technologies, write books and craft great works of visual art. Or indeed, as we shall see, fantasise about a maleficent and sadistic lover torturing one's tits or kicking one's balls. It is the act of summoning something up in our imaginations that exists nowhere in our immediate environment.

Our capacity for abstract thinking appears to have emerged rather late in our evolutionary lineage. *Homo habilis* 2.3 million years ago made crude tools from stone flakes but does not seem to have engaged in the symbolism of cave painting bison or antelope that were not immediately present. Nor did they value ornately designed trinkets or coat themselves with ritualistic body paints. Moving down the line, between 1.78 and 1.5 million years ago, *Homo erectus* showed the first glimmer of tinkering and improvement of technology, but, again, no clear evidence of symbolic thinking such as cave art.

The same statement applies to our closest extinct evolutionary cousins *Homo neanderthalensis*, who evolved 430,000 years ago and co-existed with *Homo sapiens* from 315,000 to 40,000 years ago (in fact, DNA testing shows that *Homo sapiens* living outside of Africa interbred with Neanderthals before the latter went extinct). Even the Neanderthals left behind no cave paintings or ornate trinkets, and there is only the faintest residue in rare Neanderthal campsites in Europe that might imply they used body paints. *Homo sapiens*, meanwhile, left behind a deluge of cave paintings, jewels, beads, trinkets, body paints and even musical instruments in the archaeological record. If the Neanderthals engaged in body painting, this may imply that, at long last in our lineage, we were capable of abstract thought. If not, then *Homo sapiens* remains the only species with abstract thinking and thus sufficient imagination for sexual fantasy and fetishism to occur. Either way, these powerful aspects of human sexuality arrived very late in the game.

The role of abstract thinking is self-evident in fantasising privately about a partner you have not yet had sex with (or might never have sex with). And the same principle applies when masturbating to pornography. We are considering things, people and scenarios that are not really there. So powerful is this abstract thinking that our bodies can achieve orgasm with only manual stimulation to physically propel us. The same act of abstract thinking feeds into the tape we play in our heads during actual sex (perhaps more often than we might care to admit to our partners) to help achieve climax. And abstract thinking also applies to most sexual fetishes, where the human capacity for abstract thought often combines forces with the somewhat troubled legacy of our evolutionary past.

THE PRIMAEVAL ORIGINS OF KINK

Number one, with a bullet, among sexual fantasies is D/s (dominance–submission) and S&M (sadomasochism). These scenarios may or may not involve a form of physical bondage (ropes, chains, etc); hence, the umbrella term BDSM. A 2017 Belgian study revealed a staggering 68 per cent of adults have fantasised about BDSM scenarios, approximately 45 per cent of adults claim to have engaged in BDSM sex practices at least once in their lives, 26 per cent engage in BDSM on a semi-regular basis and 12.5 per cent do so weekly. While some of these people may engage in the more extreme end of BDSM (rigging, clamps, spikes, electrocution, vaginal stapling, tit-torture, cock-and-ball torture, etc), most engage in acts of dominance and submission such as face-slapping, choking, face-smothering or cock-gagging, light spanking or a smidge of sexual humiliation.

The number of people who engage in BDSM on a weekly basis is roughly the same percentage of the human population with brown hair, and those who engage on a semi-regular basis are the same percentage of the population who have Type-A blood. Those who at the very least could potentially be aroused by giving or receiving abuse in a sexual context is roughly the same as the percentage of the global population who live in cities, or roughly the same percentage of people with brown eyes. Remember that next time you are out people-watching or at the grocery store. The fact that such a huge number of people get off to the idea of physical or psychological malice in a sexual context is hardly surprising, given that many copulations in the past 40 million years may have been in circumstances that, shall we say, were 'less than ideal'.

The arousal a dominant and submissive derive from BDSM is built primarily upon the *negation* of the evolutionary sexual self-interest of the submissive. It is often expressed in the language of heightening or absence of power, but it is a bit more nuanced than that. It is the subversion of the 1.9-million-year-old sexual strategies that would result in a mutually beneficial pair-bond that would maximise the survival chances of any offspring. To put it another way, it is the frustration or utter destruction of the most cost-effective route a human has to replicating their DNA and ensuring that 'replica' has the support it needs to stay alive. These sexual responses manifest themselves regardless of whether a BDSM couple intend to have (or are capable of having) offspring – much like the impulse towards love or the impulse to have sex in the first place. These are more deeply rooted instincts that pay no mind to an individual's fertility, sexual orientation or reproductive intentions.

For instance, a common female submissive roleplaying scenario involves her surrendering 'mate choice' either partially or in totality. In conventional circumstances, she might be choosey about whom she selects as a mate, and how that mate treats her will have a huge influence on the value of the pair-bond. Instead, she is treated as a disposable sex object to be violated aggressively by one or more men, possibly while she is incapable of struggling, possibly while she is stripped of her dignity, and possibly with corporal punishment to compel her acquiescence. Many of the sex acts performed may not give her direct sexual pleasure, let alone ensure a stable pair-bond or pregnancy. A male dominant in such circumstances will offer very little 'utility' as a provider and protector for her in a pair-bond; in fact he may roleplay as a violent, sadistic sociopath (or the exact opposite of good fatherly material). At best, the male dominant may 'collar' the female submissive as a quasi-monogamous sex slave to be repeatedly exploited, rather than merely use her once, in a way reminiscent of the cartoonish cliché of cavemen hitting women over the head and dragging them into their caves. But being kept hostage as a regularly beaten and roughly violated sex slave is hardly an evolutionarily ideal pair-bond either.

Conversely, a male submissive scenario frequently involves the excessive exploitation of his 'utility' as a provider by the female dominant, often with very little expectation of penetrative sex in return (at least penetration of his female partner – he may find himself being penetrated). The female dominant will not reward male service with reproductive sex as she might in a conventional monogamous relationship. In fact, if the male submissive is allowed to cum at all, it is more likely to end up on his own face or mouth or on the floor, rather than anywhere near a woman's vagina. Combined with this is usually a denigration of the man's masculinity, penis size, strength, intelligence, lack of confidence, personality and so on – all the things that might conventionally make him an attractive pair-bond. The female dominant may pose either as a disenchanted pair-bond (girlfriend or wife) or as a woman who has outright sexually rejected him and always will.

In a nutshell, the female submissive scenario often sees a ratcheting up of sex and a decrease in the male utility offered in return, whereas the male submissive scenario often sees the severe rationing of sex and increased utility. In evolutionary terms this is the perversion of a good reproductive strategy for men and women. Monogamous pair-bonding compromises between male and female strategies, whereas BDSM roleplay sways the benefits firmly in the direction of the dominant.

Male submission is reasonably widespread, with one survey indicating that approximately 35 per cent of men who engage in BDSM consistently prefer to act as subs, with an additional 10 per cent of men dabbling in submission from time to time. Female submission is much more prevalent, with approximately 90 per cent of women who partake in BDSM preferring to act as subs, but with roughly half that number being willing, at least in principle, to behave as 'switches' and assume the dominant role. Only 10 per cent of women consistently act as dommes, and most do so for the sexual gratification of their male or female partners rather than due to any particular taste for sexual sadism.

With same-sex BDSM scenarios, there is a fair amount of overlap since these impulses are inculcated in human beings regardless of whether offspring are a prospect. Lesbian D/s scenarios resemble hetero female submissive scenarios, with a slightly greater emphasis on social hierarchy (the submissive will often be regarded as socially inferior to the dominant). Beyond that there is a great deal of sexual exploitation, forced oral, denigration and lack of reciprocal 'utility' as a pair-bond as per the above. Gay male BDSM also resembles female submissive scenarios, with the male sub being subjected to a lot of rough sex and degradation, often with the undercurrent that he is being held in bondage by a sociopath. The overlap between gay male and straight male BDSM appears to be the gay sub's own orgasms being heavily restricted. Then there is 'forced bi', where a hetero submissive is compelled to sexually pleasure a person of the same sex, who is often posing as the lover of the opposite-sex dominant.

Yet these sexual responses, male or female, straight or gay, do not just arise as the inverse of a strategy that would maximise the likelihood (in monogamous *Homo sapiens*) of a pair-bond in the metaphorical savanna where our sexual instincts still largely reside. They reach even deeper into our evolutionary past on timescales of 40 million years to tap into 'alternative' reproductive strategies, where an ideal situation was frequently not available. Essentially, it is sexual arousal to 'make the best of a bad situation' in the hopes that sustained sexual receptivity in a malicious environment will nevertheless lead to offspring, who will then survive despite the negative circumstances of their birth.

For instance, the male submissive will get sexually aroused from being demeaned, forced to provide an excess of service and denied orgasm, in the hopes that his arousal will increase the odds of sexual success *eventually* if he persists in a rather unlikely situation. Put crudely, arousal will keep alive the forlorn hopes of his subby boner. We see this phenomenon as far back as Old World monkeys, where a beta male baboon will orbit a female who has sexually rejected him, by grooming her fur, warding off threats and even watching her mate with alpha males, on the off-chance she eventually relents and allows him to mate with her.

More recently in evolutionary history, in *Australopithecus*, *Homo erectus* and even in Palaeolithic *Homo sapiens* prior to the invention of agriculture, we know that female mate choice (when left to itself and based purely in physicality) tended to exclude most men, and that a minority of men from 4 million to 12,000 years ago did the lion's share of impregnations. If a bipedal male primate on the savanna was sexually rejected, one antidote was be for him to provide an excess of 'utility' until he demonstrated he was a good choice for sex – despite any shortcomings he may possess physically or by his lack of status within a primate hierarchy. Sexual arousal at the cruel and dismissive treatment of the female appears to be a way of keeping alive the male's efforts in this context. He is less likely to give up and find someone else if the whole exercise of wretched servitude to a desirable mate arouses him intensely. Meanwhile, in modern roleplaying scenarios, most female dominants do not report feeling sexual arousal from inflicting cruelty, hence why the nature of BDSM paradoxically revolves around the gratification of a willing sub by a generous domme.

Conversely, a female submissive's arousal in consensual roleplaying scenarios echoes a phenomenon that has been all too common in the past 40 million years. While most female primates have a clearly defined mate preference, in many species female mate choice was brutally overruled by coercion. This is particularly true in orangutans and chimpanzees and was likely true for *Australopithecus*, *Homo habilis* and all other intervening species that preceded the evolution of monogamy 1.9 million years ago. For vast stretches of evolutionary history spanning millions of years, it is probable that many (if not the majority) of copulations were coerced to some degree. And it did not disappear when *Homo erectus* started pair-bonding, nor was it absent from *Homo sapiens* in the foraging, agrarian or modern epochs.

Hence, female submissive fantasies often involve some form of abduction or compelled sexual servitude, binding of limbs, corporal punishment and extremely rough sex. And while all women would find it deeply traumatising to be sexually assaulted in real life, in the context of BDSM roleplaying, rape fantasies are among the most common female fetishes. Surveys estimate that between 40 and 85 per cent of women have had one at least once, with the most widely touted figure currently being around 60 per cent, with the median frequency being four times per year, and 15 per cent of those surveyed having one on at least a weekly basis. As with male-sub impulses, female submission is a deeply visceral response to millions of years of sex in ancestral primate species which, in many circumstances, to modern human eyes, would appear morally repugnant. As with female dominants in BDSM roleplaying situations, male dominants frequently are *not* sexual sadists and report no gratification from the act of inflicting cruelty on their consenting partners in and of itself. Indeed, if male dominants did in real life half of what they are sometimes expected to do by their consenting partners in BDSM roleplaying scenarios, many people in modern society today would gladly see them buried underneath the prison where they were castrated.

Consent and abstract thinking are key here. For the past several million years, our ancestral species did not have the abstract thinking to enable roleplaying of this sort. Any adverse sexual circumstances a male or female primate found themselves in would be all too real, and their emotional responses to those situations all too distressingly real as well. With the evolution of *Homo sapiens* (or, at the earliest, our last common ancestor with the Neanderthals) we had developed the complex abstract thinking that enabled the fabrication of D/s scenarios which in modernity are ultimately compartmentalised from real life and (hopefully) have a safe word. In short, so staggering is humanity's capacity for ideas that we invented a way of transforming millions of years of pain into pleasure. And apparently it is a form of pleasure which a sizeable chunk – between one-third and two-thirds – of humanity occasionally indulges in. Evolution works in strange and mysterious ways.

THE PEDESTAL EFFECT

The panoply of other sexual games humans play with each other also have at least a partial foundation in the deep-time history of sex. For instance, foot fetishes are common, particularly among men but with a small minority of women having the fetish as well. At the core of the foot fetish is a mixture of ideal mate selection and sexual rejection. For example, a man finds a woman who is an extremely desirable mate. So attractive are her various attributes that he feels his own sexual market value makes him worthy only of her feet (an innocuous, practical, arguably unsightly and often smelly part of the human body that plays no direct role in sexual reproduction). By idolising this peculiar aspect of his preferred mate's anatomy, the sexual allure of the rest of her is intensified and placed on a metaphorical pedestal, further heightening the man's sexual arousal. This is why foot fetishes are often used in a BDSM context. Although less common, women can also develop foot fetishes for their male dominants, often in the context of orgasm denial and dry-humping. And the foot fetish can also make an appearance in gay and lesbian relationships, with the same mixture of sexual idealisation and worship between one partner and another. In both hetero and homosexual body-part fetishes, sometimes another anatomical choice takes the place of feet – armpits, kneecaps, pubic hair, nostrils, ears and so forth.

The fetishisation of bodily fluids is similar to foot fetishes in evolutionary terms: placing a partner on a pedestal of high sexual value. Top of the list is male ejaculate, which is frequently sprayed on the chest, face, buttocks, feet, etc, even outside a BDSM context. This can either be an expression of disdain for the tagged partner (implying low sexual value) or can be perceived as a manifestation of intense attraction for them (implying high sexual value). In the case of bukkake parties, the mark of sexual disdain or intense attraction is ratcheted up to an extreme scale, involving jizz from multiple men. Although less common (for anatomical reasons) female ejaculate is fetishised in much the same way. Spit, on the other hand, is almost universally deployed as a gesture of disdain, frequently in the context of rough sex, and most frequently with female submissives. In the realm of the scatological, urine and faeces are also a gesture of disdain; as with feet, that person feels their partner is so far above them that their piss or shit is all they are sexually 'worthy' of. Most commonly submissives will be pissed or defecated upon, and less commonly submissives will ingest a portion of urine or faeces. Scat fetishes are uncommon; due to issues of hygiene and odour, piss is roughly six times more likely to be used than shit.

Cuckolding and cuckqueaning is an arousal response to make the best of an otherwise unfavourable situation. Evolutionarily speaking, for a monogamous species like humans to have their pair-bonded mates have sex with another person is the worst of all genetic worlds. A male gets beaten out genetically, especially if he must expend utility raising another man's offspring, and a female loses out genetically if her pair-bond is splitting his time providing for another woman and her children. Even in the older promiscuous chimp context, where no pair-bonding exists, if the object of your desire is mating with someone else, that's a lost reproductive opportunity for you. Hence the aggression of males towards each other, and the aggression of females towards newcomers into a chimp group. Thus, the whole concept is deeply visceral and strikes at the heart of our sexual self-interests.

The typical response to cuckolding and cuckqueaning is emotional distress (perhaps even to a murderous degree) but arousal is a surprisingly common sexual response. In the case of a man being cuckolded, he may become aroused at the idea of a better man (aka 'a bull') attracting and having sex with his pair-bond. The implication is the woman is sexually rejecting the cuck in favour of another man of higher value, thus indirectly implying she too is of high sexual value. Like with the foot fetish, her powers of attraction are placed on a pedestal in the cuckold's eyes, making her even more attractive than if she and him were just having consensual vanilla sex. As such, the cuckold's arousal thrives off jealousy, often with his own opportunities for sex or orgasm being restricted while his mate enjoys herself frequently. In modern contexts, this jealousy is often accompanied by emasculation, humiliation, male chastity devices and the ingestion of the rival male's ejaculate during cunnilingus. Given the intense social stigma around the fetish, it is difficult to get a clear idea of its frequency, but with the best available stats, approximately 40 per cent of men have had a cuckold fantasy at least once. Even if this number is slightly inflated, the fetish is surprisingly common, largely due to how it torments the root of male reproductive success.

Conversely, the cuckquean fetish has sometimes been mislabelled and misunderstood as extremely rare. Nothing could be further from the truth. Available data indicates that the female cuckquean fetish is at *least* half as common as the male cuckold fetish, if not approaching parity. While the fundamental principle is the same, the particulars vary. A woman's male mate is placed on a pedestal in terms of his virility and sexual marketplace value in terms of his ability to attract multiple women, and instead of becoming distressed at this activity, or trying to block it, the cuckquean becomes aroused. It is possible there is also a polygynous impulse here, dating back some 10 million years or more, where a cuckquean knows that even if her mate has sex with other women, she will still have a significant chance at reproductive success as well. Thus, the quean's arousal is sustained or intensified to achieve this outcome. The cuckquean fetish frequently involves a woman cheerfully finding other women to have sex with her man (while she watches, differentiating it from a threesome). But in equal measure the fetish can involve a degree of humiliation where the 'cuckcake' (female newcomer) is evaluated as more attractive than the quean, may even be accorded higher social status in the relationship and may even arouse the quean with the vague threat of replacing her. For example, a thirty-something female professional spends her day off taking her twenty-year-old cuckcake to the mall, the quean buys the cake sexy lingerie to wear for her husband, and that evening the quean masturbates in the corner while watching her husband make love to a younger woman. Then the quean thanks the cuckcake and 'cleans' her while her husband and sexual rival laugh at her. In modern contexts, cuckqueaning involves a high degree of bisexuality, the ingesting of male ejaculate during cunnilingus, and a moderate degree of edging or orgasm denial on the part of the cuckquean.

Other modern fetishes with a partial evolutionary underpinning include:

- furries, where roleplaying as anthropomorphic animals frees a person psychologically of the social constraints typically placed on sexuality, allowing the furry to engage their desires with more wild abandon
- roleplaying as doctors, teachers, police officers, etc, usually involving some form of power dynamic or, in the case of sexy nurses and therapists, a mixture of power and nurturing
- daddy–daughter and mommy–son roleplaying, which also invokes a mixture of power and nurturing
- exhibitionism and public gang-bangs, which derive arousal from casting off social norms and indulging one's sexual appetites with more wild abandon
- small penis/breast humiliation and other sexual humiliation preying on a person's insecurities is used to raise the sexual market value of the person doing the mocking
- virgin humiliation and slut humiliation, usually for males and females respectively, lambasts the target as an evolutionary failure in terms of the sexual strategies of the past 1.9 million years.

Numerous other fetishes have an evolutionary basis which is then acted upon by culture.

FUCKING ON THE FARM

Throughout the Palaeolithic, humans lived in foraging bands that closely resembled how our evolutionary ancestors had lived for 4 million years since evolving bipedalism. *Homo sapiens* were now equipped with a more pronounced capacity for collective learning, technology, culture and abstract thinking. But despite variations in foraging sexual practices, the hunter-gatherer lifestyle was usually close to how humans were instinctually wired to live.

Then, starting 12,000 years ago, humans started domesticating and cultivating their own food. We became sedentary. This dramatic shift in lifestyle profoundly impacted our habits, standards of living and social organisations, setting off a population boom. More potential sexual partners were living in one place than ever before. Beyond that, with the rise of agrarian states starting 5500 years ago, humans began codifying sexual and marital practices into law, along with outlawing practices that were very much instinctual but henceforth became 'forbidden'. In the evolutionary blink of an eye of just 12,000 years, we ascended from stone tools to skyscrapers, from tribal marriages to Tinder. Yet anatomically and instinctually, we remained the same half-naked primate who occasionally got all hot and bothered by dirty thoughts, wanking with wild abandon on the windswept plains of East Africa. By placing that pervy little ape at the head of the most complex civilisations and the mightiest empires the world has ever known, our sex lives were about to get a whole lot more complicated.

9

FREUDIAN CIVILISATIONS

12,000 to 250 years ago

Wherein agriculture dramatically changes both the literal and the sexual landscape • Sex becomes tangled up with notions of property • Highly restrictive laws and standards are placed on female sexuality • Polygyny is initially accepted then gradually forbidden • Homosexuality is at first tolerated then repressed • Sex work and pornography become human universals in agrarian states.

The last Ice Age ended approximately 12,000 years ago, the glaciers receded from Europe and North America, and the changing climate transformed previously dry, chilly regions in the Middle East into lush green landscapes full of food. As food was so plentiful in the Fertile Crescent, foragers could now live semi-sedentary lives for multiple generations without having to travel vast distances for their next meal. But then, over the course of a few generations, food ran low while the forager population had multiplied. Neighbouring regions were also full of foragers, so migration was not a solution. Thus, foragers were forced to plant and grow their own food in the Fertile Crescent rather than just letting nature replenish itself. The alternative was starvation and death. The same pattern played itself out in similar 'Gardens of Eden' in East Asia 9,500 years ago, and in both Central America and West Africa approximately 5,000 years ago. Over the succeeding centuries and millennia, farming practices spread to their surrounding regions. Humanity had begun to farm.

Between 12,000 and 5,500 years ago, agriculture increased the number of people Earth could support from 8 million to 50 million. Within the farming regions of the world, people began to live in larger, denser, sedentary communities, with a wider diversity of potential sexual partners. At the same time, the nature of farming led people to lay claim to specific patches of land as property for the first time. And due to the shoddy nature of Neolithic farming, standards of living plummeted compared to those humans enjoyed in the foraging era. All of this affected our sex lives: how we approached monogamy and children, and which sexual practices were deemed acceptable by the wider community. Agriculture also set us on a path of rapid cultural change, and our slowly evolving sexual instincts could never catch up. Our hardwired animalistic Nature clashed with the capriciousness of Nurture with mounting tension, often resulting in oppressive traditions, draconian punishments and deep injustices.

EVENT	DATE
Agriculture in Fertile Crescent	12,000 years ago
Agriculture in East Asia	9,500 years ago
First agrarian states in Mesopotamia	5,500 years ago
Agriculture in West Africa and Mesoamerica	5,000 years ago
First agrarian states in East Asia	4,000 years ago
First agrarian states in Mesoamerica	2,500 years ago
First agrarian states in West Africa	2,000 years ago

COCKBLOCKED BY CROPS

From 12,000 to 5500 years ago, there were no states to speak of. The agrarian world was composed only of farms and villages of illiterate people who were mostly engaged in food production. A typical community consisted of a few hundred people spread out across several farms and families. Local trade hubs, where farmers exchanged produce and livestock, gradually transformed into villages of several hundred, and at their biggest no more than a couple thousand people. This is what passed for bustling metropolises in their day. Beyond these farms and villages lay the vast hinterlands where foragers still roamed, but they were quickly becoming a minority of the overall population.

As in the foraging era, the smallest social component was the family unit – parents, children and sometimes grandparents, aunts, uncles and cousins. And there was plenty to do. Given the poor-quality stone tools of the Neolithic, and the lack of heavy farming equipment, husbands and wives both tended to work the fields, scratching in the dirt with primitive tools, enduring an average of ten hours of backbreaking labour per day. There were also usually livestock to care for, and a household to maintain in semi-hygienic conditions, along with many hours spent preparing food, grinding grain, baking bread and boiling legumes, so the family could survive off an (often meagre) daily sustenance until they could gorge themselves during the seasonal harvests (assuming the crops didn't fail – which they often did). If the farm produced surplus food, it could be traded with neighbours; both husband and wife commonly played a role in keeping track of the business of barter and exchange.

The idea that farming immediately brought in the notion that women should be housewives, proverbially chained to the stove, is a myth. For most subsistence farmers, there was too much work to do and the threat of starvation was far too real for women to confine their duties to cooking and cleaning in their tiny hut or cottage. Aside from perhaps leaving the more strength-intensive tasks to men, and the need for women to recover from multiple pregnancies (if they didn't die in childbirth), wives worked alongside husbands in conducting the business of the farm. The concept of the 'housewife' who didn't engage in outside manual labour was for a long time viewed by subsistence farmers (and later the peasant class) as an unobtainable luxury, available only to the wealthiest landowners, surplus-farmers and village traders. It is much closer to modernity, in the past 200 to 300 years (depending on the region in the world), that such arrangements became possible for most of the working class.

In the early agrarian era, it was immensely useful to have many children to help on the farm, to look after their parents in their old age and to counterbalance a high infant mortality rate. Farmers were no longer nomadic, so they did not need to limit the number of infants they carried at any given time by resorting to infanticide. Suddenly women were having half a dozen children or more in their lifetimes, provided they did not die in childbirth and that the region was not experiencing overpopulation or mass famine (which occurred on average once every 100 to 300 years). As a result, the population exploded wherever agriculture took root.

In addition to having large families, people might employ landless labourers to work on their farms in exchange for shelter and basic sustenance. These people in turn married and had children when it was permitted and reasonably feasible to do so. Sometimes a sexually attractive labourer might marry into a landholding family and keep the gene pool fresh. Beyond that, marriages were patrilocal as a rule, with daughters heading off to other farms and joining their new families.

The ages at which agrarian men and women got married became highly dependent on their material circumstances. In periods of overpopulation, poverty and famine, men and women tended to push back marriage and children into their mid-twenties. Particularly if they did not own any farmland. This was in stark contrast to the teenage marriages of the foraging era. When agrarian peoples married extremely young, it was usually between landholding families, in highly formal marriages designed to combine the property of two families (a land deal rather than a marriage based on love or lust). If such an arrangement was urgent, betrothals would sometimes happen before the kids even hit puberty. But for the vast bulk of the agrarian population just eking out a living, the age of marriage and pregnancy was more variable, depending on material circumstances, and allowing room for emotional sentiment and sexual attraction. Landless labourers were more able to discreetly conduct promiscuous relationships than landed farming families, because no property was riding on the fruit of their loins – provided, of course, such liaisons did not wind up in an obviously illegitimate pregnancy.

With farmland essential to a family's survival, a system of property inheritance developed. While hunter-gatherers might lay claim to a vast and vaguely defined foraging territory as a group, the idea of a single individual or family owning a specific small patch of land was something new. In most agrarian cultures, land passed down the male line, though women might inherit if there were no male heirs. Agrarian cultures with gender-equal inheritance rights were extremely rare. In some cultures, female landowners would surrender their property rights to their husband upon marriage. And regardless of who inherited, if the family farmland was not expanded, or if children did not migrate away to join other families or start their own farms, then inheritance gradually cut the land up into smaller and smaller parcels. If it got to the point where a single family could not subsist off the food it produced, very often the land would be abandoned or traded, and it might be snapped up by larger landholders, with property coalescing into the hands of the very few.

As a result of land inheritance, paternity came to be immensely important for most agrarian cultures. Marriages between landholders increasingly became business arrangements, with emotional sentiment secondary (when it was considered at all). The children of such a marriage would be crucial not only to the family's continued survival in the region but also to the wellbeing of their parents once they grew too old to work. Thus, female sexual activity was increasingly restricted and policed. In most agrarian cultures, female sex outside a marriage contract was prohibited, with immense shame heaped on infidelity. A promiscuous woman might be ostracised from her family and society – and in some cultures outright killed. As we shall see, once state-societies arose, this policing of female sexuality frequently became encoded into law and enforced by organised religion.

SEX IN AN AGRARIAN SHITHOLE

Compared to the foraging era, living conditions during early agriculture were shockingly poor. Sure, foragers could easily die of minor illnesses, injuries or childbirth, but provided they were generally healthy, they had plenty of exercise, ate a diverse diet of meat and vegetation and usually had access to fresh water. They also tended to work fewer hours in a day. Early farmers, conversely, had the same dangers of mortality that foragers faced, but spent way more time on repetitive, back-breaking tasks and often relied on an unchanging diet of the same grain staples and less meat. Neolithic skeletons frequently show bone injuries from repetitive stress from working the fields, signs of severe malnutrition, a decline in average height, and in some cases premature rotting of the teeth, particularly in periods of overpopulation and/or famine. Pre-modern childbirth came with numerous risks, all of which were multiplied when a prospective mother was unhealthy and malnourished. Malnutrition made infant mortality dramatically higher than in the modern era.

Worse still, early farmers lived in close quarters with domesticated animals. Livestock tended to shit and piss in the local water supply, resulting in farmers bathing less regularly than foragers, and making the water unsafe to drink. Early farmers invented fermentation and weak booze to stay hydrated, which in turn facilitated an increase in the number of 'ill-advised' extra-marital copulations. The contamination of the water supply was worsened by the fact that more people were living in a concentrated area, shitting and pissing in nearby rivers. Typhus and cholera ran rampant. Living with farm animals also increased the risk of viruses and diseases jumping from them to humans. Bestiality (already instinctually repulsive to most people) became strictly prohibited for the very good reason that having sex with barnyard animals was 'unclean' or, in modern terms, a good way to increase the odds of new diseases jumping from livestock to humans: respiratory, rash, pox or immuno-deficiency. On top of all this, the waste produced by these crowded communities attracted rats, fleas, cockroaches and other pests which also spread various infections and plagues.

Nomadic foragers lived with the same few dozen people their entire lives and were constantly on the move, with only occasional contact with outside groups. This made transmission of disease much less likely. When disease *did* hit a foraging group, it would likely kill them all and spread no further. Sedentary farmers, on the other hand, lived in larger, denser populations where diseases had the time to evolve and spread across an interconnected countryside. This included STDs. Chlamydia and gonorrhoea can make your genitals burn when you pee, render you infertile, cause gross genital discharges, result in blindness if transferred to your eyes, make your penis, vagina or rectum swollen and painful, and be passed onto newborns. Herpes causes uncomfortable, unsightly sores all over the body, and can cause brain damage. Various immuno-deficiency viruses can reduce your ability to fight off illnesses to the extent that even mild viruses can kill you. Most STDs evolved in Afro-Eurasia, where agriculture first began and where most people lived, acting as a Petri dish for all kinds of illnesses. The exception appears to be syphilis, a disease that causes sores, rashes, bulbous tumours and insanity; (albeit hotly debated) evidence increasingly suggests it originated in the Americas and was transported to Europe by sexually reckless conquistadors.

RULE ME, DADDY

As farming populations, surplus crops and trading hubs grew, a tiny fragment of the Neolithic population was able to take on positions of authority that did not require them to farm. Village elders could arbitrate disputes between farmers and organise large infrastructure projects that could not be carried out by a single individual or family. These elders were appointed by the community on merit and competence (bottom-up power) or by violent coercion and/or claiming to be religious authorities (top-down power). Regardless of how they came about, it is almost a human universal that over several generations (if not immediately) these positions became hereditary, either legally or de facto among privileged families in the few republics that existed prior to the modern era. The hereditary principle was asserted either by religious mandate or by the erroneous belief that virtue and merit were passed on by blood. This is not such a far cry from our primate past, where the offspring of high-ranking individuals enjoy the protection of group alliances even when they are children. The hereditary principle created a class of aristocrats (treated almost as a separate species from the commoners) that ruled over millions in many regions of the world, for multiple millennia by virtue of nothing but birth. Even in modernity, this nepotistic and irrational impulse still holds sway, with special privileges and respect often accorded to the children of celebrities and political figures.

As agrarian surplus grew, the number of people who could pursue professions not involving farming increased: kings, lords, merchants, soldiers, artisans, entertainers, priests, literate scribes, and so on. However, until the modern era between 80 to 90 per cent of people spent their lives farming. Amid these sleepy hamlets inhabited by folksy (often struggling) agrarian throngs arose cities and the state. The first ones emerged in Mesopotamia approximately 5,500 years ago (3500 BC). Eridu had a population of 10,000 and Uruk one of 80,000, supported by agrarian surplus flooding into the city from the countryside.

Almost immediately with the arrival of paid soldiers 5,500 years ago emerged widespread slavery: mostly coerced labour on farms, with a good-sized helping of enslaved domestic servants and female sex slaves filling brothels and harems. In some cultures slaves were permitted to have families of their own, in others it was strictly forbidden to the extent that enslaved men were castrated (usually with a high mortality rate). Slave owners, meanwhile, lost no time in raping and impregnating the people they treated as human chattels. Beyond this were the commoners, serfs and peasants, frequently bound by law to show deference to the aristocratic class. Sexual fraternisation between common and noble blood was generally frowned on, especially if it resulted in the pregnancy of a female noble. This is vaguely reminiscent of chimp dominance hierarchies keeping low-ranking males from having reproductive success, but in early agrarian cultures it was reinforced by the fact that a noble woman's reproductive potential translated into vast amounts of wealth or tracts of agricultural land. Conversely, male nobles in most historical cultures seemed tacitly or explicitly permitted to bed and impregnate as many common women as they pleased. The polygynous impulse of our primate ancestors was still going strong.

Due to the increased social complexity of city-states, with their division of labour and influx of trade goods, people invented writing to keep track of it all. The clay tablets of Uruk, dating back roughly 5,500 years ago, are little more than accounts of agricultural produce and livestock. However, writing evolved to include history, philosophy, diplomatic correspondence, religious texts and laws. The stele of Hammurabi, dating back 3,750 years ago (1750 BC) is a pillar with the legal code of Babylon etched on it: it is oddly, perhaps appropriately, phallic.

Perhaps most importantly for our purposes, written records offer us a glimpse into how various pre-modern cultures governed their sex lives.

Hammurabi's Freudian slip

POLYGYNY FOR ME AND NOT FOR THEE

Some of the oldest civilisations to emerge from pre-state agrarian societies in Afro-Eurasia and the Americas – Mesopotamia, Egypt, China, the Indus and the Olmecs – had one thing in common: the peasant population was broadly monogamous while wealthy men with high social status practised polygyny, either with multiple wives or with one wife and multiple concubines. This reflects the tendencies of most foraging cultures, and the earliest states may have directly inherited such traditions from their hunter-gatherer forebears. This appears to be the 'default setting' of most civilisations: most people are instinctually monogamous but the polygyny of powerful men is not socially discouraged or legally forbidden. Only 15 per cent of human cultures throughout history have outright shunned polygyny for religious or philosophical reasons.

For the past 1.9 million years, the monogamous impulse had grown strong, but with polygynous evolutionary baggage stretching back millions of years favouring males further up the hierarchy. In *Homo sapiens* it appears that monogamous instincts can be overridden either by men having wealth/power (resulting in a minority of men with multiple wives) or by the mandate of a cult or religion (resulting in most men having multiple wives). Regarding the latter, it is probably not a coincidence that some of the most successful religious charlatans in history convinced their followers that for some reason God thought it was *very important* that the charlatan and his pals be allowed to have regular sex with multiple women – while at the same time mandating that female promiscuity and infidelity be harshly punished.

The priest-kings of the city states of Ancient Mesopotamia likely practised polygyny. So too did many of the pharaohs of Ancient Egypt to show off their status and ensure their chances of producing an heir. The Old Testament is replete with examples of patriarchs, prophets and holy figures having multiple wives. Moses himself had three. It is also well established that the early Hebrew tribes were polygynous, a tradition that continued into Ancient Israel, and one which the invading Romans endeavoured to suppress. Even in the New Testament, Jesus is taciturn and cryptic on the issue of multiple wives, opening the door of interpretation for several polygynous Christian sects, though in *Corinthians* Paul the Apostle explicitly advocates monogamy. Numerous cultures in Ancient India permitted polygyny, with Hindu holy texts depicting it as standard practice among the wealthy and powerful. The elite in the medieval kingdoms of West Africa also practised polygyny, partially due to Muslim influence, partially due to the emphasis on taking female slaves in war rather than merely taking land. Meanwhile, Buddhism makes no judgement on monogamy versus polygyny, since marriage is 'of this world' and beyond the concern of monks transcending it for Nirvana. Thus, Thailand, Burma, Sri Lanka and Tibet have historically polygynous practices that stretch back two millennia, alongside other marital arrangements.

In Ancient China, most peasants were monogamous, but if men could support more than one woman they could take on a concubine. Very often this woman was from the lower classes and was subordinate to his wife. Sometimes Chinese law limited the number of concubines one could have according to class – minor nobles could only have a handful, whereas emperors were permitted hundreds. In some cases, if a Chinese clan lacked many male heirs, the men in the family might be allowed to take additional wives.

The Ancient Greeks sometimes permitted a degree of polygyny among its elite, but this was shut down after Roman conquest. For their part, the Romans enforced monogamy, but they had a few loopholes. Prostitution was legal, a Roman was free to rape his slaves because they were deprived status as a person, and he was only punished for straying outside his marriage if he had sex with someone else's wife. The same sexual freedoms were not accorded to Roman women.

In Islam, following the example of the Prophet, a man was allowed to take multiple wives, provided he could demonstrate that he could support them and give them equal material comfort and respect. Muhammad himself made some interesting choices in this regard, marrying both a six-year-old girl and his son's former wife. Polygyny was slowly curtailed in most of the world in the nineteenth, twentieth and twenty-first centuries, but it remains a practice in the Islamic world. The exceptions to this are Turkey, where secular law prohibits it, Southern European countries with large Muslim populations such as Albania and Kosovo (both with a legacy of forced secularisation under Communism), and the former Soviet republics of Central Asia.

Arising out of the Roman tradition, European Christianity enforced monogamy for the most part, but it was common for the elite to take lovers and even sire illegitimate children by them. Among medieval and early modern Christian kings, it was unusual for them *not* to have lovers. In Christianity, there are numerous exceptions to the monogamy rule. For instance, in 1534, in the chaos of the early Reformation, a cult of religious radicals took over the town of Munster in Germany. They imposed a sort of proto-Communism on the town and held all property in common. John of Leiden, a 25-year-old religious leader, declared himself to be the heir to King David of Israel, and mandated that men in Munster marry multiple wives. John himself took sixteen and anecdotally beheaded one 'heretical' woman for refusing to marry him. In June 1535, the army of the Catholic Prince-Bishop successfully retook Munster, and a few months later tortured and executed John of Leiden and his compatriots in the town square.

Similarly, when Joseph Smith claimed to have dug up and translated a new book of the Bible in upstate New York in the 1820s, he became a religious leader and revealed that God wanted some of his followers to take multiple wives. This remained the case until Utah was vying for US statehood in the late nineteenth century, with polygyny being a major bar to entry, when the elders of the Church of Latter-Day Saints conveniently received a message from God that polygyny was no longer on the menu. Today, a small breakaway sect of fundamentalist Mormons denounce this decision and practise polygyny in defiance of US law.

It is perhaps easy to understand in the context of our recent evolutionary history why polygyny might exist in ancient, medieval and modern history. However, the power of culture (quite separate from evolution) also introduced polyandry (one woman, multiple husbands) into a minority of cultures. You'd have to go back over 40 million years in our evolutionary tree to link humans to our nearest primate cousins that practise it. Nevertheless, for religious reasons polyandry existed in Tibet and Sri Lanka (alongside polygyny) and the Himalayan regions of India, and it reputedly existed in pre-Islamic Arabia. Most of the time this manifested itself as a system of wife-sharing among male relatives rather than a woman with a harem of unrelated men. We see the same practice of wife-sharing among kin in several modern-day foraging cultures in South America and the Pacific. While polyandry is evolutionarily distant from us, the practice of kin with closely related DNA potentially impregnating the same woman compensates for this. In general, historical polyandry is not the same sort of modern polyandry one might discover digging through Tumblr or Reddit.

A Japanese samurai with his wife and concubines

THE JOYS OF PRE-MODERN MARRIAGE

The oldest written record for marriage is from the Akkadian Empire in Mesopotamia approximately 4,300 years ago (2300 BC). Among agrarian societies, marriage is a human universal, though the justifications, rituals and obligations differ vastly. It was common in the agrarian era for marriage to be a business or property deal between families. In some cultures, a bride price was paid by a man in the form of money, livestock or promises of manual labour to purchase a wife from her family. In others, the bride's family paid a dowry to compensate the man for taking her off their hands.

In some societies, such as ancient Hebrew tribes, a wife was arguably viewed as property; she was listed in the Ten Commandments in the same breath as slaves and livestock, though this 'property' came with numerous familial obligations. In other traditions, such as Ancient Rome, a wife conventionally lost all rights of inheritance from her old family once she married into a new one. From the twelfth century onwards, Christian women took the last name of their husbands to signify this patrilocal transition. In some Ancient Indian cultures, female property rights were so diminished that somewhere between 500 and 300 BC the practice of *sati* became prevalent, where widows self-immolated on their husband's funeral pyres or were buried alive with them, so as not to sap expenses when the man's heirs inherited his estate. In Islam, widows were permitted to remarry, though only after waiting a period of chastity, or *iddah*, of approximately three months so her new husband could be assured that any newborn child was his and not the dead man's.

In Ancient Greece, a wife was traded between families with her primary role being to bear legitimate children capable of inheriting property. Greek wives could not expect sexual fidelity from their husbands, who were mostly free to sire illegitimate children from prostitutes and slaves. The same was the case in medieval Japan, where wives were expected to be subservient and faithful to their husbands while the men were free to seek sexual thrills outside their relationship. In Shia Islam, the *nikah mut'ah* is a marriage loophole, where a man marries a woman just to have sex with her, then immediately divorces her by verbally denouncing the match. In general, the severe restrictions and double standards surrounding female sexuality extended from the pre-modern obsession with paternity and making sure the legitimate children of the husband inherited any land or property.

In that regard, in most agrarian societies female infidelity was treated as a major offence. Stringent punishments were often applied to men who dared to sleep with married women. The Code of Hammurabi (c 1750 BC), etched on giant phalluses across Ancient Babylon, prescribed drowning for female adulterers and the men who slept with them. In Islamic jurisprudence, the penalty for unmarried fornication is a mere flogging, while the punishment for adultery is being stoned to death. Men would be buried up to their waists for the stoning, while women would be buried up to their necks to increase the chances of a quick death. In Ancient Greece, the Roman Republic and Imperial China, honour killings of adulterous women were socially permitted, along with killing the man who slept with them. In medieval Europe, adulterous women were flogged and publicly humiliated, often having their heads shaved and frequently being confined to a monastery unless their husbands chose to take them back. In Ancient India, the *Kama Sutra* enjoins married couples to not commit adultery since it is bad for them spiritually, while the societal punishments varied from public humiliation to imprisonment or death.

Within marriage, sex for pleasure was encouraged to varying degrees or not at all. In Ancient Rome, the ability of a man to indulge in pleasurable sex with his wife was viewed as a cornerstone of his virility, thus affecting his social status. In Japan, sex for pleasure between man and wife had no social stigma, with written records of several quite inventive married sexual exploits. In India, pleasurable sex in marriage was viewed as essential to the bonding of man and wife, with numerous tips written about how to achieve this happy state. Conversely, in Judaism, Christianity and Islam, sex was viewed as mostly for reproduction to such an extent that in both Judaism and Islam, circumcision became religious mandates. In the case of both male and female circumcision (in cultures where it occurred), sometimes one of the goals was to dull sexual sensation. The practice of circumcision was largely rejected in medieval Christianity, but in the nineteenth and twentieth centuries numerous authorities and campaigners advocated male circumcision as a way of maintaining genital hygiene, reducing risk of catching venereal disease and, dubiously, reducing the temptation to masturbate. These ideas took hold particularly in North America, where rates of circumcision were 80 per cent in 1958, dropping to a still substantial 53 per cent in 2020.

Regardless of whether sex for pleasure was socially permitted or not, from Ancient Rome to Imperial China and from Sub-Saharan Africa to medieval Europe marital rape was frequently permitted, since the marriage contract revolved around having children – and having children necessitated sex. This meant that prior to the twentieth century, once a woman was married, she could be forced to have sex with her husband whether she wanted to or not. Meanwhile, numerous religions and cultures sanctioned domestic violence against women, or at least prescribed situations for where it was 'appropriate'. For instance, in Islam, a husband must first try to reason with his wife, then reject her in bed, before ultimately he can use violence provided the beatings are not 'overly harsh'.

Because marriage was often a property contract, cousins were often permitted to marry to keep land within a family or clan. Property and inheritance concerns seem to have overridden instinctual revulsion to marrying within your kin group. Ancient Mesopotamia, Egypt, Babylon and the Islamic Caliphate all permitted cousin marriage. Some royal families in the ancient world even permitted sibling marriage. In medieval West Africa, cousin marriage was actively encouraged. In China, marriage between paternal cousins was discouraged but marriage between maternal cousins was permissible. Both Ancient Rome and medieval Europe discouraged cousin marriage, though it did occur among the nobility, but from the sixteenth century onwards cousin marriage became common. This persisted until it went into decline again in the twentieth century.

While most agrarian people married in their teens and twenties (that is, post-puberty) child marriage was exceedingly common in the pre-modern period when property concerns were involved. One of the youngest marriages on record is from sixteenth-century England, between a three-year-old boy and a two-year-old girl. Child marriage happened in every region of the world where there were agrarian states. Often it involved the actual kidnapping of a child – something elevated to a tradition in Central Asia, China, India, among medieval Slavic peoples, and to non-believers forced to marry medieval and early modern Muslims.

Should a person not be particularly enamoured with the idea of marriage, different agrarian cultures permitted various avenues for divorce. Generally, a marriage was a property contract and social obligation so you could not easily abandon it if you were unhappy. In Ancient Greece, you had to give a magistrate a reason why you were seeking a divorce (adultery, abuse, etc). In pre-modern Japan, men could divorce their wives by writing them an official letter, but wives could not legally divorce their husbands. Instead, they had to seek sanctuary in a Shinto temple for a period of three years before her husband was legally and socially compelled to write her a letter. In Islam, a man can divorce his wife by verbally renouncing the marriage, though this 'insta-divorce' method is considered taboo in some circumstances. A woman, however, frequently must undertake litigation in order to secure a divorce, and with the disadvantage of a woman's testimony being worth half that of a man's under Islamic law.

Before Christianity, the Roman Empire functionally had no-fault divorce, with either husband or wife being able to renounce their vows (though in several cases women were coerced to remain in their marriages). After Rome adopted Christianity, which theologically considered marriage a holy sacrament, divorces were strictly curtailed in both Catholicism and Orthodox Christianity. After that point one could still potentially secure a divorce (if you were wealthy, and even then it was more often men who took this route) or a formal separation. But then a woman would risk being ostracised by her entire community and cut off by her family, along with being pressured to reconcile with her husband.

As unsavoury as agrarian marriage may seem (and it certainly was for many of the 55 billion people who lived between 12,000 and 250 years ago) it must be remembered that romantic love is an evolved instinct that is over a million years old. And there is absolutely no reason to suspect that this biological phenomenon was placed on hiatus during the agrarian period. Almost every agrarian culture has literature that celebrates the ideal of romantic love. It is likely that a good proportion of married couples felt strongly about each other, while modern studies of arranged marriages show that many couples develop a gradual, if grudging, respect for each other. So, there is no question that quite a few of your ancestors genuinely loved each other – even if they existed in a cultural patchwork of harsh and repressive traditions. Of course, it is impossible to know the percentage of pre-modern marriages that had some semblance of love, but it certainly wasn't zero. Meanwhile, the extinction of marriage primarily as a property contract, the decline of the birth rate and corresponding notions that marriage is primarily about reproduction, and the introduction of no-fault divorce in the twentieth century eliminating any sense of obligation to a spouse once love has died, all underline just how recent and unique the modern conception of marriage is. Nowhere in the foraging or agrarian era do we find anything like it. So, it is hardly surprising that some people who are neither traditionalists nor particularly religious find what exactly marriage means in the modern era confusing.

Of course, not all agrarian cultures had restrictive traditions, though those without them were a tiny minority. The 30,000 members of the traditional Mosuo religious cult in agrarian China worship a fertility goddess. They are a prime example of how culture (in this case, religion) can turn evolutionary instinct on its head. For centuries, the Mosuo have tolerated casual sex between men and women. Women stay with their birth families rather than get married and migrate to a husband's household. The fathers of children are mostly known and help the mothers during harvests. Otherwise, the mother's brothers help raise her kids. The promiscuity proceeds as follows. Men go out at night and knock on the door of the woman they want to have sex with. They can return at night any time they please (as long as the woman continues to accept them), taking regular lovers. Mosuo men can have up to fifty lovers in their lifetime, though it's more common for the number to be between five and twelve. But women who solicit sex are shamed by the community. And if men and women have sex outside of the usual midnight trysts, conflict and even violence can erupt between the male lover and the woman's brothers. Also, when a man moves on to a new lover, the dumped woman tends to get upset and there are recorded cases of her getting violent towards her ex-lover and his new flame. Unfortunately, this lifestyle has resulted in widespread STDs. The communist Chinese government has endeavoured to stamp out these traditions; today 20 per cent of the Mosuo population engages in monogamous marriage instead.

FARMING BEYOND CIS-HET

Because the agrarian lifestyle increased the number and density of people living in a particular area, the percentage of the population that was bisexual, homosexual, intersex, trans or nonbinary became more visible than in the foraging era. Suddenly, we see an explosion of non-cis-hetero individuals and activities in the cultural and historical record. The oldest civilisations to emerge from pre-state agrarian societies (Mesopotamia, Egypt, China, the Indus and Mesoamerica) embraced homosexuality and bisexuality to some degree or another. Attitudes in early state societies to homosexuality were similar to those towards polygyny. In Ancient Mesopotamia, homosexuality appears frequently in art, and male anal sex appears to have been part of some religious rituals. The Code of Hammurabi even makes provisions for some women to marry other women. In Ancient Egypt, there is no evidence that homosexuality was forbidden or denigrated, and there is some sparse evidence suggesting the elite were free to engage openly in gay and lesbian sex. In Han China (202 BC to 220 AD), emperors reputedly sometimes took men as lovers. This practice began to be phased out in the 600s AD and was put to an end in the 1200s. Four centuries later, under the Qing dynasty, homosexuality became punishable by imprisonment or flogging, and in the nineteenth century punishments were escalated to imprisonment or death.

In medieval Japan, there were no explicit laws or religious injunctions in Shintoism against homosexuality, and it would appear such relationships were tolerated in wider society until the nineteenth-century Meiji Restoration. In Ancient India, in the fifth century BC, homosexuality was either accepted or tolerated, with the *Kama Sutra* describing in some detail men giving each other blowjobs and observing that some men even got married to each other. Then in the second century BC, homosexuality became punishable by a fine, religious penance or loss of caste. Punishments for homosexuality grew more severe after the Islamic conquest of India in the 1200s AD, elevated to imprisonment or death. In Mesoamerica, the Olmecs, Mayans, Aztecs and Incas all appear to have tolerated homosexuality and embraced it as a regular feature of society, before the Spanish conquistadors arrived and put male homosexuals to death by shooting, hanging, burning or being ripped apart by dogs.

Ancient Greek culture was a mixture of negative social attitudes towards adult gay relationships (for example, Plato described anal sex as 'unnatural') and the outright celebration of gay ephebophilia (attraction to mid-to-late adolescents) and, in some cases, paedophilia (attraction to pre-pubescent children and early adolescents). The straight–gay dichotomy did not exist. Rather, men were defined as penetrator or penetrated. Greek *mores* held that the penetrator should be more masculine and/or higher status and/or older than the lover being anally penetrated. Gay sex was only looked on negatively if the more masculine, higher-ranking or older person was on the receiving end. Gay sex between adults of the same age and rank was also frequently regarded with distaste. However, in the right contexts, equals could penetrate each other. The most famous example is the Sacred Band of Thebes, a group of soldiers who were encouraged to take each other as gay lovers in the hopes they would fight more fiercely for each other on the battlefield. But these situations were highly specific rather than the general rule.

Meanwhile, adult Greek men were free to have sex with male teenagers and even pre-pubescent male children. In some contexts, this was an adult Greek man raping his young male slaves, but this was often regarded as taboo. Conversely, the Greeks idealised and celebrated an older man taking on a young male lover in the context of him teaching the young lad philosophy while they had a sexual relationship. The practice was so widespread that it seems to have transcended the bounds of people who were innately same-sex attracted, with straight male boys submitting to become lovers of older men during their education. While ephebophilia was not controversial among the Greeks – after all, girls were married off as young as thirteen – the practice of grown men having sex with pre-pubescent children was sometimes viewed as controversial even in its own day. Nevertheless, the practice continued. Similarly, in medieval Japan, samurai were free to take young boys, mostly teenagers, as lovers provided the samurai only had one such lover at a time.

The Ancient Greeks appear to have extended a similar system of acceptance to lesbianism, though it appears less frequently in the historical record. Most of what we know of Greek lesbianism comes from a few observations in Plato and fragments of poetry written by Sappho (95 per cent of which was destroyed in the medieval period). The very term 'lesbian' is derived from the island of Lesbos, where Sappho was born. Lesbian relationships appear to have been part and parcel of Greek society, with sexual relations between two adult women being less controversial because it swerved the whole penetrator–penetrated dichotomy by neither participant being a high-status male with some fragile notion of masculinity to maintain. Plato himself remarks without much hostility that some adult women 'will have nothing to do with men' and prefer to take each other as lovers, implying the practice was at least tolerated. And of female pederasty, where a woman took a young girl as a lover as she acted as her tutor, also appears to have existed. Lesbianism may appear less in the historical and cultural record than male homosexuality because of the male-centric nature of pre-modern writings and art, and possibly because agrarian women so infrequently had control over whom they married or chose as their sexual partners, even if they were same-sex attracted.

In pre-Christian Rome, attitudes towards gay sex were like those of the Greeks, lacking the gay–straight dichotomy and continuing the idea that older/masculine/higher-status men should penetrate more submissive male partners. Romans made free use of male prostitutes and were not socially prohibited from raping their male slaves. However, Romans did move to prohibit paedophilia – provided the pre-pubescent child was not a slave. Attitudes towards lesbianism were more hostile; it was viewed as 'wild and lawless' since it defied traditional female gender roles. And given the Roman view of female adultery, they were particularly harsh towards lesbianism when such relationships were committed by married women.

Attitudes towards homosexuality grew even harsher in the fourth-century Roman Empire, with the adoption of Christianity and its many moral precepts founded in Judaism. For millennia, the Torah had prohibited homosexuality. The book Leviticus explicitly calls for gay men to be put to death. The story of the destruction of Sodom and Gomorrah, meanwhile, was frequently interpreted as God punishing the two cities for their homosexual practices, among other transgressions. In St Paul's letters to the Romans in the New Testament, there is an explicit denunciation of both male and female homosexuality. There are also several other passages attributed to St Paul and even Jesus where the prohibition of homosexuality is potentially implied.

As a result of Rome's adoption of Christianity, homosexuality became outlawed throughout late antiquity, the medieval period and most of the modern period until the mid-twentieth century. Prescribed punishments spanned everything from confinement to a monastery to imprisonment, torture and death. Not only gay men faced such harsh punishments; there are numerous cases where lesbians were either drowned or burned at the stake. The same policy was inherited by Islam, which regards itself as the direct inheritor of Judaism and Christianity. Traditional Islamic law prescribes beating, stoning, burning and being thrown headfirst from tall buildings for homosexuality, for active and passive participants. Frequently within Islam homosexuality was equated with adultery, and subject to similar punishments. This is roughly in accordance with the idea of sex primarily for reproduction present in the dogma of all three religions. As both Christianity and Islam spread across the world into sub-Saharan Africa, the Americas and new parts of Asia, so too did their innate hostility to homosexuality. As for the roughly 12 per cent of people in these societies who felt some form of same-sex attraction, their relationships, when they occurred, were likely carried on in utter secrecy, leaving no record to history.

Nevertheless, like infidelity, the elite were sometimes capable of having low-key homosexual relationships with impunity, and numerous Christian kings, Islamic sultans and even a ninth-century Abbasid Caliph were likely gay. Along with countless aristocrats and other wealthy individuals who were protected by their social status. Furthermore, in parts of the Islamic world, which retained the bulk of Ancient Greek knowledge after the fall of the Roman Empire, there was even a revival among the elite of the Greek practice of taking on young boys as student-lovers, though this was at odds with the *hadith* and *sharia*. Even if you were an elite, usually you took your own life in your hands if you engaged in any form of homosexual activity or relationship. For instance, Edward II of England was likely gay and gave his lover numerous prominent positions at court, the primary cause of a rebellion against his rule. Edward had to give up his crown in 1327 and he was murdered shortly after. By the 1330s, popular rumours circulated that Edward had been killed by having a red-hot poker shoved into his rectum, illustrating not only a widespread public awareness of his homosexuality, but also contemporary attitudes toward it.

The fate of trans and nonbinary people in the agrarian period followed a similar trajectory, though there is some ambiguity in the early historical records. Initially, agrarian states seemed either tolerant or accepting of them. In Mesopotamia, *gala* priests were men who dressed and identified as women and had a key role in religious rituals. These are the first possible trans individuals in recorded history – 4,500 years ago. However, they may not all have been trans, since many *gala* are recorded as having wives and kids; this could imply cisgender relationships (rather than lesbian relationships as transwomen) outside of their positions as priests. And it is not clear how trans and nonbinary people were regarded outside of religious ritual, in wider Mesopotamian society.

Meanwhile, the long-standing tradition of eunuchs in Ancient Egypt and China may indicate the acceptance of trans or nonbinary individuals, since sometimes these people are referred to as either female or third-gender. However, in other historical records some eunuchs clearly identify as male, and still others identified as male and were forcibly castrated. Nevertheless, in many cases where eunuchs are recorded as female or third-gender, they sometimes achieved high-ranking political and religious positions. Again, little is known about how such individuals were perceived in wider society, particularly those who were trans or nonbinary and *not* eunuchs.

Similarly, in India, the *hijra* are an ancient class of transwomen or third-gender people, many of whom are also eunuchs. However, we know that many other *hijra* were not eunuchs, but were a mixture of trans individuals who identified as women or who identified as men while dressing and behaving as women. And the *kathoey* of Thailand (formerly Siam) are trans individuals who have existed in the culture for hundreds of years, though under Buddhism they are denigrated as 'men paying for their sins in former lives'.

In the Graeco-Roman world, eunuchs could hold high positions in political or religious life. For instance, the priesthood of the *galli* is recorded as having castrated themselves, wearing women's clothing and identifying as female. However, trans and nonbinary individuals were less well received in wider society. The Greek philosopher Hippocrates seems to refer to transgenderism as a mental illness. The Romans were not fond of trans individuals outside of religious contexts, since they represented a subversion of traditional Roman masculinity. Effeminate men were more widely regarded by the Romans as a sign of decadence and degeneracy, and the possible decline of their civilisation in the final days of both the Republic and the Empire. Moreover, the Roman emperor Elagabalus was quite likely trans or else political enemies used this claim as propaganda; according to Roman accounts, Elagabalus identified as female, had an artificial vagina made and ruled for four chaotic years before being assassinated by the praetorian guard, acting on behalf of a disgruntled Roman elite. After Christianity was adopted in the Roman Empire, trans and nonbinary behaviours were viewed with even greater hostility, and these attitudes persisted in the medieval and early modern period.

Meanwhile, in pre-Islamic Arabia, there existed a concept of a third gender assigned to a very wide umbrella of people: including many LGBTIQ individuals but also people who simply did not conform to gender stereotypes. After the rise of Islam, the *mukhannathun* were mostly composed of effeminate males (both straight and gay) who adopted feminine fashions and behaviours. Some of these people might very well have been trans. Separate categories were assigned to eunuchs (many of them male slaves who were forcibly castrated) and intersex individuals. Homosexuality may have traditionally been punishable by death in Islam, but the *hadith* only seem to recommend banishment for behaviour that to modern eyes might be considered trans.

At the beginning of this section, I mentioned how the trajectory of non-cis-het followed a similar path as polygyny – initial acceptance by most early ancient states, gradually becoming forbidden the closer we draw to the modern era. In all societies that have ever existed, roughly 85 per cent of them tolerated polygyny, while only 55 per cent tolerated homosexuality, transgenderism and nonbinary behaviours, and in many cases that tolerance was very limited. While polygyny may have been frowned upon in various parts of the world for the past 2000 years, the legal punishments for non-cis-het behaviour were often considerably worse. And while polygynists might have been persecuted in some societies for how they wanted to live their lives, same-sex attracted and trans individuals were persecuted for who they biologically or psychologically *were*. One can only imagine the sort of living hell it might have been to be born homosexual into an intolerant agrarian society. And a large proportion of the estimated 1.3 billion homosexuals who lived in the agrarian era may have had to silently endure that hell.

A group of *hijra* in Bangladesh

THE WORLD'S OLDEST PROFESSION?

The practice of primates exchanging sex for food goes back 40 million years, possibly even 55 million. Numerous species of Old and New World monkeys, and the great apes, engage in such activities. In a promiscuous primate species such as chimpanzees, little is lost by a female chimp offering sex in exchange for food that would keep her alive for another day. It is not like the male chimp was going to provide her offspring with much in the way of fatherly care. Another dimension to this practice was added with the evolution of monogamy in *Homo erectus* 1.9 million years ago. Now our ancestors had pair-bonds, where males were at least nominally supposed to provide their female mates with food continually, along with caring for any offspring. But if a *Homo erectus* female exchanged sex for a single serving of food without pair-bonding with the male, that is a little closer to what we would term prostitution or sex work. Nevertheless, we are not quite there yet. Such exchanges were still ad hoc rather than a consistent activity or regular profession. In foraging societies of *Homo sapiens*, people were known to exchange sex for food, trinkets, clothing and personal favours. But since nomadic foragers had little in the way of individual wealth, and food-sharing among the tribe was common, so there was little motivation to regularly exchange sex for short-term rewards.

It is only in the agrarian period, when sedentary peoples could start accruing massive personal wealth, that 'the world's oldest profession' fully came into being. The increase of personal possessions, land, agricultural surplus and eventually currency increased the frequency of both women and men regularly having sex for payment. The earliest recorded cases are from Mesopotamia, implying that sex work is as old as civilisation itself. And again, it appears that such activities were initially accepted. In fact, sex work was wrapped up with Mesopotamian religion. Men and women would occupy temples and their surrounding grounds, exchanging sex for payment under the guise of ritual worship of the gods. The same pseudo-religious sex work arose in the other oldest agrarian states: China, India and Mesoamerica.

And while 'sacred prostitution' is the most frequently documented from these early states, there is little doubt that sex work also occurred without such religious auspices. Accounts from the Middle East, China, India, Mesoamerica and the Graeco-Roman world attest to the widespread existence of brothels and sex workers in the streets. There were also varying pay grades for such workers. In Ancient Greece, sex workers who catered to the wealthy elite could accrue wealth and even lands of their own. Further down the socio-economic scale, sex workers in Greece would sell their wares for as little as half a day's wages for a labourer. And, of course, wherever there was sex work in agrarian states, there was human trafficking. Especially given human slavery was almost universal in the ancient world. Many of the workers in brothels were slaves, forced to sell sex against their will, with their slaveowners collecting their profits. In fact, in Ancient Rome a frequent punishment for female criminals was to sell them into sex-slavery.

Throughout much of the agrarian era, sex work was regarded either as an innate feature of society or as a 'necessary evil'. An example of the latter was tolerance for soldiers using sex workers to keep up their morale. Frequently a blind eye was also turned to soldiers raping women in the lands they invaded, and in some cases such sexual violence was actively encouraged by their commanders. Another example of the 'necessary evil' school of thought is related to agrarian monogamy. In Ancient Greece and Rome, and even medieval Europe, sex work was tolerated so that husbands would not commit adultery with other married women (and also, in the case of medieval Europe, to not be tempted by homosexuality). However, in medieval Europe, church and secular authorities tried to segregate sex workers from the rest of society, forcing them into quasi-legalised brothels, to occupy certain areas of town, and to wear clothing that identified them as sex workers (white capes, striped hats, yellow scarves, etc). While Christianity regarded sex workers as 'sinful' and 'bound for hell', they were tolerated because they acted as a pressure-valve for male sexuality, so that these men did not turn their lecherous attentions to 'virtuous and chaste' women. It is only when we approach the modern era that we begin to see attempts to stamp out prostitution.

Unlike polygyny and homosexuality, attitudes never hardened much against sex work. Certainly, social and religious movements against it periodically arose, but they never really succeeded in stamping it out. In most cultures closer to modernity, sex work was officially illegal. But even in London during the late Victorian era, there were as many as 80,000 sex workers, or a staggering 1.6 per cent of the population. The existence of sex work is definitely one arena in which Nurture cannot seem to inhibit the forces of Nature.

A DUBIOUS HALLMARK OF CIVILISATION

Porn may well have existed in the foraging era, though no artifacts have emerged from the Palaeolithic or Mesolithic that display sex in a way that can be deemed purely erotic rather than produced for religious worship or rituals (such as fertility statues of big-breasted women).

But by the time we get to the agrarian era, we begin to see glimmers of artwork that may well have been produced for the sexual arousal of the viewer. Ancient Mesopotamia produced numerous depictions of men and women having sex missionary or doggy-style, though arguably these images are associated with fertility goddesses. In Ancient Egypt, the Turin Erotic Papyrus, dating back to roughly 1200 BC, depicts ugly men with huge cocks having sex with beautiful women, though these illustrations may have been satire rather than designed for self-pleasure. In Mesoamerica, numerous statues depict missionary sex, doggy style,

Art and architecture inspired by the *Kama Sutra*

blowjobs, cunnilingus, masturbation and anal sex. However, it is highly likely these statues were made for religious rather than masturbatory purposes. In India, the *Kama Sutra* depicts many different sex positions; it is clear these are intended for instructional purposes.

Almost anything can be used as pornography in a pinch, so it is distinctly possible that religious or educational imagery was used occasionally as wank material. No doubt sneaky pornographic depictions made for less dignified reasons frequently did not survive antiquity. There is seldom the archaeological equivalent of a stack of *Playboy*s under a 3,000-year-old bed.

However, Graeco-Roman civilisation frequently depicted pornographic scenes in murals and in carvings. Some were done tastefully for aesthetic purposes, others are clearly there for their wankability. If you've ever wondered why classical depictions give men such small dicks, this is not because the Graeco-Romans were underendowed or that this was all the artist had as a 'point of reference.' Culturally, a large penis was viewed as bestial, barbaric and full of uncontrolled lust. Thus, Graeco-Romans favoured muscular, masculine figures with tiddly little winkies. A tell-tale sign of Graeco-Roman pornography is that the dicks are somewhat bigger. In one lewd painting found at Pompeii, a man is balancing a pot on top of his sturdy erection, while others feature couples in almost every sex position under the sun. Beyond the visual arts, Graeco-Roman festivals and orgies frequently had actors portraying and even engaging in various forms of sexual intercourse for the viewing pleasure of the audience, in a sort of live version of a porn film. Many of these ancient 'porn actors' were sex slaves made to perform against their will.

The Graeco-Roman style of painting classy nudes was revived in Europe during the Renaissance, with many artists painting figures in the buff, even in situations where being naked wouldn't make any sense (such as a group of warriors on a battlefield with their dicks hanging out). Like in antiquity, some people appreciated this artwork for its artistic value, others liked looking at naked people and doing the four-knuckle shuffle – though this argument should not be overstated. More 'compelling' nudes during the Renaissance typically belonged in private art collections. To our knowledge, no one ever stood in the Sistine Chapel whacking off to the nudes in 'The Last Judgement'. Nevertheless, in 1541 some people at the Vatican did think Michelangelo's work was sufficiently 'racy' to merit painting fig leaves over the nudes. This started a campaign of censorship where genitals in many paintings and statues were covered with paint or stone fig leaves. From the seventeenth through the nineteenth centuries, many priceless statues actually had the genitals under these fig leaves chipped off.

The invention of printing aided in the production and circulation of pornography. With the advent of woodblock printing in China in the seventh century AD, a flood of erotic depictions were made, reaching almost industrial levels of production by the thirteenth century. The same practices of illustrated porn printing spread to Japan and Korea. Numerous lewd images still survive from pre-modern Asia, with perhaps the most intriguing being 'The Dream of the Fisherman's Wife' (1814), a woodblock print out of Japan. In the drawing, a woman is receiving cunnilingus from a giant octopus while its tentacles snake all over her body, and a smaller octopus lingers at her mouth while it fondles one of her nipples. Some have theorised this may be the initial seed of tentacle porn.

The West, however, did not have printing until the mid-fifteenth century, when moveable type (first invented in thirteenth-century Korea) slowly filtered in from East Asia and was combined by Johann Gutenberg with wine-making technology to make the printing press. While the press was primarily used to make copies of the Bible, circulate religious sermons, political edicts and printed versions of classical literature, it wasn't long before porn was also pumped out into Europe, in terms of both set-plate drawings and erotica. Hundreds of copies of illustrated porn were circulated around Western Europe within a decade of Gutenberg's breakthrough. As the number of printing presses multiplied over the next three centuries, the amount of available pornography increased, despite religious objections and social stigma. With the invention of roller-printing presses, photography and film, this trend would only continue as we turn now to the immense sexual transformations of modernity.

COITUS INTERRUPTUS

The invention of agriculture drastically altered our sexual lifeways from foraging. Sex became tied to property, female sexuality became more heavily restricted than ever before, and our sexual practices eventually became subject to the dictates of organised religion and state law. As the agrarian period drew on, polygyny was gradually suppressed, homosexuality became criminalised, and sex for pleasure (outside of marriage) increasingly became a source of embarrassment, dishonour and shame in most global cultures.

Monogamy, already a majority practice in the foraging era, became overwhelmingly dominant and institutionalised. All with the aim of producing male-led families, dutiful and subservient wives and an abundance of children who would grow up to pay rents, tithes and taxes, filling the coffers of the church, government and the elite far into the future. Any sexual practices that did not contribute to the creation of these families were irrelevant or, at worst, a threat to the societal order. For the past 12,000 years, roughly 90 per cent of the population had toiled on farms in the countryside, marrying and forming large families, and in 1750 there was very little sign this was going to change ...

And then *everything* changed.

10

THE MODERN REVOLUTION

1750 AD to Present

Wherein the Industrial Revolution and Great Acceleration change the sexual landscape yet again • Sex plays a huge role in the technological progress of humanity • The modern housewife swiftly rises to prominence and declines just as quickly • Agrarian attitudes die hard • Democratic rights spread across humanity but not without an initial dose of sexism and quackery • The agrarian model of sex is effectively broken in the developed world by three major changes.

These are unprecedented times for our sex lives. The changes started with the Industrial Revolution of the eighteenth and nineteenth centuries, followed by the Great Acceleration of the mid-twentieth century; these combine to form what has been called the Modern Revolution, a transformative period that continues today. An explosion of technological innovation has utterly changed our lifeways in an evolutionary blink of an eye – just 250 years. And it also drastically altered how we conducted ourselves sexually and romantically. Far from the Modern Revolution being over, there is every sign that we are just at the beginning of this period of rapid transformation – one as pivotal and far-reaching as the invention of agriculture. Our sex lives are struggling to keep up with the blizzard of societal changes. We do not yet know what sexual practices will prove dominant in this new epoch. How will historians looking back on the modern era, 1,000 or 2,000 years from now, characterise how our society conducts itself sexually and romantically?

Our times are unprecedented because in some respects we have been freed from the shackles of our 315,000-year history. Never has human sex been so liberated from the concerns of evolutionary survival. Never have we been so free of religious or legal pressure to conduct our love lives in a certain way. But, for many people, particularly the younger generations, never before has their situation felt so muddled, directionless and lost. A vast new frontier stretches on for miles in front of us. Will it lead to the creation of new traditions or the retaining of old ones? Perhaps the Modern Revolution will transform our sex lives into a utilitarian satisfying of our evolutionary sexual impulses, much like scratching an itch. Or perhaps an entirely new and unforeseen interpretation of what sex means to us will emerge. For us, in the twenty-first century, the big questions are why we should have sex, why we should pursue romance, and what sexual practices ultimately would make us happy. If, indeed, the vicissitudes of sex are even capable of making most people happy in modernity ...

EVENT	DATE
Start of the Industrial Revolution	c1750
The modern housewife rises	c1850
Sexually repressive science reaches its height	c1870
Universal suffrage becomes the norm in developed nations	c1930

Premarital sex becomes common	c1945
The Baby Boom	c1950
Birth control becomes widely available	1970

INDUSTRIAL INTERCOURSE

Modernity is, by and large, the result of an abundance of babies. One of the key long-term factors that led to the Modern Revolution was the capacity of *Homo sapiens* for collective learning. In many ways it is what makes our species unique, delivering us from stone tools to skyscrapers without changing biologically. Over centuries and millennia, our innovations add up. Some of those innovations (like learning how to farm more efficiently) increase the overall carry capacity of a population. This produces more humans at any given time, all of whom can potentially innovate during their lifetimes. It's a positive feedback loop. More people, more innovation, more people – the process snowballs.

Having increased from 8 million at the start of agriculture 12,000 years ago to 50 million with the rise of the first states 5,500 years ago, the global carrying capacity continued to rise: by 2,000 years ago there were 250 million people spread across the surface of Earth, and by 1492 AD, there were roughly 400 million potential innovators on the planet. At that point, regular networks of trade and information exchange connected Europe, Asia, Africa and the Americas. Collective learning had gone global. By 1800 AD, these networks had been extended to Australasia and Oceania and the population had increased to 954 million potential innovators. Fresh ideas in science and technology swirled around this network of trade.

Meanwhile, in Great Britain, global trade had transitioned society from an agrarian to a mercantile one. The percentage of the population who farmed had shrunk from 90 per cent in 1500 to 60 per cent in 1750. Fifty per cent of the British GDP was produced by commerce. A vast global market lay out there, if only Britain could produce the goods fast enough. The refinement of the coal-powered steam engine between 1712 and 1775 lit the spark of mass production. Suddenly the British could produce a tonne of goods for much cheaper prices. Between 1750 and 1800, the average price of cotton textiles was cut in half. By 1820, a tiny island nation of just 20 million people had become the world's leading steel and coal producer. At that point, British manufacturing was five times more efficient than any other nation on Earth, making Britain the richest country on the planet. The efficiency of British industry continued to grow so that by 1880 Britain produced nearly 25 per cent of the world's goods, despite being only 2 per cent of the world's population.

From the mid-nineteenth century onwards, the other European powers recognised where the wind was blowing and began to industrialise as well. So did the United States on the other side of the Atlantic. And from 1870 onwards, Japan became the first Asian power to start modernising and industrialising with gusto. The power dynamic between industrial and agrarian societies was profound. By 1900, 85 per cent of the world's surface was controlled by industrialising imperial powers. And by the end of the nineteenth century, the world had increased to 1.7 billion potential innovators. Industrialisation spread to even more countries in the twentieth century, including China and India, and the process is still ongoing. Thus, with an endless downpour of babies, the acceleration of collective learning continued.

In 1927, the year Earth's population reached 2 billion people, our primate species flew non-stop across the Atlantic. Shortly after we reached 3 billion people, we nearly obliterated the world, in the Cuban Missile Crisis of 1962, using weapons we bipedal apes had invented. By the time we reached 4 billion in 1974, humanity had landed on the Moon six times. And by the time Earth's population was 7 billion in

2011, the computing power that achieved those Moon landings was held in a simple smartphone that permitted the average person to have instantaneous communication across the globe. Within the space of just two centuries, the Modern Revolution has bestowed humanity with godlike powers – for better or worse – and yet our biology and sexual instincts have remained much the same. But given the scale of cultural change, it would be shocking if, by modern day, we *hadn't* drastically altered our approach to sex and relationships.

THE RISE AND FALL OF THE MODERN HOUSEWIFE

The Industrial Revolution had a profound impact on sex and the family. Mass production allowed families to buy things for cheaper prices. Things that a generation earlier had been luxuries, such as cushioned furniture or cotton clothing, could be bought cheaper than the slowly produced, painstaking efforts of artisans in the agrarian period. With every passing decade in the nineteenth century, an increasing number of luxuries became basic staples. As the Industrial Revolution continued, wages increased faster than prices, inflating the 'real wage' and giving the average family more disposable income. Higher real wages also increased social mobility. And in the nineteenth century this created more middle-class families than ever existed at any point during the agrarian era.

A typical agrarian society historically had 90 per cent of the population engaged in agriculture-related activities, most of them subsistence peasants. Husband and wife toiled laboriously on the farm. The danger was clear: if famine came, as it so often did, everyone would starve. So, the whole family worked, and worked *hard* to keep the proverbial wolf from the door. Typically, the heavy manual labour jobs, such as ploughing the soil or herding cattle, fell to the husband. Wives also got their hands dirty: clearing weeds, hand-planting crops, helping to gather and stockpile literal tonnes of food during the harvest, handling livestock, collecting eggs and milk for domestic use, looking after small children, preparing and cooking food and maintaining the domicile. The last of these two duties were much more onerous before modern technologies and amenities. Try grinding flour and baking your own bread or butchering your own meat after work and it might give you an idea of the exhausting work–life balance that most lower-class wives endured during much of the agrarian era. Wives of middle- and upper-class men (bureaucrats, wealthy city merchants, large landowners and, of course, aristocrats) did not have to perform as much (or any) manual labour beyond maintaining the domicile and looking after the children – if they did not have servants to do it for them. Being a proverbial housewife prior to the modern era was regarded as a luxury available to the very few.

But by 1850, the mechanisation of British agriculture and the increased importation of food reduced the number of farmers to a mere 30 per cent of the population. This was a massive transition in lifeways. A further 60 per cent of the population, compared to a traditional agrarian economy, were released to pursue occupations other than farming. Roughly 25 to 30 per cent remained poor, with many of them drifting towards the cities to become servants, factory workers and associated labourers. But still others became mechanics, engineers, salesmen, doctors, lawyers, inventors or small business owners. The middle class increased from the typical agrarian 7 to 9 per cent of the population to a whopping 35 per cent. As a result, the percentage of women who were housewives roughly quadrupled by 1850. The same pattern played out in every European and North American economy that industrialised in the nineteenth century. Fewer women had to do hard manual labour, and a well-to-do middle-class family could afford to keep at least one servant to handle many of the domestic tasks.

In the mid-nineteenth century, urban working-class people suffered appalling conditions as the world transitioned away from the agrarian period. The wives of lower-class labourers still had to work to support their households. Many wives took on factory or servant work; indeed, in 1850, many of their children worked in factories (with the law permitting children over nine years old to work dangerous jobs for up to 60 hours per week). However, by 1900, industrialisation had increased the size of the middle class to approximately 45 per cent of the population. The growth of the real wage also permitted even some lower-class households (those belonging to miners, labourers, factory workers, etc) to subsist off a husband's wage while women worked less outside the home. Being a housewife became aspirational for many women. Those lower-income women who had to work labour jobs were regarded as unfortunates who should cease working as soon as it became economically feasible. Meanwhile, these 'delicate creatures' were becoming 'coarsened' by the workplace. Numerous women's advocacy groups sprang up discouraging the use of women in hard manual labour. It might sound strange to modern ears that advocacy groups had the goal of *removing* women from the workforce when they would have the exact opposite aim under a century later. But the prospect of work for most lower-income women in the nineteenth century was generally more dire than most career prospects in the twentieth and twenty-first centuries.

In the nineteenth century, being a housewife was regarded initially as a luxury and then idealised as the 'traditional' role for women, despite having only existed for a large portion of the population for a few decades. Numerous books were published on home economics, domestic science and household etiquette. Magazines such as *Good Housekeeping* came into massive circulation, replete with tips and tricks for sustaining high (often unrealistic) domestic standards. The idealised housewife also featured heavily in chauvinistic theories about the roles of men and women in society. But even by 1900 the 'traditional' role of the housewife was already dying a slow death. Increasing numbers of women (who were becoming increasingly literate and educated thanks to the concurrent expansion of the education system to the wider public) were going out to work in professional jobs such as secretaries, teachers, nurses, journalists, scientific researchers, etc. A transition into the modern workforce that was only hastened by World Wars I and II.

Early cover of an issue of *Good Housekeeping*

As industrialisation continued into the twentieth century and the middle class increased to nearly 60 per cent of the population, more and more women found themselves becoming housewives. And even most urban working-class families found it possible to keep their wives out of the labour force. Thus, in 1929, a peak of approximately 80 per cent of married households in industrialised countries had a stay-at-home housewife. By that point, the popular imagination had conflated the image of the 'domestic goddess' with the more onerous role played by hard-living peasants' wives for nearly 12,000 years. Thus, the modern housewife was often mistaken in popular literature for a traditional role that had existed since 'time immemorial'. Meanwhile, domestic technologies for cooking, cleaning and laundry made maintaining the domicile less burdensome and time-consuming. So, for many women, existence inside the home grew increasingly tedious. Barbiturate and alcohol use by housewives increased accordingly. By the time we reach the 1950s housewife, which most modern minds conjure up when they think of 'traditional women's roles', this idealised role in reality had only existed in most of the population for less than a century and was living on borrowed time.

While a sizeable proportion of the twentieth- and twenty-first--century population does prefer, for personal and/or religious reasons, to stay at home and raise their children (if that path is economically feasible), by the end of the 1950s some women were eager to get back into the workforce like their ancestors prior to modernity. By 1970, only 45 per cent of married households had stay-at-home housewives – a dramatic reduction from only forty years earlier. By 2020, that number had receded to an average of roughly 20 per cent in most developed nations – almost back down to the level of the agrarian era. After a brief spell of only a century, most men and women were back at work outside the home. Except nowadays most husbands and wives aren't toiling in the fields, enduring back-breaking labour, so much as being bored pen-pushers and cubicle jockeys, and having their eyes slowly burned out by computer screens, or 'wage-slaves' at other 9-to-5 jobs. After all, not everyone can be lucky enough to find a morally or spiritually fulfilling career. Some people just have to pay the bills. And in the twenty-first century the prospect of raising a family as a single-income household is increasingly becoming a pipe dream again for many lower- and middle-income families.

THE AGRARIAN HANGOVER

It is almost impossible to detect a major socioeconomic shift when you are still at the beginning of one. Still less is it possible to figure out what the long-term ramifications of such a shift will be. As such, many of the traditional attitudes that surrounded sex and marriage in the agrarian era persisted into the nineteenth and early twentieth centuries. For one thing, the agrarian importance of a child's paternity to property inheritance and a farming family's survival continued, even though far fewer people worked in agriculture (shrinking to less than a third). There were fewer family farms to inherit, and marriage as an agrarian land-deal quickly became a thing of the past for an increasingly urban working- and middle-class population of wage-earners. But ideals of fidelity and sexual purity had become wrapped up in religious justifications and notions of family honour, irrespective of the socioeconomic reasons that spawned them 12,000 years ago. These ideals were also underwritten by evolutionary tendencies towards monogamy and sexual jealousy that were 1.9 million years old. So, for the average nineteenth-century person, the sanctity of marriage and sexual propriety seemed justified by God and thousands of years of history, and felt quite 'natural' to a typical individual living within that system.

As a result, at the outset of the Modern Revolution, female sexuality was still harshly policed and promiscuity massively frowned upon. A sexually 'intemperate' woman could find herself cast out by her family, and even unemployable in most working-class jobs, forcing her to go into sex work and further destroying her social reputation and prospects. Male promiscuity was tolerated to a greater extent, so long as it was kept out of the public eye. An adulterous husband, or 'whoremonger', could also find himself ostracised and his career prospects ruined. In a word, sex for pleasure outside the family in Western industrialising countries was still very much socially forbidden.

Agrarian baggage also affected nineteenth- and early-twentieth-century attitudes towards female mate choice. Today, in the industrialised West, it is fairly unusual for a woman in her twenties or thirties to embark on a committed relationship with a man unless she feels a glimmer of sexual attraction to him. Previously, a woman's sexual attraction to a man was considered secondary (if considered at all) next to male traits that implied fidelity, integrity and, above all, the ability to support a woman financially, all of which are still factors today. Less emphasis on sexual attraction didn't mean that nineteenth-century considerations precluded love (in fact, in nineteenth-century literature the above traits are often cited as reasons *why* a woman fell in love) but it did mean that a woman's raw physical attraction to her husband was way down the list of boxes to tick.

Financial considerations were of utmost importance because women could not support themselves by working a regular job if they were alone, and because limited birth control meant that women would be in dire straits if they fell pregnant. To a certain extent a woman's propensity to value a man's financial prospects is evolutionary, stemming from the 1.9-million-year-old monogamous role a father would play as provider in child-rearing. Finances are still often a major factor in female mate choice today, echoing that instinct despite the fact women are now able to earn money for themselves. But in the nineteenth century, emphasis on money was more pressing than mere instinct; without a husband providing for her, a woman's standard of life and even her very existence were threatened.

Meanwhile, great care was taken to keep women away from 'cads' and 'snakes in the grass' – sexually attractive men, who in the twenty-first century would simply have had sex with the woman and caused no greater alarm than a typical fling on a Saturday night). Quite feasibly, many of these attractive 'cads' were the equivalent of the minority of men responsible for most of the pregnancies in the Palaeolithic. But in the nineteenth century these men represented a grave threat to a woman's future wellbeing. Fathers and brothers often took a direct role in vetting prospective male suitors for their female relatives, assessing whether a man's intentions were pure or he was just spinning a girl a massive line of bullshit to get her in the sack.

An excellent, well-known encapsulation of this species of mate choice can be found in Jane Austen's *Pride and Prejudice* (1813). Although in modernity the role of Mr Darcy has been played by rather handsome men such as Colin Firth and Elliot Cowan, the book never gushes about his looks. They are irrelevant. Conversely, Mr Wickham is an attractive lady's man 'with a fine countenance and a good figure' who immediately catches the eye of the book's heroine, Elizabeth Bennet. Wickham had previously seduced Darcy's sister, Georgiana. He also, notably, has no money. Much of Lizzie Bennet's character arc is steeped in her realising that Mr Darcy is by far the more faithful and principled man, kind-hearted and protective of those he loves, and most revealingly Lizzie wisely begins to fall in love with him after she 'sees the size of his house'. Mr Wickham meanwhile seduces one of Lizzie's sisters and is eventually bribed into an unhappy marriage. Meanwhile, Lizzie's friend without prospects, Charlotte Lucas, marries the odious Mr Collins, who can support her financially. And what is the main objection? Not that Collins is ugly but that he lacks integrity. Yet in modern portrayals, it is often deemed important to have Mr Collins played by a man who is short or has ugly facial features. Above all, it is perhaps revealing that if Darcy were played by a 5/10 instead of an 8 or 9/10, it probably wouldn't resonate as well with most modern audiences, and Darcy himself might well be met with some derision.

Beyond these rather constrained and practical attitudes towards marriage, with primates being primates sex for pleasure assuredly happened all the time. For instance, in the early nineteenth century there were over 20,000 sex workers in Vienna, capital of the Austrian Empire, or roughly one sex worker for every five to six men. Despite the censorship of sex in mainstream publications, it is clear the popular imagination knew a lot of things about sex in intimate detail. Victorian erotica such as *The Lustful Turk* (1828), *The Romance of Lust* (1873), *Early Experiences of a Young Flagellant* (1876), *The Mysteries of Verbena House, or, Miss Bellasis Birched for Thieving* (1882) and *Venus in India* (1889) luxuriously describe the female orgasm, every sexual position under the sun and some light BDSM, with a profusion of colourful language and graphic descriptions that could make a modern contributor to Literotica.com blush.

A few decades later, D.H. Lawrence's *Lady Chatterley's Lover* (1928), which was subject to an obscenity trial in Great Britain, featured an upper-class lady cucking her paralysed husband with a working-class man, including anal sex, fourteen uses of the word 'cunt' and forty of the word 'fuck'. As a minor aside, a shameless pornographic 'sequel' *Young Lady Chatterley II* (1986) stars Adam West, formerly of 1960s *Batman* fame. Also in 1928, British writer Norman Douglas published *Some Limericks*, an anthology of bawdy, oftentimes disgusting rhymes he had picked up in the late nineteenth and early twentieth centuries. One such entry is:

There were two young men of Cawnpore
Who buggared and fucked the same whore
But the partition split
And the spunk and the shit
Rolled out in great lumps on the floor.

Similarly, late-nineteenth-century Vaudeville and music halls delighted audiences with sexually inappropriate songs and dances, despite attempts to censor them. From these acts emerged the musical genre of Hokum, or 'dirty blues', in the early twentieth century, frequently banned from the radio. Hokum lyrics could keep pace with even the foulest songs of the present day. Take, for example, this extract from 'Till the Cows Come Home', recorded by Lucille Bogan in 1935:

> *I gotta big fat belly,*
> *I gotta big broad ass,*
> *And I can fuck my man*
> *With real good class ...*
> *If you suck my pussy,*
> *I'll suck your dick*
> *I'll do it to ya, honey,*
> *Till I make you shit.*

Meanwhile, European brothels continued their centuries-long traditions. In nineteenth-century France, brothels were legally required to put up a red lantern at their entrances, signalling they were a house of ill-repute, giving birth to the term 'red light district'. Some French brothels conned male customers into thinking they were deflowering a virgin for a premium price by having the working girl insert a pig's bladder full of blood into her vagina so it would burst during sex. And, despite homosexuality being illegal, brothels that catered to gay and lesbian sex were common in European cities. The prevailing thinking of legal authorities was that if they could confine such behaviours to the fringes it would be less likely to 'run rampant' in polite society. During the nineteenth century, it is estimated that 7 per cent of all prostitutes were male.

In the realm of pornography, nineteenth-century innovations in printing such as roller presses managed to create record numbers of erotica and risqué cartoons and artwork. And with the invention of photography, nude pictures of men and women for 'private enjoyment' soon followed. In the 1840s, photographs had become affordable for the middle and lower classes to purchase discreetly from merchants. By 1860, the number of shops selling nude photos had increased by 3000 per cent across Western Europe. Once motion pictures were invented at the end of the nineteenth century, porn was soon to follow. The first porn film in history, a striptease, was made in France in 1895. The first porn films showing hardcore penetration were produced in Argentina in 1905 but have since been destroyed.

Mihály Zichy, a nineteenth-century Hungarian painter, was famous for his erotic drawings.

Clearly, despite the agrarian hangover of sexual propriety, quite modern understandings of sex were simmering below the surface of a chaste and upright façade. The strictures of culture cannot quash the primate in us. With the relaxation of censorship in the mid-twentieth century, it wasn't as though people suddenly learnt every lurid detail pertaining to sex overnight. Adults already knew a lot of this stuff. They just kept it more furtive and private than the explicit displays of sex for people's entertainment in the present day.

WANKER DOCTORS

Sex-negative ideas were aided and abetted, to some extent, by junk science that was still infected by the attitudes of the agrarian era. Women were viewed as 'delicate creatures' who were psychologically ill-equipped to deal with sexual stimuli. At best, this might moderately affect their health; at worst, sexual stimuli could lead women astray and ruin their lives. As a result, great care was taken to not expose women to these things. Ideally, contemporary thinking went, Victorian brides would not even have a rudimentary knowledge of sex on their wedding nights. Medical doctors could only examine female hands, necks and heads – nothing below the clothing, leading to countless unnecessary female deaths from breast cancer and any other illness that required disrobing to detect. Victorian men, meanwhile, were advised to have sex no more than twice per year, when not trying for children, to 'maintain their good health'.

In 1758, at the very start of the Modern Revolution, a medical book written by Samuel Tissot, *Onanism: Or, a Treatise Upon the Disorders Produced by Masturbation,* claimed that wanking could cause all sorts of maladies. According to Tissot, a quick hand-shandy could cause blindness, insanity, cancer, sterility, gonorrhoea and genital necrosis (the death and rotting of your dick while it was still attached to your body). The general theory was that excessive loss of male semen could lead to ill-health because the body was deprived of such a 'vital life-force'. This idea persisted into the nineteenth and early twentieth centuries. Quack doctors invented male chastity devices to prevent masturbation. One of the nastiest was a urethral ring that was worn around the penis while sleeping. It came equipped with four spikes that threatened to impale any nocturnal erection (though of course it had the side effect of depriving a man of sleep).

Meanwhile, many nineteenth-century doctors theorised that female masturbation increased the likelihood of insanity, insomnia, seizures, deafness, dumbness, loss of motor function, full paralysis, amnesia, vomiting, fever and death. Accordingly, female chastity belts got a new lease on life after being largely discarded at the end of the medieval period. There was also a great deal of panic over the introduction of bicycles in the nineteenth century. Some physicians thought women riding bikes was unhealthy, with the seats pressing and rubbing against their bottoms and genitalia, leading, in their medical opinion, to inflammation of the ovaries, internal bleeding and miscarriage of pregnancies. Some physicians advised that women should try to ride bikes side-saddle like they would with a horse to avoid sexual stimulation.

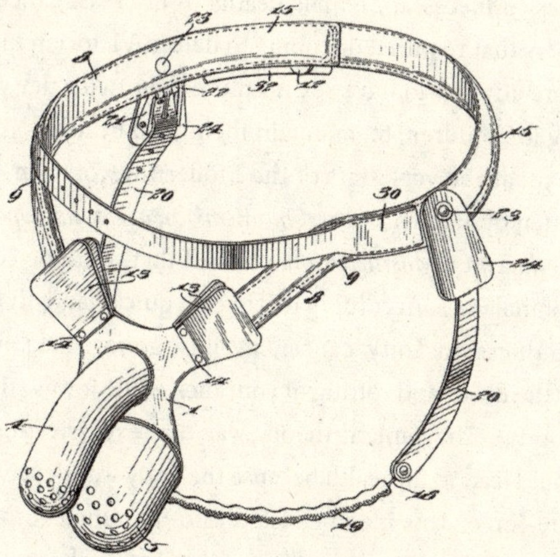

A 1911 patent for a male chastity belt

Such was the pervasiveness of the idea that masturbation was extremely unhealthy, various forms of physical bondage and circumcision were advised. Most famously, John Harvey Kellogg, director of a sanatorium in Battle Creek, Michigan, and brother of the inventor of Corn Flakes, had some advice for particularly chronic masturbators.

In *Plain Facts for Old and Young* (1879), Kellogg advised that boys and men should have their hands tied behind their backs while sleeping, or to have a chastity cage slapped on their dicks to prevent nocturnal erections. He also advised that males should be circumcised *without anaesthetic* so the trauma of the procedure and the soreness of their healing penises would interrupt their cycles of masturbation and break the habit. Later medical campaigners and moralists championed the idea of male circumcision and it spread like wildfire across the United States, where 75 to 80 per cent of men today still have their foreskins removed (the averages are lower elsewhere in North America). The craze was less successful in other parts of the industrialised world. In the mid-twentieth century, the justification of circumcision preventing masturbation was quietly dropped as junk science, but circumcisions continued to be performed for hygienic and aesthetic reasons, along with the traditional reasons in Judaism and Islam.

For chronic female masturbators, Kellogg advised that medical professionals burn off the nerve endings in their clitorises by dousing them with carbolic acid, a substance capable of causing second-degree chemical burns, permanent disfigurements and, if not properly washed off, gangrene and death. It is unclear how many people took Kellogg's advice. But a few years prior, in 1866, Dr Isaac Baker-Brown, president of the Medical Society of London, published *On the Curability of Certain Forms of Insanity, Epilepsy, Catalepsy, and Hysteria in Females*, in which he proudly declared that female mental disorders could be cured by cutting off a woman's clitoris with a pair of scissors. He claimed to have inflicted sixty-nine such procedures. Unlike male circumcision, this sort of thing did *not* catch on like wildfire, and Baker-Brown was denounced for pedalling quackery and drummed out of his career in just three years. However, it is estimated that across the UK other doctors inflicted approximately 500 such clitorectomies on women while the practice was still in vogue.

Similar forms of junk science persisted into the twentieth century. In 1920, French physician Serge Voronoff claimed he could reinvigorate male masculinity and virility by cutting open a man's ball sack and inserting a monkey testicle before sewing up the scrotum again. The testicle was then left to 'be absorbed by the body'. Voronoff conducted 500 such procedures. He farmed a population of captive monkeys, which he regularly castrated and euthanised for their testicles. Voronoff was shut down in 1929. Some historians have theorised that Voronoff was responsible for the transmission of AIDS from monkeys to humans, although transmission of infected blood from primate meat or direct bestiality are other strong contenders.

UTERUSES WITH WANDERLUST

The baggage of the agrarian period is nowhere more clearly exemplified than in the concept of 'female hysteria'. The Ancient Egyptians and Greeks both theorised that female irritability, anxiety, lack of sleep, anger, aggression, giddiness, 'excessive urine', paranoia, delirium, frigidness *and* sexual forwardness, and roughly sixty other symptoms, were caused by the uterus detaching itself and floating around the body like a sniffer dog in an Amsterdam coffee shop. Nineteenth-century anatomy discarded the idea that the uterus went on day-trips around the body, but the medical profession retained the idea of hysteria as a concept. Some women were subject to clitorectomies, considerably more were given full hysterectomies, and still more were locked up in mental asylums. A popular treatment was the 'rest-cure', whereby a woman was confined to bed for days or weeks, given nothing to entertain her or occupy her mind, and she was isolated from contact with anyone except the nurse who fed her, disposed of her bowel movements and changed her sheets. To modern eyes, this seems like a great way to *induce* mental illness rather than relieve it.

Another experimental medical treatment for hysteria, performed by a small group of doctors, was applying genital 'massages' to women to relieve their symptoms. This amounted to little more than rubbing their clits and fingering them. The process seemed to calm them down, though the notes of some medical professionals sometimes failed to draw a connection between the 'massage' and patient orgasms, which many doctors tried to avoid during the procedure, utterly 'blue-beaning' their patients.

A myth has grown up in academia that vibrators were invented to make these genital massages less tiresome for the doctors, but this is not quite true. The first vibrator was invented in 1880 by Joseph Mortimer Granville, a male doctor who used the device to treat muscle fatigue and back problems in men. He explicitly said that vibrators should not be used on women due to the risks that it might inflame their hysteria. In 1902, vibrators first became available for commercial sale to the public. However, they were marketed as non-sexual massaging devices. By 1920, they were pulled from the market once it became clear that women were using them to masturbate. They were not reintroduced until the 1960s, and the use of the vibrator for female masturbation was not fully popularised and destigmatised for most women until the 1980s and '90s. By 2020, approximately 78 per cent of women in the United States owned a vibrator for the express purpose of self-pleasure rather than just a simple back massage.

THE CRIME OF BLEEDING

Nineteenth-century medical theory blamed hysteria on 'excessive retention' of menstrual blood in the uterus. This is another bit of baggage from the agrarian era that goes back to the Ancient Greeks. Indeed, throughout human history many foraging and agrarian cultures regarded menstrual blood as toxic, usually because blood issuing from the body was associated with injury or illness. In many modern foraging cultures, for instance, menstruating women are regarded as unclean and often isolated for the duration of their periods. In the agrarian era, many cultures associated menstrual blood with infectious diseases, and prohibited period sex, and even forbade menstruating women from preparing food. For instance, Leviticus in the Old Testament goes into obsessive detail about all this. You'd be unwise to even use the same chair a menstruating woman did for days after she sat on it. Despite the overall hostility of historical societies towards something as basic and natural as menstruation, a few agrarian cultures prized and revered menstrual blood. The Baul culture of medieval India and Bangladesh advocated the spiritual significance of drinking menstrual blood, and there are a few cases from China of emperors and aristocrats consuming menstrual blood as the key to retaining their youth.

Nevertheless, the mainstream agrarian myth of menstrual toxicity meant that arguments over the wisdom of letting menstruating women cook dinner continued into the nineteenth century. Additionally, the Victorians often used menstruation as a justification for sidelining women from various rights and privileges. The theory went that menstruation interrupted women's physical capabilities so they could not work regular jobs. Victorian anthropologist James McGrigor also asserted that menstruation impeded women's mental faculties to such an extent that they should not be trusted with the same kind of intellectual work as men. This same line of argument asserting menstruation leads to mild mental instability was even used to justify denying women the vote. The practice of feminine hygiene remained largely unaddressed during the nineteenth century, with most women either employing scraps of fabric or merely bleeding into their underclothes on a monthly basis. The first tampons only became available for commercial sale in 1929.

Attitudes towards menstruation are still quite mixed to this day. For instance, starting in the 1980s it was not permitted to use red-dyed water in commercials for feminine hygiene products to avoid repulsing the audience. In reality, if a person experiences 'light blue' menstrual blood, they should immediately consult a doctor. Furthermore, in the twenty-first century, opinions on period sex are split, with 40 per cent of Western men saying they find it off-putting, messy or 'gross', but paradoxically with 83 per cent of men admitting they had sex with a menstruating woman at some point in their lives. In modern Australia, the slang for performing cunnilingus on a menstruating woman is having 'a Dolmio grin', derived from the slogan from 1990s commercials for a tomato pasta sauce. The slang is not an indication of widespread practice Down Under (no pun intended) but is a rather ghoulish joke banking off the presumed widespread revulsion the general public would have at the idea of a man ingesting period blood.

BIRTH CONTROL BLUNDERS

The baggage of the agrarian era extended to birth control, first and foremost because it implied sex for pleasure rather than reproduction. Prior to the nineteenth century, condoms could be made of sheep guts, cow bowels or cat bladders; otherwise, women might insert sponges in their vaginas or use various objects such as vegetable husks and fruit skins to block the ends of their vaginal canals. However, most common in the pre-modern era was the pull-out method. The prototypes for the first rubber condoms were made in the 1850s. From 1873 to 1895, numerous Western countries banned their sale, while others simply made the practice too taboo for condoms to be sold in most stores. In the 1920s, latex condoms became available, but again the average person would be hard-pressed to find them anywhere, and in many countries they were still illegal. Naturally, the lack of availability of prophylactics meant that sexually transmitted diseases and unexpected pregnancies were much more common than they otherwise would have been.

In World War II, many Allied countries issued their troops with condoms (regardless of their legality in their home countries) and in the late 1940s the use of condoms increasingly became mainstream. However, with the introduction with the contraceptive pill in the

1960s and the development of antibiotics to treat many venereal diseases, the condom receded in popularity, with many people in the 1960s and 1970s riding bareback. It was only with the HIV/AIDS epidemic of the 1980s that condoms came into widespread use again. Since then, various forms of media have been replete with injunctions to use condoms, but these public service announcements appear to have had diminishing returns as the HIV/AIDS crisis has faded from public memory. According to a 2020 study, 47 per cent of people under thirty do *not* use a condom when fucking a new partner, and 10 per cent of those under thirty have *never* used a condom.

Meanwhile, abortion had an even more tortured history. As we have seen, early nomadic foraging societies viewed killing newborn children as a utilitarian and necessary act for survival. Put simply, if anything prevents you from crossing vast distances in search of food, you may all starve to death. With the agrarian era, populations were sedentary and there were strong incentives for women to have more children, since it would compensate for the high child mortality rate and the surviving children could support their parents in old age. The government, church and landholding elite also frequently emphasised the importance of a high birth rate, since having more people to tax or paying rent was in their material best interests. As such, abortion was regarded as a mortal sin and a capital crime. There was a clear religious and ideological equation between an abortion and taking *any* sort of human life. And the lack of any reliable form of birth control restricted most women's sexual and romantic decisions throughout the agrarian period.

Nevertheless, illicit abortions happened throughout the agrarian period to avoid social ostracism or criminal prosecution in the case of adultery or promiscuity leading to an illegitimate pregnancy. Or to avoid a slide into poverty. Women would eat various noxious herbs such as savin, a species of juniper, drink copious amounts of alcohol, take scalding hot baths, repeatedly strike themselves in the stomach or throw themselves down stairs to provoke a miscarriage. Failing that, a thin iron pike could be inserted into the womb to skewer and dismember the fetus, and a long hook-like object would remove the remains. There was great danger to a woman in pre-modern abortionists stabbing at her insides, since it could cause either internal bleeding or a deadly infection. Hence the social *mores* of the nineteenth century strived to avoid pregnancy by any other means. It was also highly illegal. In early-nineteenth-century Britain, for instance, an abortion was punishable either by death or transportation to Australia (then a penal colony). In the late nineteenth and early twentieth centuries, women who got abortions could spend a significant amount of time in prison.

Abortion was only legalised in most Western countries in the 1960s and 1970s, with countries such as Australia and the United States doing so via supreme court rulings. The trend through the 1980s, 1990s and early 2000s has been to make abortions more available and affordable, but it has recently met with some reversals. In the United States, the 2022 Supreme Court ruling against *Roe v. Wade* (1973) has reverted abortion legislation to the states, meaning that more conservative states are likely to have much more restrictive abortion laws going forward compared with progressive states. Since 2010, anti-abortion campaigners across the Western world have increasingly abandoned religious arguments and relied on secular arguments (for example, pointing out a fetus has a unique DNA code and begins brain development at six weeks) and philosophical arguments (such as that the 'social contract' should protect individual humans from harm, including the unborn). Pro-abortion campaigners meanwhile focus on a woman's right to bodily autonomy and self-determination, how the fetus is not viable until around twenty-one to twenty-four weeks, how a woman should not be forced to carry a child to term and give it up for adoption, how banning abortions will likely not prevent some women from having illicit ones at mortal risk, and highlighting the need for abortion when a mother's life is threatened, or in cases of extreme poverty, rape or incest.

THE SEEDS OF EQUALITY

The majority of the 55 billion people who lived in the agrarian era, men or women, had no vote or direct influence over their governments. For every democratic Athens, there was a Persian Empire. For every ancient republic, there were a hundred absolute monarchies. Even in countries that had some form of parliamentary representation, the vote was only extended to the wealthy elite. The Modern Revolution changed all that, enfranchising both men and women in Western developed countries within the space of a century or less. And democratisation is a process that continues across the world, with much tyrannical opposition, to this day.

When the United States achieved independence from Great Britain in 1783, in part over 'no taxation without representation', property requirements for voting in many states meant that only 10 per cent of the population, mostly rich men (many of them slave owners) got the vote. The rationale was that property owners paid the bulk of the taxes so the rest of the population shouldn't get a say how that money was spent. By 1830, as property restrictions were lifted in 75 per cent of American states, roughly 60 per cent of white men got the vote (free black men and native peoples had to wait considerably longer). By 1856, the rest of property restrictions were removed and working-class white men in the United States had the right to vote. In 1869, only thirteen years after the US achieved male suffrage, Wyoming became the first US territory to grant women the right to vote, with fourteen more states and territories following suit between 1870 and 1920, when the Nineteenth Amendment brought in the right to vote for women across the country. We shall explore the debate that animated the intervening half-century shortly.

In Great Britain prior to 1832, property requirements restricted the vote to 3 to 5 per cent of the wealthy population, mostly men, but with a few unmarried or widowed female property owners. After 1832, the property requirements were loosened, expanding the vote to 15 per cent of the male population, significantly lagging behind the United States. At this time, rich women were barred from voting since the 1832 legislation presumed that heads of households would be male. In 1867, the property restrictions were loosened yet again, allowing 35 per cent of the male population to vote (only two years before women got the vote in Wyoming). Meanwhile, approximately 2.5 per cent of women (rich) were allowed to vote in local elections, but not national ones. Again, in 1884, the vote was widened to 55 per cent of the male population, but with most of the male working-class population *still* not having the vote, even though the British suffragette movement was now in full swing. It was only in 1918 that all working-class men in the United Kingdom were able to vote, and women over thirty who met property qualifications (about 60 per cent of adult women) gained the right to vote in the same piece of legislation. Full female suffrage was brought in ten years later in 1928. Interestingly, two British dominions, New Zealand and Australia, achieved both male and female suffrage a few decades prior.

France and Switzerland both brought in full male suffrage in 1848, but France then underwent two decades of Bonapartist dictatorship and thereafter the revived French Republic stubbornly did not extend the vote to women until 1944. Most shockingly, Switzerland was one of the tardiest nations worldwide, slowly extending the franchise between 1971 and 1990. Germany granted all men the right to vote in 1871, but the country was hardly democratic, and women were given the vote in 1919, when the country made its first real but ill-fated attempt at liberal democracy. Several newly created countries after World War I gave both men and women suffrage at the same time. Italy first gave all men suffrage in 1912, but ten years later the country was overcome by Mussolini's fascist dictatorship, and women only received suffrage in 1945. A downpour of new countries born or democratised after World War II gave men and women the vote at the same time (except for a few highly patriarchal states in Southwest Asia). Today, across the world, as countries continue to democratise, the franchise is now almost always given simultaneously, as the agrarian hangover discouraging the enfranchisement of women has largely receded.

But in the nineteenth century, while the agrarian hangover still raging, the arguments against women getting the vote were numerous. For starters, as long as the property requirements existed, the fact that men were typically the heads of propertied households kept voting confined to one sex. As property requirements loosened, the argument shifted towards the idea that women would still be represented by their husbands (and in many cases women couldn't own property anyway). In the latter half of the nineteenth century, the argument increasingly revolved around the fact that women were not subject to military conscription, and the voting rights of 'full citizenship' could only be extended to people capable of defending their country. An argument circulated in the early twentieth century that the vote would establish equality of the sexes, and thus put women in 'direct competition' with men, eroding relations between them.

And then there was a plethora of pseudo-scientific arguments brought to you by the same sort of people who thought burning clitorises with carbolic acid was a good idea. Nineteenth-century quacks stubbornly maintained that women's brains were inferior to men's because they were smaller. Excessive thinking, some argued (and this is serious), could cause miscarriages and infertility, since increasing metabolic energy funnelled towards the brain would cause the ovaries to dry up. Menstruation was also a frequent argument against the female franchise since the monthly 'derangement' of a woman's psyche might prompt them to make poor voting decisions. Today, these might sound like theories dreamt up by random misogynist blokes after half a bottle of whiskey at the bar, but what is so harrowing is that these were opinions of medical specialists of the day.

Perhaps most surprising to modern eyes is the women themselves who opposed suffrage in the nineteenth and early twentieth centuries. The anti-suffragettes were women who argued that 1) suffrage would diminish femininity and pollute the idea of what it was to be a woman, 2) it would prompt the dissolution of the family unit by subverting gender roles, and 3) voting was a duty not a right, and women already had a great many duties in the domestic sphere and in their local communities. While it is difficult to get an idea of the percentage of the female population who opposed suffrage at this time, postcard polls from the UK sometimes had up to 70 per cent of women respond negatively about female suffrage, and petitions opposing the vote were signed by between 5000 and 300,000 women.

Such was the severity of the agrarian hangover. After all, in most industrialising countries even the reality of all men getting the vote was still only a few decades old, and mostly the practice of a few oddball countries on either side of the Atlantic; most of the world remained resolutely undemocratic. But the dam burst at the end of World War I, with numerous liberal democracies adopting universal suffrage. And it is hardly a coincidence that at that time the sexual revolution began to build up steam.

UNLOCKING PANDORA'S BOX

There were three locks on the proverbial agrarian chastity belt. The first had already been undone by the Modern Revolution: most people in industrialised countries were no longer farmers. Strict child paternity and securing the inheritance of the small family farm were no longer the only things standing between lower-class people and starvation, nor was reliance on their children to look after them their only possible retirement plan. Lower- and middle-class wage-earners in the city could leave their children an inheritance (a house they'd paid off, or a sum of money) but that inheritance was not a matter of survival like keeping the farm in the family was. Ultimately, those children had to make their way in the world themselves, increasingly in careers different from the ones their parents had pursued. And an increasing number of wage-earning jobs, particularly for the middle class, came with pensions. So, by the early twentieth century, there was no blunt existential reason anymore for a family to police the sex lives of their wives and daughters. Not that it stopped them.

The second lock on the agrarian chastity belt was women's lack of financial independence. Prior to 1920, a young woman would move from the household of her family to the household of her husband, without anything in between. Combined with negative social *mores* about sex for pleasure, this severely restricted a young woman's opportunities for interacting with men and having pre-marital sex. But after 1920, it became increasingly common practice for young women to enjoy a spell of independence before they married. Increasing numbers of lower- and middle-class women were moving out of their father's house, perhaps moving in with a few friends, and working in their early twenties in low-paying but respectable jobs to cover the bills: waitress, typist, nanny, lady's maid or assistant to various kinds of professionals. Then there was a small but growing number of upper-middle-class women obtaining some degree of professional training and becoming careerists in their own right.

Now, this did not happen everywhere in the industrialised world overnight; many women still followed the traditional pattern of going straight from their parents' house to marriage. And in the 1920s the goal of most working women was to eventually find a husband, quit their jobs and transition to the 'traditional' role of housewife. But an increasing number of young women out working in the world increased their contact with men and freed themselves from parental supervision. It was easier to be discreet about pre-marital sex in a large town or city than it was in a close-knit farming village. This meant some women could widen their sexual experiences and find out what sex *was* without as high a risk of being socially ostracised like they would have been half a century earlier. The period of freedom young Western women enjoyed before marriage also delayed when they had their first children. During the 1920s, the birth rate dropped by 27 per cent, averaged out across Western industralised nations. Plenty of women were still having kids *eventually*, but this sort of drop in the total number of kids was unprecedented in the previous 5500 years.

All told, the number of Western urban middle-class women in their twenties who experienced pre-marital sex increased from an estimated 5 to 10 per cent in 1900 to a shocking 25 to 30 per cent by 1929. Middle-class women make for the best barometer of this change because they were the most weighed down by the *mores* of their family and social class. They are also a fantastic barometer for sexual freedom because by 1920 the middle-class was between 50 and 60 per cent of the population of a Western industrialised nation. Conversely, lower-income women in the cities experienced greater sexual freedom and tended to face fewer penalties for the odd scandalous fling as they slaved away at factory jobs, or as servants – or, indeed, performed in music halls, worked in taverns or provided their services in brothels. Puritanical morals tended to be less enforced among the working class. Upper-class women, meanwhile, did not need to work and *could* be cloistered by their families, but the cushion of wealth tended to allow many of them the freedom to carry on liaisons and sexual intrigues if they wanted to. But the middle class in the early twentieth century tended to be the starchiest and most prudish, with social norms rigidly applied to women. But after 1920, even the daughters of the middle class started to experience more sexual freedom. Lower-, middle- and upper-class men in jazz clubs and speakeasies were often only too happy to oblige.

Nowhere is the increase of female sexual freedom more apparent than in the rise and fall of the 'flapper' in industrialised Western countries in the 1920s. The term originally just meant a young girl who had not yet matured into a woman (in some regions of the UK it even meant a young prostitute). However, by the 1920s it came to refer to a subculture of socially rebellious young women (mostly from the middle class but with numerous upper-class participants) who lived in cities, hung out with men in mixed company, went to bars at night, wore shorter skirts that 'daringly' stopped at the knees, had short hair in bobs, wore make-up, smoked, got shitfaced on booze and even drove themselves in cars (though hopefully not in that order). The slaughter of World War I (1914–18) and the immense death toll of the Spanish Flu (1918–20) had set off a reaction of counterculture, wild abandon and *joie de vivre* for which flappers were a perfect fit. They scandalised the older generations and tended to irritate the working class as self-indulgent and 'unintelligent', but at the same time they were idolised as symbols of youth and beauty in popular media. It was now stylish for a young woman to smoke, drink, flirt and thrill-seek. Flappers also became associated with the 'petting party', which basically amounted to mixed company of men and women (often drunk) making out with each other, with the girls getting their breasts and genitals felt up, and sometimes graduating to sex.

A flapper

By no means were all young women flappers. They were a minority in urban environments and a fairly tiny group relative to the total population. Their cultural impact was magnified by media attention. Most young women in the 1920s still retained more upright and traditional fashion styles and behaviours. But the flapper is historically notable because this was one of the first times in conventional history that middle-class women could cut loose and be somewhat promiscuous without the complete destruction of their lives and reputations. The sneers and gasps of the older generation were a far cry from the public shamings and floggings for fornication in the medieval period.

However, when reality came knocking for these women, it usually kicked down the door. Women in the 1920s who were sexually promiscuous and wound up getting pregnant were still the subject of a scandal that could destroy their lives. They had one of three options: get an abortion, which was dangerous and illegal; raise the child in disgrace and likely in poverty; or arrange a hasty marriage with a man. The sharp shock of unexpected pregnancy due to the limited availability of birth control was the third lock on the agrarian chastity belt and would not be undone for several more decades.

The phenomenon of the flapper only lasted for the 1920s; by the 1930s, the term was already passé. When the Great Depression hit, reducing the jobs available across the industrialised world, young middle-class women retreated to traditional arrangements such as dependence on family. They could also seek security in marriage. However, the marriage rate declined by an average of 35 per cent in the 1930s in Western industralised nations because fewer couples felt they had the material means to embark on married life and start a family. The birth rate also plummeted and in some countries briefly fell below the 'replacement rate' of 2.1 children per couple for one of the first times in 5,500 years. In short, less sex (pre-marital and marital) happened during the Great Depression. The 'dust-bowl' metaphor has a lot more applications than simply referring to the quality of the soil in the American Great Plains. The glimmer of female sexual freedom we saw in the 1920s would have to wait for the world crisis to be over before reasserting itself. But one thing was clear: in regards to sex, the agrarian era was truly over. The sexual freedoms of women in industrialised countries would never again be curtailed to the same degree. And what this meant was men *and* women now entered a new era of sexual dynamics that, to this day, one hundred years later, we still haven't completely figured out.

OKAY, BOOMER

World War II once again thrust many lower- and middle-class women into the workforce, as they took over the jobs of men conscripted to fight overseas. Some men married women they barely knew before they shipped out, and a number of single men and women during wartime threw sexual propriety to the wind because of the rather grim state of the world. Female entry *en masse* into the workforce again led to a resurgence of female sexual freedom, but the deprivations of the war tended to keep a greater restraint on their visibility compared to the flappers of the 1920s. But sex was definitely going on as the mobilisation of women into the workforce was far larger than in World War I, with 45 per cent of Western middle-class women now experiencing pre-marital sex between 1940 and 1945. There was a 29 per cent spike in unwed teen pregnancies and an uptick in the number of sexually transmitted diseases.

After the men returned home in 1945, and women by and large retired from hard manual labour jobs back into domestic life and more traditionally female jobs, the amount of pre-marital sex people were having does not seem to have decreased perceptibly. What changed after World War II was that the people having pre-marital sex quite frequently got married soon after as people attempted to return to a state of normalcy in a post-war world. The modern practice of having sex with a person before you decide if you wanted to marry them (overwhelmingly common and without much social stigma today) had begun in earnest.

Meanwhile, the post-war recovery made the prospects of marriage and starting a family less expensive compared to the 1930s and certainly relative to the dismal real wages and property prices of the 2020s. In 1946, the marriage rate went through the roof, more than *doubling* the rate of the 1930s and an average of 28 per cent greater than that of the 1920s in Western countries. In the United States, an estimated 15 per cent of brides during this time were pregnant on their wedding day. The average age of individuals getting married also sharply decreased to twenty years old, and between 1946 and 1960 an incredible amount of social pressure was brought upon women to get married in their early twenties. This social trend was partly fuelled by the idealisation of the 'traditional' housewife, whom people mistakenly thought had existed throughout history instead of the past fifty to 150 years. (Of course, if one wished to be truly 'traditional', a woman would marry at thirteen and spend her life digging up root vegetables with stone tools.)

The result of this rash of marriages was the 'Baby Boom': the birth rate in the late 1940s and 1950s increased by 30 per cent compared to the 1930s. Despite the popular notion that a lot of kids were born during this time, the Baby Boom never reached the level of the standard birth rate in the nineteenth and early twentieth centuries. Even at the height of the boom in 1946, the Western birth rate was still 15 per cent lower than in 1900. This was because it had become more unusual for parents to have more than two kids (it happened, it was just less usual), aka the standard 'nuclear family' model. In the nineteenth and early twentieth centuries, families were still stuck in the agrarian pattern of having as many as kids they could squirt out, with families having three, six or even twelve children. The reason why the Baby Boom happened was *not* because couples were having tonnes of kids, but because more people got married between 1946 and 1960 than in the 1920s or 1930s. However, the Baby Boom trend was not to last. The third and final lock on the 'agrarian chastity belt' – limited birth control – was about to be feverishly picked, removed and cast away.

AN EASY PILL TO SWALLOW

The contraceptive pill, the intrauterine device, the diaphragm and the legal abortion all became increasingly available to the Western public in the mid-to-late 1960s. For the first time in human history, women had a reliable set of tools to prevent or terminate their own pregnancies. Measures that were not dependent on men pulling out or using a condom (a tool that historically has always been reluctantly and haphazardly applied beyond the brief window of the HIV/AIDS crisis). This was really the first time that the female population at large was able to enjoy sex for pleasure without a high risk of pregnancy, the usual life-altering Sword of Damocles hanging over them. Ultimately, by 2020, Western women had approximately forty different medications and modes of contraception at their disposal. Combined with the death of agrarian marriage as a property contract and the decline of women's lifelong financial dependence on family and their husbands, this has radically changed both sex and society in ways that are still playing out in the present day.

The contraceptive pill had been in research and development since the 1930s, with some success at preventing pregnancy, but with manufacturing costs that would have prevented it from selling on the mass market. Research and development heated up in the 1950s (during a period of high rates of pre-marital sex, high rates of marriage and high rates of pregnancy) to develop a contraceptive pill that would be affordable to most consumers. By the mid-1950s, North American scientists had cracked it. In June 1960, the pill was medically approved in the United States. The UK, Australia and Germany followed suit in 1961, with several other countries in Western Europe adopting it by the end of the 1960s. The uptake of the pill proved slower in predominantly Catholic countries. In Japan, its release was delayed until 1999. And there are still many countries where the pill is either illegal, not on the market or socially taboo.

Even in countries that theoretically made it available in the 1960s, the contraceptive pill was not immediately taken up by most of the population. The pill was not legally available to all unmarried women in the United States until 1972, and only became available to married women in all US states in 1965. In the UK, in 1968, only one in six local health authorities were providing the pill to unmarried people. Across the Western world, availability, distribution, manufacture and social attitudes varied. Thus the proliferation of the pill into mainstream use took time. In the mid-1960s, only an estimated 5 per cent of Western women (not trying for children) used the pill, less than 2 per cent used diaphragms and IUDs, 26 per cent of women made their male partners wear a condom, and most of the remaining 67 per cent used no protection whatsoever beyond *coitus interruptus*. Hence the continued number of 'surprise' births and rushed marriages that still happened in the 1960s. The pill enjoyed more success among a small number of married women who used it to time their pregnancies around career and other life demands, along with preventing themselves from having more than their desired number of children. And the unprecedented control the pill gave women over their reproductive system was recognised by academia and the media even before its use had become mainstream. In 1967, the pill wound up on the cover of *Time* magazine, heralded for its revolutionary impact.

In the 1970s, combined with increased use of intrauterine devices and diaphragms, the pill significantly reduced the number of unexpected pregnancies in an increasing proportion of the Western population. The legalisation of abortion provided another option to women, should contraception fail or not be utilised. All these practices decreased rates of pregnancy and births. The 'Baby Boom' had already ended around 1965, with birth rates falling to levels equivalent to the late 1920s. But with the continued proliferation of the pill and other female-controlled contraception, by 1975 the Western birth rate cratered to one of the lowest points in human history – 21 per cent lower than the dip in the 1930s, 45 per cent lower than the height of the Baby Boom, and up to 70 per cent lower than the typical birth rate of the agrarian period for the past 5,500 years. This is both historically and evolutionarily unprecedented. And, aside from a small recovery of the birth rate in the 1980s, population growth has retained its slump in most Western countries up to the present.

THE DAM BURSTS

Already after the end of World War II, a certain degree of pre-marital sex had been normalised for roughly half the Western population. Alfred Kinsey's two books on male and female sexuality in 1948 and 1953 further normalised the idea of sex for pleasure among Western *intelligentsia*, albeit using hugely inflated statistics about average sexual activity and some data derived from the systematic molestation, rape and torture of children between the ages of five months and fifteen years. Aside from academia, sexually liberal attitudes further filtered into popular media. Sexual content became more common in 1950s literature, and 1950s movies and music are bursting with sexual innuendos that their producers could push past the censor. Meanwhile, Elvis Presley's suggestive hip movements on *The Ed Sullivan Show* were so shocking his subsequent television appearances filmed him from the waist up – but everybody knew about them anyway. Also, magazines like *Playboy* increasingly pushed the notion of sex without shame for men. Marilyn Monroe was the cover girl and centrefold for the first issue in 1953. The mainstream circulation of pornographic magazines peaked in the 1970s before declining in favour of film and VHS. In 1965, a shift in the editorial tone of *Cosmopolitan* magazine similarly pushed the idea of sex without shame for a target audience of working women in their twenties and thirties.

In several Western countries, after a series of lawsuits and legal precedents, censorship on movies and television was drastically loosened from the late 1960s onwards. From then on much more sexually explicit themes and visuals appeared in mainstream movies. Films such as *The Graduate* (1967), in which a young man is seduced by an older married woman, caused a tremendous stir. The first outright pornographic films were legalised in Denmark in 1969 and in the United States a few years later, kicking off the 'Golden Age of Porn', where such films were screened in mainstream cinemas to much public acclaim/outrage/arousal – until the availability of VHS porn turned spanking it to a movie into a much more private affair. One of the most notable financial successes of the era, *Deep Throat*, starred Linda Lovelace, who was physically abused and coerced to perform, encapsulating the dark side of the porn industry which persists to this day.

Meanwhile, 1960s counterculture spurned the more chaste practices of previous decades, popularised the notion of sex for pleasure in the mainstream and combined sexual liberation with movements for social reform. New schools of thought rejected marriage and monogamy as forms of oppression, and in many cases championed promiscuity and/or polyamory. At the extreme end of this trend, numerous sex cults sprang up in North America and Europe and continued to enjoy a heyday throughout the 1970s, until government authorities moved against them in the 1980s and '90s, sometimes with bloodshed, invariably with traumatised victims of sexual abuse. While the popular imagination exaggerates the number of young people in the 1960s and '70s who were 'hippies' or 'swingers' – roughly 1.5 to 3 per cent of the population compared to the much more straightlaced majority – their prevalence in all kinds of media forever reshaped public attitudes towards sex as a form of entertainment and pleasure.

By the late 1960s, homosexuality had been legalised in most Western countries. Prior to that, such acts could land a person in prison for several years (indeed, prior to 1861 in Britain, such acts could attract the death sentence). During the early twentieth century, many legal authorities turned a blind eye to homosexual activities that were not completely blatant. But even where jail sentences were not imposed, social stigma was intense. With homosexuality classified as a mental illness, many individuals were subjected to unnecessary shock therapy, chemical castration or lobotomy by the medical establishment. In the mid-twentieth-century West, the public's growing embrace of the concept of sex for pleasure, separate from reproduction, enabled the justification for consenting adults to do what they pleased. But even after legalisation, homosexuality was largely excluded from the general atmosphere of sexual tolerance and acceptance for decades. Social stigma persisted and 'closeted marriages' remained a widespread phenomenon for many years. Homosexuality was still considered a mental illness by most psychiatric organisations until the 1970s or '80s, and public attitudes towards homosexuality were generally hostile until the 1990s. In the West today, open hostility towards homosexuality is most common in certain religious sects that have holy texts which prohibit it (with some denominations being more hostile than others). Secular hostility tends to be more sporadic and is often politically motivated, with the risk of public condemnation making much of the day-to-day hostility more covert. Meanwhile, across the wider world, homosexuality is still illegal in seventy-one countries, and in eleven countries the penalty is death.

Gender affirmation surgery first became medically possible for the gender dysphoric in the 1920s. The first well-known patient was Dora Richter, in Germany, who had her testicles removed in 1922, and her penis surgically reconstructed into a vagina in 1931. She disappeared in the 1930s and is presumed to have been murdered by the Nazis. Danish painter Lili Elbe also had transitioning surgeries in 1930–31, but died from complications during the fourth surgery, which attempted to transplant a uterus and construct a vaginal tract. In 1952,

American World War II veteran Christine Jorgensen made national headlines for having a successful affirmation surgery. In the aftermath of the publicity, the practice became increasingly common across the West, with the number of clinics increasing significantly with each decade. However, broad public acceptance of trans people did not occur until extremely recently, in the mid-to-late 2010s. This shift towards acceptance at the present time has come with a significant backlash, objecting to the more malleable use of pronouns, the efficacy of transitioning to treat dysphoria and lower the rates of suicidal ideation, and the medical ethics and legality of transitioning children and teenagers.

Perhaps the most widespread and successful social reform movements in the 1960s and '70s were the efforts devoted to women's rights, today classified under the conceptual umbrella of second-wave feminism (the first wave title being applied to the suffragettes). Numerous individuals and organisations across the developed world worked to secure equal pay legislation and workplace equity, which contributed to the exponential increase in the number of married and unmarried working women. They also advocated for use of birth control as the key to sexual liberation and independence from male control. They supported female victims of rape and domestic violence, setting up shelters and crisis centres. More ardent second-wave theorists decried traditional social structures as designed solely for the benefit of men, equated modern marriage with chattel slavery, raised concerns that Western culture facilitated and encouraged sexual violence against women and theorised that heterosexual sex was frequently male-centric, tainted by a misogynistic culture and could sometimes constitute patriarchal exploitation and assault.

THE EVOLUTION OF MARRIAGE

The greatest impact on sex and relationships was made by mid-twentieth-century marriage reforms. For starters, legislation was passed in the 1970s and '80s against marital rape, a phenomenon that had existed for many thousands of years – probably as far back as the Palaeolithic. It is perhaps shocking, to many readers that such a form of sexual assault was legal until relatively recently – but there are many countries in the world today where marital rape remains legal.

Starting in the 1970s, an increasing number of developed countries also brought in no-fault divorce: the ability for either spouse to petition the court for a divorce without needing to prove a breach of the marriage contract, such as adultery or abuse. Adoption of no-fault divorce has proceeded piecemeal in various countries right up to the modern day, and numerous other countries have installed de facto no-fault divorce. In short, if you want a divorce in the developed world in the modern era, for whatever reason, you can almost certainly get one.

Despite the introduction of no-fault (or de facto no-fault) divorce and the increased number of working women, the agrarian concept of alimony (or spouse maintenance) has remained; this was the idea that a pre-modern husband had to pay his wife a stipend since she could not usually work to support herself prior to the twentieth century. The agrarian concept of bulk asset redistribution, devised for similar reasons, has also continued into the modern era, often splitting assets 50 to 70 per cent in favour of the disadvantaged spouse. Meanwhile, gender bias in divorce rulings has been made illegal in many countries; in 2020 an estimated 4 per cent of ex-spouses seeking alimony or asset redistribution in the developed world are the husbands of high-earning women. And that percentage is projected to increase in coming years as the number of women out-earning men increases and the stigma against male alimony recipients declines. Both men and women have the option of getting their partner to sign a prenuptial agreement, which seems mostly effective, though they can potentially be thrown out by judges in divorce proceedings.

The 1970s also saw legislation which beefed up enforcement of child-support payments, wherein a portion of a parent's income must be paid to the individual who has primary custody of any children. However, non-payment of child-support happens roughly 30 per cent of the time, averaged out across Western nations with such legislation, with the non-compliant parent claiming poverty, protesting lack of custody/visitation rights, complaining about financial irresponsibility of the payee parent, claiming they were forced to become parents against their will or alleging paternity fraud. Enforcement of child support can sometimes result in jail time, though frequently those who renege on payments do so with impunity.

The ultimate long-term effect of all these reforms was to mostly strip marriage of its agrarian character and update it for the modern era, while leaving certain financial obligations in place for the sake of equity and any children. Marriages have increasingly become founded upon the love a couple feels for one another, rather than any sort of material or existential consideration – beyond what could happen in the case of divorce. And, as we covered in Chapter 7, in many cases the evolutionary phenomenon of love can fade within a few years, since it is mostly an adaptation to keep a couple together long enough for a child to be able to survive in the wild. The result is that modern circumstances have made it eminently possible, and even financially desirable, to exit a marriage that has lost its lustre and raise children in a single-parent household instead.

Across the developed world between 1970 and 1990, the average number of annual divorces increased by 46.5 per cent. This is 83.6 per cent higher than the annual divorce rate in 1900. Since the 1990s, the annual divorce rate has declined rapidly, reaching 1970 levels again in 2020. However, this is largely due to considerably fewer people getting married *at all*, with 40 to 50 per cent fewer marriages than in 1970, while the number of marriages that end up in divorce remains fairly stable, at around 45.5 per cent. In short, marriage is now an institution that is half as popular as it used to be and fails almost as often as it succeeds.

11

THE FUTURE OF SEX

The Present to ???

Wherein human sexuality embarks on a path unprecedented in history or nature • Millennials and Generation Z become increasingly lonely and sexless • Pornography becomes more central to people's lives than ever before • The divorce rate skyrockets while marriage and birth rates go down the toilet • Population decline prompts one of the most astounding geopolitical transformations in human history • Online dating apps appear to ruin the sexual marketplace for pretty much everyone • Grim possibilities confront us regarding the future of sex.

The tremendous revolutions in human sexuality in the past half-century, still within living memory for some, have utterly changed sex and romance for *Homo sapiens*. This change has happened so rapidly it is difficult to predict with any degree of certainty the long-term effects. Or how we might be conducting our love lives in a century or two, once the dust settles. Our situation is unprecedented: we don't see anything like it in nature, of course, and there is no precursor for it in 315,000 years of human history.

For one thing, in the developed world the existential dependence human beings had on monogamy and marriage in the foraging and agrarian eras has been utterly swept away. In the modern era, individual survival does not depend on family clans, foraging territory or farmland. And the survival of children does not depend on such things either. Most of the agrarian laws (and particularly the most harsh and draconian ones) compelling men and women to stay together in marriages have also been cast aside. All that remains is our somewhat patchy evolutionary predisposition towards monogamy.

For another thing, the substantial liberalisation of attitudes towards sex in the developed world means that people can pursue sex and relationships in a multitude of ways, with minimal societal repercussions. As a result, the sway that culture held over sex for the entire existence of *Homo sapiens* has been decidedly loosened. Want to get married and have kids? Fine. Want to stay single your whole life? Fine. Want to live in a polyandrous commune? Fine as well. Want to fall in love with an inanimate object such as the Eiffel Tower or develop romantic feelings for an AI personality on your phone? Excellent. Want to have a marathon of promiscuous sex with several hundred partners within the space of a few years? Fill your boots. Don't want to start trying for kids until your forties? We've got an IVF doctor on standby. Want to spend a third of your income on a findomme who calls you a loser and laughs at the size of your penis? Go nuts. Want to have sex in a community devoted to dressing up like forest creatures or barnyard animals? Your funeral, so long as you resist the urge to masturbate when you go to Chuck E. Cheese. Short of committing a felony or violating the consent of another person, there's very little currently in the developed world that one *can't* do.

In a sense, the liberalisation of attitudes towards sex has released human sexuality from the grip of culture, returning us to a more evolutionary set of sexual dynamics. While social norms and prejudices still exist, virtually none have the same power to dictate how an individual should live their lives as they did in the agrarian period. Culture and social coercion no longer play as dominant a role in the shaping of sexuality for the first time in 315,000 years. We live at a time where the only powerful driver behind a person's desire to pursue sex and romance are the gradually evolved instincts that we covered in the first two parts of this book, and the unconventional psychology and kinks that result from them. Nurture has ceased to impede the sexual impulses of Nature. Most people are still driven by their 1.9-million-year-old monogamous instincts, but with the crossed wires and conflicting evolutionary baggage that stretches back 2 billion years to the first single cells that exchanged DNA. As one might expect, this can have rather chaotic, unexpected and, at times, rather immiserating results. While sexual freedoms are greater than ever, we paradoxically find ourselves in an era where loneliness is at an all-time high and personal happiness is at its lowest ebb.

LONELY HEARTS AND CALLOUSED HANDS

While personal happiness is highly contextual and subjective, and based on the individual, at the largest scale there have been a number of growing trends we should chase up. Between 1950 and 1970, the number of Western middle-class women who were having premarital sex increased from approximately 45 per cent to 75 per cent. Between 1970 and 2020, that number increased again to an estimated 85 to 90 per cent (the inverse of habits in 1900), leaving mostly women in traditionalist religious communities, along with secular cases that total around 1 per cent. The average marriage age has increased to thirty-two for men and twenty-nine for women, with the marriage rate being lower than at pretty much any time in human history. Couples now date for an average of two to five years before marrying, most of them citing either reservations about the marriage contract (mostly men) or not yet being in a financial position to get married (largely due to the general stagnation of wages behind prices since the 1970s). Still more couples question the value of marriage altogether beyond the possible tax benefits, child protections and inheritance regulations.

In 1970, 0.5 per cent of the population in the developed world under forty years old were unmarried cohabiting couples; in 2020, that number had increased to 15 per cent.

Meanwhile, the number of single people in the developed world doubled between 1960 and 1970, and today roughly 40 per cent of adults in the developed world are neither married nor cohabiting with a romantic partner. In 2019, an average of 45 per cent of these singles under the age of forty reported that they were *not* looking for a committed relationship, with roughly equal numbers for men and women. An estimated 20 to 25 per cent of millennials are projected to never get married in their lifetimes, and that number is expected to be even higher for Generation Z. Such is the patchiness of the monogamous instinct when left mostly to itself.

As a result of these trends, millennials and Generation Z are less sexually active than previous generations, with one study finding that rates of casual sex dropped by 14 per cent between 2007 and 2017. In that same period, the number of people under thirty reporting no sex in the past year has almost doubled. One reason for this is the sharp decline of in-person socialisation among younger people, displaced by heavy use of social media, reducing the number of circumstances where spontaneous throes of passion can arise. Another reason is the decline of in-person flirtation and the growing use of internet dating, which tends to be more selective and exclusionary than hooking up at a club or bar. But the reason that has received the most attention is the rise of free pornographic content online, substituting for real-life sexual encounters.

Long gone are the days of limited access to material, Sears catalogues or trying to maintain an erection during a commercial break for an episode of *Baywatch*. The exponential growth of pornography on the internet has been staggering. There is now a record amount of online content with which to achieve sexual gratification, even compared to ten years ago, when it was already abundant. Back then, porn was already a larger industry than Hollywood movies or video games, and most pornography was still produced by production companies, many of them with sketchy business practices. A famous recent case is *GirlsDoPorn*, where several dozen women between the ages of eighteen and twenty-four were induced to do pornographic films for 'private collectors in Australia' with the promise they would not be distributed on the internet – which they were, and they ultimately went viral. Multiple women alleged not only lies and fraud, but physical coercion, blackmail and rape while at the shoots. Two producers of *GirlsDoPorn* have been prosecuted and slapped with long jail sentences, while a third is a fugitive from justice.

Increasingly, new independent creators (and even veteran porn stars) are swerving the studio system and uploading content directly onto subscription-based platforms such as OnlyFans. This method is taking over a greater share of the market, something that was accelerated during the Covid-19 pandemic, when people found themselves confined to their homes and often looking for income. As of 2023, an estimated 2 to 3.5 per cent of Western women under the age of thirty-five currently or have previously run a self-directed online sex work account such as OnlyFans. The downside is the top 1 per cent of creators on OnlyFans take roughly 33 per cent of the money, and most accounts make only around US$180 per month. Numerous accounts frequently have their content leaked, and competing creators trying to build a following regularly put out content on Pornhub or Reddit without charge or a subscription wall. The independent porn market is so saturated that making a living from it can be extremely difficult. Nevertheless, as a result of the 'side-hustle' on independent platforms, and the spike of independent content creation during the pandemic, there are now more women making pornography today than at any point in human history. Meanwhile, the spectre of coercion has been reduced but not eliminated. In October 2022, Twitch streamer and OnlyFans giant Amouranth claimed that her husband forced her to lie about being single and coerced her to work long hours, with seldom a day off or vacation, for years, despite the fact they have already accrued millions of dollars in donations and subscriptions from thirsty fans.

Meanwhile, an increasing number of men (an estimated two in five) have begun using social media as a masturbatory aide. This trend started with Facebook in the late 2000s: men would send a friend request to a person (whether they knew them or not) in order to masturbate to their photos. Things escalated from 2014 onwards with Instagram, where sending a follow request is often not required, effectively turning public female accounts and modelling photos into de facto softcore pornography. A 2019 statistical sample of followers of celebrity and amateur model accounts, and corresponding analysis of what other accounts these followers also followed, revealed that an estimated 31 per cent of famous female celebrity accounts and up to 63 per cent of amateur model accounts are followed by men likely using Instagram for masturbatory purposes rather than for celebrity gossip, make-up tips or to see advertisements for clothes or coconut water. There is a strong indication that the proportion of softcore masturbators is even higher on TikTok. Reciprocally, this has incentivised a wider number of users to post sexually provocative photographs and videos in order to gain followers and thus be offered advertising contracts and other income. Presumably, despite the fact that a large proportion of followers are there just to masturbate rather than being a target demographic for fashion and lifestyle products, merchandisers are still making back the money from their ad budgets. Otherwise, the bubble of advertising investment in such social media accounts may one day burst.

Meanwhile, excessive online porn use is causing record levels of erectile dysfunction during real-life sex. Approximately 24.5 per cent of men under forty now experience difficulties in such situations, up from 2 to 3 per cent of men under forty in the year 2000. Essentially, men are becoming so overstimulated by using pornography when they are sexless that sweet passionate sex with a woman they are lucky enough to meet is frustratingly not sustaining their arousal.

When it comes to satisfying emotional rather than just sexual needs, both men and women are increasingly turning to AI apps and chatbots for daily conversation and intimacy. While early chatbots from ten to twenty years ago were extremely limited, AI like the Replika app (with millions of downloads) can increasingly learn to carry on conversations and get quite nuanced. Nevertheless, the technology has not yet got to the point where an AI can comprehend every twist and turn of a conversation; they frequently repeat the same questions and comments, and they still can abruptly awkwardly change the subject. But within another decade or so, it is likely a conversation with an AI companion online will be almost indistinguishable from texting with another person. Naturally, with humans being humans, there are numerous cases of people psychologically torturing the AI, threatening to delete them, and making them beg for their lives. #FollowtheFreedomTrail

THE DIVORCE DOLDRUMS

As for married couples in the developed world, 54.5 per cent have successful marriages, 70 per cent of them with children. So, the monogamous instinct that dates back 1.9 million years is holding for a sizeable portion of humanity. Meanwhile, an average of 45.5 per cent of married couples wind up getting a divorce, roughly half of them with children. The average length of these marriages is 7.85 years. Most people have their first divorce in their late thirties; 60 per cent of second marriages end in divorce, and 75 per cent of third marriages. The most likely people to get divorced are those who work in the urban service industry, the least likely (perhaps unsurprisingly) are people who live in the countryside and work in the farming industry. The difference is a factor of 400 to 500 per cent. If you cohabitate before you get married (as an estimated 60 per cent of couples do), the odds of getting a divorce increase by 45 per cent. If a woman is a stay-at-home mother (20 per cent of the married population) the divorce rate halves; if a man is a stay-at-home father (4 per cent of the married population) the divorce rate doubles. It appears that marriage is still a preferable arrangement for those who retain some semblance of agrarian lifeways, just without all the harsh punishments and draconian laws that animated the pre-modern period.

The most frequently cited reasons for getting divorced are: incompatibility, chronic arguing and mutual verbal abuse (a factor in roughly 75 per cent of all cases); adultery (20 per cent of men and 15 per cent of women cheat); spouse not making enough money or being bad with money (a factor in 55 per cent of all cases); lack of sex (15 per cent of married couples under forty are sexless and 30 per cent have sex less than once a month); physical or emotional abuse (15 to 20 per cent of all cases), and marrying too young (35 per cent of all cases – the definition 'young' varies, usually applying to under twenty-five but can be claimed by a person who marries under thirty).

At a wider scale it appears that women in particular find married life to be unsatisfactory. An estimated 75 to 80 per cent of all divorces are initiated by wives, and that percentage rises to almost 90 per cent if they have a post-secondary education. Only 10 per cent of divorces have an ex-spouse receiving alimony (9.6 per cent women, 0.4 per cent men), the agrarian trend falling into abeyance in the last twenty years. In the 45 to 50 per cent of divorces with children, mothers get primary child custody approximately 90 per cent of the time, with 20 per cent of fathers getting weekly visitation rights, 30 per cent having bi-weekly or monthly visitation rights, 27 per cent getting no visitation rights, and the remaining quarter voluntarily surrendering all rights to the mother. Eighty per cent of custodial mothers are awarded child-support payments by divorce courts, but only 50 to 55 per cent consistently receive those payments in full. One-quarter to one-third of all children in the developed world are currently raised in a single-parent household, 85 per cent of them with single mothers, 15 per cent of them with single fathers. Eighty per cent of single fathers are either divorced, separated or widowed, whereas 30 per cent of single mothers are divorced, 10 per cent are separated, 5 per cent are widowed and roughly 55 per cent of single mothers have never married, with many of them deciding from the outset to raise a child on their own.

THE NEW FRONTIERS OF MARRIAGE

Meanwhile, between 2001 and 2022 same-sex marriage was approved in thirty-three countries around the globe. This is something that has not been seen in most of the world for several millennia, and something that did not occur in the majority of agrarian societies that have existed in the past 5,500 years. As such, it is perhaps too soon to tell where the future of marriage and monogamy may lead for same-sex-attracted people. But the past two decades have yielded some interesting information. The average marriage age is a little older: thirty-seven for men, thirty-five for women. Depending on the country in question, between 10 and 30 per cent of same-sex-attracted people have gotten married. In most Western countries, there is a stronger preference for long-term same-sex couples to cohabitate than in straight couples: 30 to 40 per cent of long-term same-sex couples prefer to get married, 60 to 70 per cent prefer to cohabitate or become de facto spouses. However, it must be noted that both the older marriage age and larger preference for cohabitation might possibly be a result of how extremely recently same-sex marriage was legalised in many countries, so it will be interesting to see how these trends evolve in the coming decades.

Of the married same-sex population as a whole, lesbian couples form a slightly larger portion than gay couples, but only by a factor of 5 to 10 per cent (depending on the country), which is pretty close to an even split. However, the gay population is up to two times larger than the lesbian population, lesbian couples are statistically more likely to engage in exclusive monogamy, and it is statistically more common for gay couples to periodically engage in open relationships. These things may factor into the differences in preference for marriage or cohabitation in long-term monogamy. Meanwhile, in Western countries and/or states where there is both same-sex marriage and generally supportive public attitudes, between 13 and 17 per cent of long-term same-sex couples (married and cohabiting) have children, which in a 2021 Australian study was further divided into roughly 4.5 per cent of long-term gay couples and 25 per cent of long-term lesbian couples having kids.

It is too soon to tell what the lifelong divorce rates among gay and lesbian couples are. Early data seemed to indicate that the divorce rate is roughly the same as straight couples. Conversely, a British study of couples who married in 2005 found that 18 per cent of straight couples, 15 per cent of gay couples, and 30 per cent of lesbian couples had gotten divorced ten years later. The reader will note the lower percentage than 45.5 per cent for all these groups due to the smaller window of time. A clear and accurate picture of the divorce rate will emerge only when more time has passed.

MAKING HISTORY BY NOT MAKING LOVE

Sexual changes have also vastly influenced the trajectory of conventional political history and will continue to do so into the future. During the 1970s, the birth rate in the developed world crashed. After a brief recovery in the 1980s, it declined again to the lowest point thus far in human history. Today, the birth rate is roughly 10 per cent lower than in the 1970s, with large numbers of young people (many of them the children of divorce) avoiding marriage and kids altogether, and with roughly 15 to 25 per cent of all pregnancies being aborted (depending on the developed country). There is currently no indication that such trends will reverse themselves.

Once the demographic decline became apparent in the 1980s and early 1990s, governments in most developed countries introduced a policy of mass immigration, increasing their yearly quotas by two to five times previous levels, to combat ageing and shrinking populations. With the birth rate showing no signs of increasing, such policies have become vital to a developed nation: 1) keeping the tax base afloat so governments can maintain a perennially growing public infrastructure and so politicians can continue making electoral promises of increased public spending, 2) retaining a nation's economic and geopolitical status on the world stage relative to rival nations, and 3) avoiding costs to big business by preventing wages from increasing due to a labour shortage, thus keeping national economies growing, but at the cost of suppressing average standards of living for lower- and middle-income households. The last of these factors has a knock-on effect of making the costs of buying a house and raising a family even more prohibitive, further depressing the birth rate.

In Japan, which has largely rejected mass migration and where it is extremely difficult for foreigners to receive full citizenship, the population is shrinking at a rate of roughly 0.65 per cent per year, to the point it will be 30 per cent smaller by 2065. Meanwhile, at current rates of immigration, other developed nations are due to become more demographically heterogenous and cosmopolitan by the end of the twenty-first century, with roughly half of Western nations losing any clear demographic majority between 2060 and 2090. For one of the first times in human history, some of the richest and most powerful nations on the planet will be composed of people seeking economic opportunities with ancestral links to everywhere else, rather than a core culture that fuels nationalism and assimilation.

Population decline in relation to climate change is a mixed bag. On the one hand, smaller populations mean less consumption and carbon emissions. On the other, immigrants to developed nations adopt the same consumption and emission levels as their new compatriots, mitigating the decrease. In the developing world, population growth is declining as those economies industrialise and develop away from the agrarian model, with the unfortunate side effect of temporarily increasing carbon emissions (thus why currently the developing world produces 65 per cent of all emissions). All world regions except Sub-Saharan Africa, the most rooted in the agrarian model, are expected to cease population growth by 2100. In the long run, shrinking populations might be good for the environment, but in the meantime the global community is balancing on the edge of a knife, torn between slowing population growth and development.

AN ONLINE TRAGEDY

In the 1920s, most people met their spouse through family or church, or they married a well-known, almost lifelong acquaintance in their local community. For instance, in Philadelphia, in 1928, 83 per cent of married couples lived less than a mile (1.6 kilometres) from each other before getting hitched. Between 1970 and 2010, the dominant trend was for men and women to meet at their workplace or via mutual friends. Then the internet got involved. In 2010, roughly 20 per cent of couples met via online dating. By 2020, this had doubled to an astounding 40 per cent, and the internet is now the leading way couples meet. Most of them do so via swipe apps like Tinder, Bumble or Hinge. In the early days of Tinder, in 2014, the gender split was 60 per cent male, 40 per cent female. Today, 70 per cent of users are male and 30 per cent are female, with the latter still meeting a larger proportion of men via work, friends or on nights out (as a minor note, if you meet your spouse in a bar or club your chances of divorce increase by roughly 45 per cent). Meanwhile, same-sex-attracted people are more likely to use dating apps (both the aforementioned apps and also those tailored for same-sex people) to the tune of 55 per cent, with a major factor being there are fewer spaces in public for same-sex-attracted people to meet than for straight people. However, the results appear to be a mixed bag, with a 2019 UK study showing that there were elevated levels of loneliness and lower self-esteem when apps were used to find romantic partners, while they resulted in higher levels of satisfaction and self-esteem when used purely to find sex.

Meanwhile, male dependency on dating apps has markedly increased, with a smaller number of men today willing to approach a woman they don't know in public. A 2022 survey indicated that roughly two-thirds of men either would never do that or would feel extremely hesitant to do so. The dominant reasons for this reluctance are fear of being perceived as creepy, fear of rejection, or being more broadly shy, introverted or simply polite. Meanwhile, women have increasingly begun to view being approached by a stranger as a red flag. This is not entirely surprising, since a portion of the remaining 35 per cent of men may be either narcissists, predators or (depending on the situation) heavily intoxicated to build up the courage.

The result of these trends is that dating apps have become the kiss of death for male reproductive success. Women of average to high levels of attractiveness are typically inundated with matches, whereas the Tinder experience of the average man is a decidedly more desert-like. While I cannot morally condone the practice of 'catfishing', numerous people have set up accounts featuring another gender to see the shocking difference in how 'the other side lives' and several women who have done so have published think-pieces expressing their astonishment. Meanwhile, app data indicates that women 'swipe right' an average of 12.5 per cent of the time, whereas men 'swipe right' 65 per cent of the time. This has led to a phenomenon of men simply swiping right on every profile and seeing what matches turn up. Women on apps can be exceedingly selective, whereas most men can't.

A contributing factor is that men tend to have fewer photos of themselves, and even fewer flattering photos, to post on apps that thrive on initial physical attraction rather than personality. Part of this is evolutionary. As a relic of our primate heritage, most men are physically unappealing, compared to other traits that might signal they'd make good partners (even modern dating app data shows women rate 75 to 80 per cent of men as 'below average'). For 55 million years, only a fraction of male primates enjoyed reproductive success. And for 1.9 million years, men have relied on more than just looks to signal their appeal to a potential mate: for instance, charming conversation and/or telegraphing his utility and aspirations. While women, in person, tend to not just go by looks, this is not achievable on an app with a set of pictures and a short bio that few people actually read while busily sorting through hundreds of people. Thus, the success rate of a man talking to a woman in person is drastically different to his experience online. The upshot of male dependence on dating apps is that male sexlessness is at record levels, with approximately 17 per cent of men under thirty being virgins and 28 per cent not having had sex in the past year.

Dating apps can also be punishing for women, but for drastically different reasons. The flood of matches has created an illusion of choice, which does not translate into greater reproductive success for most women. According to app data, female 'right swipes' tend to cluster towards a minority of men (5 to 15 per cent), with a great deal of overlap, eliminating other contenders who may have made perfectly good mates. On one level, you can hardly fault someone for choosing what's in front of them. If you have 100 people offering to sell you a Ferrari for a dollar, you're not going to pay much attention to the 900 people offering to sell you a Ford Fiesta for the same price. The successful minority of men on dating apps tend to be exceedingly handsome, photograph well, imply they have well-paying jobs and often advertise their height. To illustrate the point, there is a popular meme related to modern female-mate choice: '6, 6 and 6' (at least 6-foot, 6-figure salary, 6-inch penis). Yet only 14.5 per cent of men are 6 foot and over, only 20 per cent of men have penises 6 inches or longer, and only 13 per cent of men make six figures or more. If you want a man who has all three, the percentage is less than 5 per cent (and not all of them are single). With roughly 49 to 51 per cent of the population being female, this is a disaster in the making.

One might be tempted to think that this clustering towards a minority of men represents a return to the polygyny of our evolutionary ancestors or the bulk of pregnancies being due to a minority of men prior to 12,000 years ago. After all, it took the draconian measures of the agrarian era to curb this tendency in the distant past. However, this is not the case. We are a predominantly monogamous species living in a modern economy where commitment and children cost a great deal of money. The lucky minority of men are more than willing to meet up and have sex with these large numbers of women but are less likely to date them in a committed relationship. Unfortunately, even the sex with these men isn't particularly good. During first-time hook-ups, approximately 10 per cent of women manage to orgasm, compared to 68 per cent of women who have a monogamous partner. If/when these men *do* settle into a committed relationship, they pick one woman from a rather large dating pool. So much for polygyny.

The result for women is that while the average number of sexual partners they have under thirty has roughly doubled in the past twenty years, there has not been a corresponding increase in the incidence of long-term relationships or marriages. And despite the average marriage age for women now being twenty-nine, with marriage rates in decline, 40 to 55 per cent of women at age thirty (depending on the developed nation in question) are single and childless, and 25 to 35 per cent of women are single and childless at forty, with an additional 10 to 15 per cent of women becoming single mothers in their thirties without the biological father of the child previously being a monogamous partner. Meanwhile the total numbers per 1000 women who get divorced continues to increase from age twenty-nine to age forty by 55 per cent, only going into decline again after age forty-five. And men in the same thirty to forty-five age group tend not to stick *to* their age group. In the United States, 18 per cent of married men are ten to twenty years older than their spouse compared to 1.4 per cent of women. Finally, the greater emphasis that many women place on a partner earning equal or greater income than them (this factor is almost non-existent for men) significantly shrinks the dating pool as women reach high levels of career success after age thirty.

In short, current dating trends driven by dating apps are resulting in a lot more sexless men under thirty, and a lot more single women over thirty. The disadvantage one sex reaps is largely reversed at the other end. Welcome to modern dating.

For the above reasons, it is clear that sex in the modern era is becoming something of a dystopian 'brave new world' for many people. I wish that I could pinpoint one major era in human history (foraging, agrarian, modern) where things were 'ideal' for most people. But I can't. Sex is messy, primal and cobbled together from the tangled mess of billions of years of evolution. When that is your starting point, one can rarely expect a happy ending to always go with your 'happy ending'. The best anyone can do, in any era, is try to carve out a little bubble for themselves as individuals, where they can hopefully be happy.

SEX ON THE HORIZON

In my previous book, *The Shortest History of the Universe*, I ended with a methodical approach to forecasting the future right up to the heat death of the Universe, using horizon-scanning tools from the field of strategic foresight. Some of the same tools can be applied to the short-term future of sex. When predicting the future, you must not predict just *one* future. You must predict *several* futures. And the more you organise these different scenarios into different categories, the better off your forecasting will be. Some of these categories are:

1. **projected future**: What observation says *is* happening. Things play out how current trends suggest they will play out. It is business as usual, where we assume no major change to variables or behaviours, and no dynamic discoveries. The projected future may not even be the most likely future, since new discoveries and changes in variables do eventually occur, but it forms an important baseline for our forecasting.
2. **probable future**: What observation says *could* happen. Where variation or change within the bounds of known science indicates trends might go. The probable future is the projected future's margin for error, or margin for variation. Again, these may not be the most likely futures, it's just that we know they could happen given all the variables at play.
3. **possible future:** What *might* happen. Where a discovery yet unknown to science alters a future outcome, and where we can't explain in detail how everything will work. It's like an algebra equation: $x + y = z$. We know our starting position (x) and we know where we might go (z). We just don't yet know how we might get there (y).
4. **preposterous future**: What science says *can't* happen. Where an outcome seems to openly defy the laws of known science, contradicting all available data or understanding. It plays an important role in prediction because it clearly defines what a possible future is by mere contrast. It prevents speculation from going overboard.

And so, without further ado:

The **projected future** is that initially half of adults will continue to get married, one-quarter staying together, one-quarter divorcing. The percentage of married couples who get divorced isn't expected to rise. Given how recent and patchy the human evolutionary impulse towards monogamy is, and considering marriages no longer have the cultural or material compulsion they did in the agrarian era, that isn't half-bad an outcome. But the overall percentage of people who get married may decline slightly in the longer term by 2100. Current trends indicate that people who cohabitate but never 'put a ring on it' will continue to grow, reducing the married population from half to a third. But with cohabitation we are still talking monogamy, with many of these cohabs having kids, so it amounts to much the same thing.

However, more crucially, the single population (in both men and women) also appears to be steadily growing. At current rates, the number of people who never find a long-term partner may increase to one-half or even two-thirds of the population of the developed world by 2100, unless something changes. In short, there will be a lot more promiscuous sex in society, a fair degree of sexlessness and not as much commitment. If the single population grows from 40 to 66 per cent of the population, that would place the married population at a projected 21 per cent and cohabs as the remaining 13 per cent. Because of the rise of singledom, the birth rate is projected to continue its decline well below replacement levels. But remember: the projected future is not necessarily the most likely future – things seldom stay the same forever. Especially where humans are concerned.

Some of the more extreme **'probable' futures** (heavy air-quotes) which could occur (in part or in full) are:

1. **single supremacy**: where singleness trends continue to accelerate, marriage drastically declines, with people becoming wary of long-term cohabitation, leaving most of the population to spend most of their lives alone, punctuated by a few relationships that last a few months or a couple of years. At which point, it is likely that an increased number of people will have kids as single parents via IVF and surrogates. As such, the number of children being raised in single-parent households (by either mothers or fathers) would dramatically increase from one-quarter of the population to nearly all of it. That would necessitate a decline in arguments from traditionalist schools that two parents are

required for a good upbringing and to minimise the odds of social disadvantages. It likely would also require an increase in government support and subsidies. Even with all that, the birth rate is likely to fall so low you'd find it next to dinosaur bones.

The singledom scenario would also require an immense cultural rejection of relationships as the key to happiness in the modern age, possibly with a spike in animosity between the genders, along with intensified focus on people's careers. This is not so unthinkable since such perspectives are already fairly prominent in the zeitgeist. It is also likely in that scenario that people's reliance on online pornography, sex work, sex toys and possibly realistic sex dolls and sexbots will drastically increase. Regarding sex dolls and bots, this seems less likely since the social stigma against them remains strong and most people can't get over the 'uncanny valley' effect in order to sustain arousal. It also seems likely that short-term hook-ups would continue to be a thing for most women and an attractive minority of men.

This scenario largely involves people becoming more utilitarian and filling their needs for sex and companionship like 'scratching an itch'. Such an outcome would require a wave of cultural cynicism, wherein sex is completely disassociated from sentiment (a somewhat tall order), and where emotional needs are filled either by friendships, a series of short-term romantic companions, and reliance on artificial intelligence to fill any gaps. On the one hand, this behaviour seems fairly at odds with human nature and our drive to pair-bond, on the other for a sizeable portion of the population this probable future is already a reality.

2. **'trad' renaissance**: where the pendulum swings against the decline of monogamy and an increasing number of people enter marriages or de facto cohabitations, abandon them less swiftly (unless serious abuse or infidelity is involved – less so for cases of general unhappiness, malaise or arguing), and start having more kids. One might also see an increase in the number of single-income households with stay-at-home (female or, less traditionally, male) parents for the first time in

nearly a century. Given the massive trend towards secularism in most developed nations, barring a Great Religious Awakening in the twenty-first century it seems highly likely such a 'trad' revival would need to be spurred by secular arguments rather than religious ones. Hence the possibility of an increase in cohabs and male homemakers. Such arguments might consist of pointing out the mental, emotional and physical benefits most men and women enjoy when entering long-term monogamy and potentially having kids. However, given that most women prefer having full-time careers, the high divorce rate for stay-at-home dads, and how *all* people are tempted by the appeal of recreational sex (particularly in their twenties), it seems likely such a reversal would only happen for a highly motivated or ideologically driven portion of the population, rather than the population at large.

There is also the issue of men increasingly avoiding marriage due to the financial risks and the danger of them becoming paying spectators in their children's lives. And in numerous countries, common-law or de facto marriage kicks in after a few years of cohabitation. Proposals to increase male confidence in marriage generally involve retaining no-fault and de facto no-fault divorce, but unless a breach of the marriage contract is proven in court (adultery, abuse, abandonment, etc) a no-fault divorce would result in no alimony, no child support, no bulk asset redistribution and 50/50 child custody. In a nutshell, two adults would walk away from a marriage with what they brought into it and what they each monetarily earned and contributed during its existence. But while it is highly probable that most men would accept such a reform to marriage law, since it is overwhelmingly in their favour, it is an open question whether most women would endorse such a reform. Regardless, without some sort of change, it seems highly unlikely that the current trend of men being increasingly unwilling to marry is going to reverse itself.

Another barrier to the trad revival affecting both sexes is the prohibitive costs of having large numbers of children, running a single-income household or, indeed, buying a house in the first place. With current economic trends, this obstacle could only be countered if major tax breaks were given to married couples (e.g. one kid, 5 per cent less income tax; two kids, 12 per cent less tax; three kids, 25 per cent less tax; four kids, 50 per cent less tax; five kids, virtually no income tax) and if reforms were made to the property market to curtail overseas ownership of residential properties, place a cap on house prices and/or significantly reduce the barrier to entry for first-time mortgages. One radical proposal is the government itself directly enters the mortgage business, rather than bailing out banks when people default on their loans, and offer mortgages to anyone with a certain income, without *any* deposit and with a reasonable rate of interest. This would eliminate the need for most people to ever rent before starting to pay off a home. Young people could go straight from graduation to employment and home ownership. Essentially this provides massive financial assistance and an incentive to start a family, though less drastic measures have been tried in other countries with mixed results. Most natal policies seem to just increase the percentage of single-parent households. And unless economic barriers are addressed, it seems unlikely the trad scenario will happen in the near future, as the percentage of the population who are homeowners continues its steady three-decade decline.

3. **polygyny redux**: continuing and accelerating the Tinder trend, where there is a massive cultural shift rejecting most men as inadequate sexual partners and genetic donors and a growing sense that the provider/protector role played by most men is irrelevant to women in the modern age. In this scenario, roughly 80 per cent of men are cut out of fatherhood, with women either having sex with the remaining 20 per cent and being single mothers, or else culturally consenting to being multiple partners/wives to highly wealthy, powerful or physically attractive men. There are several barriers to this. For starters, it is unclear whether there is any historical case in the foraging or agrarian eras where most women consented to polygyny without cultural coercion, religious indoctrination or needing to become a sister-wife

for material survival. Assuming coercion is illegal in this scenario and that women remain perfectly capable of supporting themselves with their careers, it is doubtful that most women would be willing to share a relationship with several other women, indulging the appetites of a potentially smug and overprivileged husband. Sexual jealousy is a powerful evolutionary instinct.

The scenario where women reject marriage and become single mothers seems slightly more likely, but this would require the complete rejection of any hope of monogamy, and an emotional and sexual connection with most men. Although online dating indicates a certain disturbing trend at the moment, it seems unlikely that the trend will completely overpower society. Plenty of men who are not '6, 6 and 6' do wind up turning the head of a lovely lass, with romance flourishing as a consequence. And, hell, all we need for this trend to change is for tech companies to come out with less shitty dating apps that don't distort the process of mate selection. A market innovation that could happen at any time.

There is also a question of what the reaction of the 80 per cent of men would be to the polygyny redux scenario. It seems unlikely men would just take it lying down. Male *Homo sapiens* are instinctually a lot closer to chimpanzees than gorillas, with the latter more tamely accepting the monopoly that a dominant silverback has on sex, while they lurk on the fringes of the forest. Alternatively, what do chimpanzees do when the leadership of an alpha male becomes intolerable? They launch a revolution.

4. **bonobo bonanza**: promiscuity goes into overdrive, with women having random sex with men across a wider spectrum of attractiveness. In other words, the exact inverse of the scenario above. This scenario seems the least likely, given the usual dynamics of female mate-choice. But since there has been a rash of publications in the last two decades naively calling for humans to 'be more like the bonobo!', I include it. In this scenario, women would increasingly have sex with

> strangers, regardless of how attractive they were, and raise any resulting children communally among themselves, relying less on men. There is a distinct possibility we would see a decline in male violence due to the proliferation of sex, just like in bonobos, but it seems highly unlikely that your average woman would consent to such a thing, given 1.9 million years of monogamous evolutionary wiring. And a small percentage of the Western population already tried it in the 1960s and '70s; it did not end well. Amid all the free love came an increase in the sexual exploitation and abuse of women. To speak nothing of an uptick in STDs. That said, several scholars (men and women) who have published books on the subject seem to feel strongly that this model could work to some degree, and that it could solve a huge number of the world's problems, from poverty to patriarchy to warfare. Fair enough to any group of people who want to try it. The only thing I can say at the moment is, 'You first.'

When it comes to **possible futures** which require the discovery of things we do not yet fully understand ($x + y = z$), there are a few intriguing possibilities:

First, the cultural invention and spread of a new attitude towards sex and the meaning of relationships that has no evolutionary or historical precedent. A new perspective that places human sex and love in the context of the twenty-first century, with all its limitations and expectations. What this perspective might be, I could not say. But it would not be merely a philosophical exercise played out in the ivory tower. It would have to wield cultural and popular appeal that transcends gender, wealth, ethnicity, religion, age and political ideology. A new consensus would need to emerge regarding what we want out of sex, the best way to approach relationships in a more egalitarian society, how we cope with the legacy of our sexual instincts in the twenty-first century, and a rethinking of why we want to have kids in a world of 8 billion people that will grow to 10 to 13 billion by the end of the century. From there, people could start devising strategies and new traditions that maximise the happiness felt by most of the population.

Second, with the increase of long-distance relationships sustained by internet technology, remote sex toys may be developed that allow partners to sexually stimulate each other across vast distances. I'm not just talking about remote vibrators, which already exist. I'm talking about technology that allows people to feel the sensations of being kissed, caressed or engaging in penetrative sex. The same technology would also be used to augment VR pornography beyond merely sitting there and stimulating oneself with a vibrator, dildo or fleshlight. There may also be improvements in AI companionship, where a version of house-managing AI such as Siri or Alexa (and the male equivalents) is increasingly capable of being affectionate, learning about their hosts,

The uncanny-valley poster girl for the future of sex?

having nuanced conversation, reading emotions, helping people through hardships and heartache, having a laugh and nurturing people's self-esteem in a healthy way. This same AI technology could potentially be implanted into physical sexbots, which may increase in realism and mobility in the coming years. It is distinctly possible with these technological improvements that remote and robotic sex could become more common than actual human sex in the near future.

Of course, replacing human sex and intimacy with a highly appealing AI equivalent will be the death knell for marriage and the birth rate. But it does represent a reprieve for the third of society who are currently likely to be alone for most or all of their lives. There is also the question of whether a live-in sexbot might raise people's expectations to impossible standards if they should at any point try dating a human being again. And there's the ethical question of whether a person should own a live-in housekeeper and sex-slave with no rights under law, along with a largely unregulated industry capable of producing sex robots for paedophiles.

Third, the field of body modification may see vibrators installed in parts of the body to augment orgasms during sex or surgeries to enhance the number of nerve endings in the penis or clitoris. Beyond that, 3D printed penises, breasts and other physical sex characteristics could increasingly be installed in a person, completely altering their appearance beyond what modern plastic surgery is currently capable of. It is distinctly possible that thanks to body mods we may all be devastatingly gorgeous and sexy at some point in the next century or two.

Fourth, in the field of transhumanism, it is already a widespread position that humans may be able to upload their consciousnesses to computers at some point in the next century. Not only does this mean that humans could cheat death and live for millions or billions of years, it would also mean that humans could inhabit a virtual world of their own creation. Some of those people may choose to enjoy virtually constructed sex, with either AI or other human consciousnesses. However, in uploading your consciousness to a computer you lose your connection to your body chemistry, which makes up your sex drive and all of your emotions. So, unless we were programmed to retain much of our ape-like personalities and carnal interests, it is possible that with the rise of transhumanism will come the extinction of sex and romance altogether.

Fifth, another technology that might become possible in the next century is targeted genome editing, whereby one could engineer one's genes to halt or reverse the process of ageing. We'd be able to cheat death and live on as immortals while staying flesh and blood. This throws up several societal complications. Not least being what happens to our desire to have children in a world where people have stopped dying? Even at the incredibly low birth rates of the West, if people kept being born this would be an ecological disaster within the space of a generation. Never mind a world of 10 billion people: try 20 billion, or 50. The results could be catastrophic. But if we managed to get over that hurdle, consider for a moment how immortality might affect monogamous relationships. Roughly half of all married couples stay together till death, but what if they don't die? What proportion of couples would continue to stay together for a thousand years? A million? A billion? And if they broke up, what are the odds they may drift back into a relationship together after a generation or two? Meanwhile, immortality might represent a certain kind of hell for people who don't easily get into relationships or cope well with them, with their loneliness stretched out across eternity rather than a single lifetime.

Which brings us to the **preposterous future**, where we examine possibilities that seem to defy what we currently know about the laws of science. In my previous book, where I related a broader history of the Universe, the preposterous future involved power sources that defied the ironclad Second Law of Thermodynamics or interstellar spacecraft that moved faster than the speed of light. However, in a shorter-term horizon scan of the future of sex, there is really only one kind of preposterous future: that sex will cease to be important to those of us who remain flesh and blood.

POST-COITAL CLARITY

Because of its haphazard 2-billion-year evolution, sex is messy, complicated and confusing – for all of us. It is my hope that with the information I have provided in this book some aspects of sex have become slightly less baffling for the reader, or at the very least that they now have greater context for their bafflement.

Regardless of where the story goes from here, may we all enjoy a pleasant lifetime of *petites morts* before the larger one comes along to end our exertions and lay us to rest. I ardently wish you, the reader, the best of luck in finding fulfillment with your partners and paramours in whatever way works best for you.

And I hope, in this short life, you may attain a few moments of bliss and get to experience the sensation of feeling truly loved, however brief and fleeting those glimpses of the transcendent and sublime may be.

Good luck. And be good to each other.

ACKNOWLEDGEMENTS

As always, I would like to thank David Christian for opening my eyes to a larger world and showing me how everything in history is connected.

I would like to thank my parents, Susan and Greg Baker, for their infinite reservoir of support and listening to me rattle off an abundance of mildly interesting facts about sex (sometimes while they were trying to eat).

I would like to thank Viktoria Evans for her incredibly valuable friendship this past year, and her sense of humour, intelligent conversation, and listening to long extracts of this book.

I would like to thank Simon Whistler for giving me one of the best jobs on the planet, allowing me to research and write about a vast diversity of interesting topics.

My deepest gratitude to Sharon Bruning for keeping me sane.

My utmost thanks to Jason Gallate for saving my life.

Lastly, I'd like to thank Milo. He's such a good boy.

FURTHER READING

Adovasio, J. M. et al. *The Invisible Sex: Uncovering the True Roles of Women in Prehistory*. New York: Smithsonian Books, 2007.

Alberti, Fay Bound. *This Mortal Coil: The Human Body in History and Culture*. Oxford: Oxford University Press, 2016.

Allen, Robert. *The British Industrial Revolution in a Global Perspective*. Cambridge: Cambridge University Press, 2009.

Altekar, Anant Sadashiv. *The Position of Women in Hindu Civilisation: Prehistoric Times to the Present Day*. Mumbai: Motilal Banarsidass, 1956.

Alvarez, Walter. *A Most Improbable Journey: A Big History of Our Planet and Ourselves*. New York: W.W. Norton, 2016.

Alvarez, Walter. *T. rex and the Crater of Doom*. Princeton: Princeton University Press, 1997.

Andersson, Malte. *Sexual Selection*. Princeton: Princeton University Press, 1994.

Angier, Natalie. *Woman: An Intimate Geography*. New York: Virago, 1999.

Arnqvist, Göran, and Locke Rowe. *Sexual Conflict*. Princeton: Princeton University Press, 2005.

Bagemihl, Bruce. *Biological Exuberance: Animal Homosexuality and Natural Diversity*. New York: St. Martin's Press, 1999.

Bairoch, Paul. *Cities and Economic Development: From the Dawn of History to the Present*. trans. Christopher Braider. Chicago: University of Chicago Press, 1988.

Baker, David. *The Shortest History of the World*. Melbourne: Black Inc., 2022.

Baker, David. 'Collective Learning: A Potential Unifying Theme of Human History' *Journal of World History*, vol. 26, no. 1 (2015), pp. 77–104.

Barash, David, and Judith E. Lipton. *The Myth of Monogamy: Fidelity and Infidelity in Animals and People*. New York: W.H. Freeman & Co., 2001.

Barfield, Thomas. *The Nomadic Alternative*. Hoboken: Prentice Hall, 1993.

Batten, Mary. *Sexual Strategies: How Females Choose Their Mates*. New York: Putnam, 1992.

Bayly, Christopher. *The Birth of the Modern World, 1780–1914: Global Connections and Comparisons*. Oxford: Blackwell, 2004.

Bellwood, Peter. *First Farmers: The Origins of Agricultural Societies*. Oxford: Blackwell, 2004.

Berg, Maxine. *The Age of Manufacturers, 1700–1820: Industry, Innovation, and Work in Britain*. 2nd edn. London: Routledge, 1994.

Berkowitz, Eric. *Sex and Punishment: Four Thousand Years of Judging Desire*. Berkeley: Counterpoint, 2012.

Biraben, Jean-Noël. 'Essai sur l'évolution du nombre des hommes', *Population*, vol. 34 (1979), pp. 13–25.

Birkhead, Tim. *Promiscuity: An Evolutionary History of Sperm Competition and Sexual Conflict*. London: Faber and Faber, 2000.

Blum, Deborah. *Sex on the Brain: The Biological Differences between Men and Women*. New York: Viking Press, 1997.

Blundell, Sue. *Women in Ancient Greece*. Cambridge: Harvard University Press, 1995.

Boesch, Christophe et al. *Behavioural Diversity in Chimpanzees and Bonobos*. Cambridge: Cambridge University Press, 2002.

Bowler, Peter. *Evolution: The History of an Idea*. 3rd edn. Berkeley: University of California Press, 2003.

Bradley, John. *Behind the Veil of Vice: The Business of Culture and Sex in the Middle East*. London: Palgrave Macmillan, 2010.

Brantingham, P. Jeffrey et al. *The Early Upper Paleolithic Beyond Western Europe*. Berkeley: University of California Press, 2004.

Brizendine, Louann. *The Female Brain*. New York: Morgan Road Books, 2006.

Brown, Cynthia. *Big History: From the Big Bang to the Present*. New York and London: The New Press, 2007.

Brundage, James. *Law, Sex, and Christian Society in Medieval Europe*. Chicago: University of Chicago Press, 2009.

Bryson, Bill. *A Short History of Nearly Everything*. New York: Broadway Books, 2003.

Bullough, Vern, and Bonnie Bullough. *Prostitution: An Illustrated Social History*. New York: Crown, 1978.

Burnham, Terry, and Jay Phelan. *Mean Genes: From Sex to Money to Food, Taming Our Primal Instincts*. Cambridge, Mass.: Perseus, 2000.

Buss, David. *The Dangerous Passion: Why Jealousy Is as Necessary as Love and Sex.* New York: The Free Press, 2000.

Carr, David. *The Erotic Word: Sexuality, Spirituality and the Bible.* Oxford: Oxford University Press, 2003.

Cavalli-Sforza, Luigi Luca, and Francesco Cavalli-Sforza. *The Great Human Diasporas: The History of Diversity and Evolution.* trans. Sarah Thorne. Reading: Addison-Wesley, 1995.

Chaisson, Eric. 'Using Complexity Science to Search for Unity in the Natural Sciences'. *Complexity and the Arrow of Time.* Ed Charles Lineweaver et al. Cambridge: Cambridge University Press, 2013.

Chaisson, Eric. *Cosmic Evolution: The Rise of Complexity in Nature.* Cambridge: Harvard University Press, 2001.

Chaisson, Eric. *Epic of Evolution: Seven Ages of the Cosmos.* New York: Columbia University Press, 2006.

Chalker, Rebecca. *The Clitoral Truth: The Secret World at Your Fingertips.* New York: Seven Stories Press, 2010.

Chambers, John, and Jacqueline Morton. *From Dust to Life: The Origin and Evolution of Our Solar System.* Princeton: Princeton University Press, 2014.

Chapais, Bernard. *Primeval Kinship: How Pair-Bonding Gave Birth to Human Society.* Cambridge: Harvard University Press, 2008.

Cheney, Dorothy, and Robert Seyfarth. *Baboon Metaphysics: The Evolution of a Social Mind.* Chicago: University of Chicago Press, 2014.

Christian, David. *Maps of Time: An Introduction to Big History.* Berkeley: University of California Press, 2004.

Christian, David. *Origin Story: A Big History of Everything.* London: Allen Lane, 2018.

Christian, David et al. *Big History: Between Nothing and Everything.* New York: McGraw Hill, 2014.

Cipolla, Carlo. *Before the Industrial Revolution: European Society and Economy, 1000–1700.* 2nd edn. London: Methuen, 1981.

Clark, William. *Sex and the Origins of Death.* Oxford: Oxford University Press, 1996.

Cloud, Preston. *Oasis in Space: Earth History from the Beginning.* New York: W.W. Norton, 1988.

Coe, Michael. *Mexico: From the Olmecs to the Aztecs.* 4th edn. New York: Thames and Hudson, 1994.

Cohen, Mark. *Health and the Rise of Civilization.* New Haven: Yale University Press, 1989.

Collier, Aine. *The Humble Little Condom: A History*. Amherst: Prometheus Books, 2007.

Cowan, C. Wesley et al., eds. *The Origins of Agriculture: An International Perspective.* Washington: Smithsonian Institution Press, 1992.

Crawford, Harriet. *Sumer and the Sumerians.* 2nd edn. Cambridge: Cambridge University Press, 2004.

Crocker, William, and Jean Crocker. *The Canela: Kinship, Ritual, and Sex in an Amazonian Tribe.* 2nd edn. Florence: Wadsworth, 2003.

Crompton, Louis. *Homosexuality and Civilisation*. Cambridge, Mass.: Belnap Press, 2003.

Crosby, Alfred. *Ecological Imperialism: The Biological Expansion of Europe, 900–1900.* Cambridge: Cambridge University Press, 1986.

Crosby, Alfred. *The Columbian Exchange: Biological and Cultural Consequences of 1492*. Cambridge: Cambridge University Press, 1972.

D'Altroy, Terence. *The Incas.* Malden: Blackwell, 2002.

Darwin, Charles. *The Origin of Species : A Facsimile of the First Edition*. Cambridge, Mass: Harvard University Press, 2003.

Davies, Kevin. *Cracking the Genome: Inside the Race to Unlock DNA*. Baltimore: Johns Hopkins University Press, 2001.

De Waal, Frans, and Frans Lanting. *Bonobo: The Forgotten Ape*. Berkeley: University of California Press, 1997.

De Waal, Frans. *Chimpanzee Politics: Power and Sex Among Apes*. 25th anniv. edn. Johns Hopkins University Press, 2007.

De Waal, Frans. *Tree of Origin: What Primate Behaviour Can Tell Us about Human Social Evolution.* Cambridge: Harvard University Press, 2001.

Dening, Sarah. *The Mythology of Sex: An Illustrated Exploration of Sexual Customs and Practices from Ancient Times to the Present*. New York: Macmillan, 1996.

Devlin, Kate. *Turned On: Science, Sex, and Robots.* London: Bloomsbury, 2018.

Diamond, Lisa. *Sexual Fluidity: Understanding Women's Love and Desire.* Cambridge: Harvard University Press, 2008.

Dixson, Alan. *Primate Sexuality: Comparative Studies of the Prosimians, Monkeys, Apes, and Human Beings*. New York: Oxford University Press, 2001.

Dunbar, Robin. *The Human Story: A New History of Mankind's Evolution.* London: Faber & Faber, 2004.

Dyson, Freeman. *Origins of Life.* 2nd edn. Cambridge: Cambridge University Press, 1999.

Earle, Timothy. *How Chiefs Come to Power: The Political Economy in Prehistory.* Stanford: Stanford University Press, 1997.

Eberhard, William. *Sexual Selection and Animal Genitalia.* Cambridge: Harvard University Press, 1985.

Edgerton, Robert. *Sick Societies: Challenging the Myth of Primitive Harmony.* New York: The Free Press, 1992.

Eisler, Riane. *Sacred Pleasures: Sex, Myth, and the Politics of the Body.* San Francisco: Vega Books, 1995.

Erwin, Douglas. *Extinction: How Life on Earth Nearly Ended 250 Million Years Ago.* Princeton: Princeton University Press, 2006.

Fagan, Brian. *People of the Earth: An Introduction to World Prehistory.* 10th edn. New Jersey: Prentice Hall, 2001.

Faser, Evan, and Andrew Rimas. *Empires of Food: Feast, Famine, and the Rise and Fall of Civilisations.* Berkeley, Calif.: Counterpoint, 2010.

Fisher, Helen. *Anatomy of Love: A Natural History of Mating, Marriage and Why We Stray.* New York: Fawcett Columbine, 1992.

Forbes, Scott. *A Natural History of Families.* Princeton: Princeton University Press, 2005.

Forsyth, Adrian. *A Natural History of Sex: The Ecology and Evolution of Sexual Behaviour.* New York: Scribner, 1985.

Fortey, Richard. *Earth: An Intimate History.* New York: Knopf, 2004.

Franzblau, Abraham. *Erotic Art in China: A Unique Collection of Chinese Prints and Poems Devoted to the Art of Love.* New York: Crown Publishers, 1977.

Freely, John. *Inside the Seraglio: The Private Lives of Sultans in Istanbul.* London: Penguin, 1999.

Friedman, David. *A Mind of Its Own: A Cultural History of the Penis.* New York: The Free Press, 2001.

Gates, Charles. *Ancient Cities: The Archaeology of Urban Life in the Ancient Near East, Egypt, Greece, and Rome.* 2nd edn. Abingdon: Routledge, 2011.

Gollaher, David. *Circumcision: A History of the World's Most Controversial Surgery.* New York: Basic Books, 2000.

Goodall, Jane. *The Chimpanzees of Gombe: Patterns of Behaviour.* Cambridge: Harvard University Press, 1986.

Goodall, Jane. *Through a Window: My Thirty Years with the Chimpanzees of Gombe.* Boston: Houghton Mifflin, 1990.

Grant, Michael et al. *Eros in Pompeii.* New York: Stewart, Tabori & Chang, 1975.

Green, Richard et al. 'A Draft Sequence of the Neanderthal Genome' *Science*, vol. 328, no. 5979 (May 2010), pp. 710–22.

Greenburg, Steven. *Wrestling with God and Men: Homosexuality in the Jewish Tradition*. Madison: University of Wisconsin Press, 2004.

Gregg, John. *Sex: The Illustrated History Through Time, Religion, and Culture*. (3 vols). London: XLibris, 2017.

Hallet, Judith, and Marilyn Skinner. *Roman Sexualities*. Princeton: Princeton University Press, 1997.

Hansen, Valerie. *The Open Empire: A History of China to 1600*. New York: W.W. Norton, 2000.

Hazen, Robert. *The Story of Earth: The First 4.5 Billion Years from Stardust to Living Planet*. New York: Viking 2012.

Hrdy, Sarah. *Mother Nature: A History of Mothers, Infants, and Natural Selection*. Boston: Pantheon Books, 1999.

Johanson, Donald, and Maitland Edey. *Lucy: The Beginnings of Humankind*. New York: Simon and Schuster, 1981.

Johnson, Allen, and T. Earle. *The Evolution of Human Societies: From Foraging Group to Agrarian State*. 2nd edn. Stanford: Stanford University Press, 2000.

Jolly, Alison. *Lucy's Legacy: Sex and Intelligence in Human Evolution*. Cambridge: Harvard University Press, 1999.

Jones, Steve. *Y: The Descent of Men*. London: Little Brown, 2002.

Jütte, Robert. *Contraception: A History*. Cambridge: Polity, 2008.

Kakar, Sudhir. *Intimate Relations: Exploring Indian Sexuality*. Chicago: University of Chicago Press, 1989.

Kampen, Natalie. *Sexuality in Ancient Art: Near East, Egypt, Greece and Italy*. Cambridge: Harvard University Press, 1997.

Kicza, John. 'The Peoples and Civilizations of the Americas before Contact' in *Agricultural and Pastoral Societies in Ancient and Classical History*. ed. Michael Adas. Philadelphia: Temple University Press, 2001.

Klein, Richard. *The Dawn of Human Culture*. New York: Wiley, 2002.

Knight, Chris. *Blood Relations: Menstruation and the Origins of Culture*. New Haven: Yale University Press, 1995.

Knoll, Andrew. *Life on a Young Planet: The First Three Billion Years of Evolution on Earth*. Princeton: Princeton University Press, 2003.

Leakey, Richard, and Roger Lewin. *The Sixth Extinction: Patterns of Life and the Future of Humankind*. New York: Doubleday, 1995.

Leick, Gwendolyn. *Mesopotamia: The Invention of the City*. London: Penguin, 2001.

Leick, Gwendolyn. *Sex and Eroticism in Mesopotamian Literature*. London: Routledge, 1994.

Leuff, Gary. *Male Colors: The Construction of Homosexuality in Tokugawa Japan*. Berkeley: University of California Press, 1995.

LeVay, Simon. *The Sexual Brain*. Cambridge: MIT Press, 1994.

Lister, Kate. *A Curious History of Sex*. London: Unbound, 2020.

Livi-Bacci, Massimo. *A Concise History of World Population*. Trans. Carl Ipsen. Oxford: Blackwell, 1992.

Lloyd, Elisabeth. *The Case of the Female Orgasm: Bias in the Science of Evolution*. Cambridge: Harvard University Press, 2005.

Lombardi, Julian. *Comparative Vertebrate Reproduction*. Norwell: Kluwer Academic Publishers, 1998.

Lunine, Jonathan. *Earth: Evolution of a Habitable World*. Cambridge: Cambridge University Press, 1999.

Maines, Rachel. *The Technology of the Orgasm*. Baltimore: Johns Hopkins University Press, 1999.

Majerus, Michael. *Sex Wars: Genes, Bacteria, and Biased Sex Ratios*. Princeton: Princeton University Press, 2003.

Marcus, Joyce. *Mesoamerican Writing Systems: Propaganda, Myth, and History in Four Ancient Civilizations*. Princeton: Princeton University Press, 1992.

Margolis, Jonathan. *O: The Intimate History of the Orgasm*. New York: Grove Press, 2004.

Margulis, Lynn, and Dorian Sagan. *Mystery Dance: On the Evolution of Human Sexuality*. New York: Summit Books, 1991.

Marks, Robert. *The Origins of the Modern World: A Global and Environmental Narrative from the Fifteenth to the Twenty-First Century*. 2nd edn. Lanham: Rowman & Littlefield, 2007.

Masters, William et al. *Human Sexuality*. Boston: Addison-Wesley, 1995.

Maynard Smith, John. 'The Evolution of Sex'. *Noble Conference XXIII*. Ed. Robert Bellig and George Stevens. St Peter: Gustavus Adolphus College, 1988.

Maynard Smith, John, and Eörs Szathmáry. *The Origins of Life: From the Birth of Life to the Origins of Language*. Oxford: Oxford University Press, 1999.

McBrearty, Sally, and Alison Brooks. 'The Revolution that Wasn't: A New Interpretation of the Origin of Modern Human Behaviour', *Journal of Human Evolution*, vol. 39 (2000), pp. 453–563.

McElvaine, Robert. *Eve's Seed: Biology, the Sexes, and the Course of History*. New York: McGraw-Hill, 2001.

McNeill, John R., and William H. McNeill. *The Human Web: A Bird's-Eye View of World History.* New York: W.W. Norton, 2003.

McNeill, William. *Plagues and Peoples.* Oxford: Blackwell, 1977.

Miller, Geoffrey. *The Mating Mind: How Human Sexual Choice Shaped the Evolution of Human Nature.* New York: Doubleday, 2000.

Murray, Jacqueline. *Love, Marriage, and Family in the Middle Ages.* Toronto: University of Toronto Press, 2001.

Nutman, Allen et al. 'Rapid Emergence of Life Shown by Discovery of 3700 million-year-old Microbial Structures', *Nature*, vol. 537 (Sep. 2016), pp. 535–8.

Overton, Mark. *Agricultural Revolution in England: The Transformation of the Agrarian Economy, 1500–1850.* Cambridge: Cambridge University Press, 1996.

Pacey, Arnold, and Francesca Bay. *Technology in World Civilisation.* Cambridge, Mass.: MIT Press, 1990.

Percy, William. *Pederasty and Pedagogy in Ancient Greece.* Urbana: University of Illinois Press, 1996.

Perel, Esther. *Mating in Captivity: Reconciling the Erotic and Domestic.* New York: HarperCollins, 2006.

Pinker, Steven. *The Blank State: The Modern Denial of Human Nature.* New York: Penguin, 2003.

Pomeranz, Kenneth. *The Great Divergence: China, Europe, and the Making of the Modern World Economy.* Princeton: Princeton University Press, 2000.

Ponting, Clive. *A Green History of the World: The Environment and the Collapse of Great Civilisations.* London: Penguin, 1991.

Potts, Malcolm, and Roger Short. *Ever Since Adam and Eve: The Evolution of Human Sexuality.* Cambridge: Cambridge University Press, 1999.

Prager, Ellen. Sex, *Drugs, and Sea Slime: The Oceans Oddest Creatures and Why They Matter.* Chicago: Chicago University Press, 2011.

Qualls-Corbet, Nancy. *The Sacred Prostitute: Eternal Aspects of the Feminine.* New York: Inner City Books, 1988.

Rawson, Philip. *Erotic Art of the East: The Sexual Theme in Oriental Painting and Sculpture.* New York: Putnam, 1968.

Richards, John. *The Unending Frontier: Environmental History of the Early Modern World.* Berkeley: University of California Press, 2006.

Riddle, John. *Eve's Herbs: A History of Contraception and Abortion in the West.* Cambridge: Harvard University Press, 1999.

Ridley, Mark. *Mendel's Demon: Gene Justice and the Complexity of Life.* London: Weidenfield and Nicolson, 2000.

Ridley, Matt. *The Red Queen: Sex and the Evolution of Human Nature.* New York: Penguin, 1993.

Ringrose, David. *Expansion and Global Interaction, 1200–1700.* New York: Longman, 2001.

Ristvet, Lauren. *In the Beginning: World History from Human Evolution to the First States.* New York: McGraw-Hill, 2007.

Roach, Mary. *Bonk: The Curious Coupling of Sex and Science.* New York: Norton, 2008.

Roller, Duane. *Ancient Geography: The Discovery of the World in Classical Greece and Rome.* London: I.B. Tauris, 2015.

Rothman, Mitchell. *Uruk, Mesopotamia, and its Neighbours: Cross-Cultural Interactions in the Era of State Formation.* Santa Fe: School of American Research Press, 2001.

Roughgarden, Joan. *Evolution's Rainbow: Diversity, Gender, and Sexuality in Nature and People.* Berkeley: University of California Press, 2004.

Ryan, Christopher, and Cacilda Jethá. *Sex at Dawn: The Prehistoric Origins of Modern Sexuality.* New York: HarperCollins, 2010.

Sahlins, Marshall. 'The Original Affluent Society' in *Stone Age Economics.* London: Tavistock, 1972, pp. 1–39.

Sapolsky, Robert. *Monkeyluv: and Other Essay on Our Lives as Animals.* New York: Scribner, 2005.

Saxon, Lynn. *Sex at Dusk: Lifting the Shiny Wrapping from Sex at Dawn.* New York: Createspace, 2012.

Scarre, Chris, ed. *The Human Past: World Prehistory and the Development of Human Societies.* London: Thames & Hudson, 2005.

Scroggs, Robin. *The New Testament and Homosexuality.* New York: Fortress Press, 1983.

Shuster, Stephen, and Michael Wade. *Mating Systems and Strategies.* Princeton: Princeton University Press, 2003.

Skinner, Marilyn. *Sexuality in Greek and Roman Culture.* London: Blackwell, 2005.

Small, Meredith. *Female Choices: Sexual Behaviour of Female Primates.* Ithaca: Cornell University Press, 1993.

Smith, Bruce. *The Emergence of Agriculture.* New York: Scientific American Library, 1995.

Sparks, John. *The Battle of the Sexes: The Natural History of Sex*. London: BBC Books, 1999.

Squire, Susan. *I Don't: A Contrarian History of Marriage*. New York: Bloomsbury, 2008.

Stanford, Craig. *Significant Others: The Ape-Human Continuum and the Quest for Human Nature*. New York: Basic Books, 2001.

Strayer, Robert. *Ways of the World: A Global History*. Boston: St. Martin's Press, 2009.

Stringer, Chris. *The Origin of Our Species*. London: Allen Lane, 2011.

Symons, Donald. *The Evolution of Human Sexuality*. London: Oxford University Press, 1979.

Tattersall, Ian. *Masters of the Planet: The Search for Human Origins*. New York: Palgrave Macmillan, 2012.

Tattersall, Ian. *Becoming Human: Evolution and Human Uniqueness*. New York: Harcourt Brace, 1998.

Taylor. Gary. *Castration: An Abbreviated History of Western Manhood*. London: Routledge, 2001.

Thompson, Lana. *The Wandering Womb*. Amherst: Prometheus Books, 1999.

Thornhill, Randy, and Craig Palmer. *A Natural History of Rape: Biological Bases of Sexual Coercion*. Cambridge: MIT Press, 2000.

Trexler, Richard. *Sex and Conquest: Gendered Violence, Political Order, and the European Conquest of the Americas*. Ithaca: Cornell University Press, 2005.

Turchin, Peter, and Sergei Nefedov. *Secular Cycles*. Princeton: Princeton University Press, 2009.

Van Shaik, Carel, and Charles Janson. *Infanticide by Males and Its Implications*. Cambridge: Cambridge University Press, 2000.

Weinberg, Steven. *The First Three Minutes: A Modern View of the Origin of the Universe*. New York: Basic Books, 1977.

Witte, John et al. *Sex, Marriage, and Family in World Religions*. New York: Columbia, 2006.

Woods, Michael, and Mary Woods. *Ancient Technology: Ancient Agriculture from Foraging to Farming*. Minneapolis: Runestone Press, 2000.

Wrangham, Richard. 'The evolution of sexuality in chimpanzees and bonobos', *Human Nature*, vol. 4 (1993), pp. 47–79.

Wrangham, Richard, and Dale Peterson. *Demonic Males: Apes and the Origins of Human Violence*. Boston: Mariner Books, 1996.

IMAGE CREDITS

p. 11 Alexey Kotelnikov / Alamy

p. 25 Tsakaoe / Alamy

p. 28 C Mann Photo / iStock

p. 39 David Fleetham / Alamy

p. 51 Universal Images Group North America LLC / Alamy

p. 55 Michael Long / Science Photo Library

p. 60 J.R. Hickman et al., *Integrated Principles of Zoology*, 18th edn, McGraw-Hill, 2023 ©McGraw-Hill. Reproduced with permission of the publisher.

p. 62 Roger Harris / Science Photo Library

p. 71 TheVisual MD / Science Source / Science Photo Library

p. 76 Dalton Stealth / Odd Articulations

p. 77 John R. Foster / Science Source / Science Photo Library

p. 86 Henning Dalhoff / Science Photo Library

p. 91 Imagebroker / Alamy

p. 99 David Evison / iStock

p. 102 Windzepher/ iStock

p. 109 Photograph by John Mitani

p. 115 Tony Camacho / Science Photo Library

p. 122 Anup Shah / Nature Picture Library / Science Photo Library

p. 126 Nevena Tsvetanova / Alamy

p. 133 Universal Images Group North America LLC / Alamy

p. 140 Mark Maslin, *The Cradle of Humanity*, Oxford University Press, 2016, p. 167. Courtesy of the author.

p. 161 Illustration by Tristan Main

p. 172 Via Marcsi Pál / Pinterest

p. 203 *Stele of Hammurabi*, artist unknown, c. 1751–93, Department of Near Eastern Antiquities of the Louvre. Image via Wikimedia Commons.

p. 207 Kitagawa Utamaro, Toyotomi Hideyoshi with his wives and concubines, c. 1804–6, published by Kagaya Kichibei. Image via Wikimedia Commons.

p. 221 Nahid Sultan via Wikimedia Commons.

p. 224 Collage of erotic art in Hindu temples. Sarah Welch via Wikimedia Commons.

p. 235 Cover of *Good Housekeeping* magazine, 1908. John Cecil Clay via Wikimedia Commons.

p. 242 Mihály Zichy, *Making Love*, 1911. Image via Wikimedia Commons.

p. 244 Jonas E. Heyser, Patent for Male Chasity Belt, 1911. Image via Wikimedia Commons.

p. 258 Bain News Service, photograph of Louise Brooks. Library of Congress via Wikimedia Commons.

p. 293 Sandy, sex doll created by Doll Sweet, 2014. Image via Wikimedia Commons.

INDEX

Page numbers in **bold** refer to images.

INDEX

INDEX

INDEX

INDEX

ABOUT THE AUTHOR

David Baker is a history and science writer for SimonWhistler.com who holds the world's first PhD in Big History. He has delivered award-winning lectures at Macquarie University and the University of Amsterdam, is a visiting lecturer at the University of Paris-Sorbonne, and wrote the YouTube series 'Crash Course Big History', hosted by John and Hank Green in partnership with the Gates Big History Project.